The Great Depression on Film

Recent Titles in Hollywood History

The Vietnam War on Film
David Luhrssen

The American West on Film
Johnny D. Boggs

The Civil War on Film
Peg A. Lamphier and Rosanne Welch

World War II on Film
David Luhrssen

The Cold War on Film
Paul Frazier

Sports on Film
Johnny D. Boggs

The 1960s on Film
Jim Willis and Mark Miller

The Great Depression on Film

David Luhrssen

BLOOMSBURY ACADEMIC
NEW YORK • LONDON • OXFORD • NEW DELHI • SYDNEY

BLOOMSBURY ACADEMIC
Bloomsbury Publishing Inc
1385 Broadway, New York, NY 10018, USA
50 Bedford Square, London, WC1B 3DP, UK
29 Earlsfort Terrace, Dublin 2, Ireland

BLOOMSBURY, BLOOMSBURY ACADEMIC and the Diana logo
are trademarks of Bloomsbury Publishing Plc

First published in the United States of America by ABC-CLIO 2022
Paperback edition published by Bloomsbury Academic 2025

Copyright © Bloomsbury Publishing Inc, 2025

For legal purposes the Acknowledgments on p. xiii constitute
an extension of this copyright page.

COVER PHOTO: Studio publicity film still from *Paper Moon*, 1973.
(PictureLux/The Hollywood Archive/Alamy Stock Photo)

All rights reserved. No part of this publication may be reproduced or transmitted
in any form or by any means, electronic or mechanical, including photocopying,
recording, or any information storage or retrieval system, without prior permission
in writing from the publishers.

Bloomsbury Publishing Inc does not have any control over, or responsibility for,
any third-party websites referred to or in this book. All internet addresses given in this
book were correct at the time of going to press. The author and publisher regret any
inconvenience caused if addresses have changed or sites have ceased to exist,
but can accept no responsibility for any such changes.

Library of Congress Cataloging-in-Publication Data
Names: Luhrssen, David, author.
Title: The Great Depression on film / David Luhrssen.
Description: Santa Barbara : ABC-CLIO, [2022] | Series: Hollywood history |
Includes bibliographical references and index.
Identifiers: LCCN 2022025792 | ISBN 9781440877131 (hardcover) |
ISBN 9781440877148 (ebook)
Subjects: LCSH: Motion pictures—United States—History. |
Depressions—1929—United States. | Motion pictures—Social
aspects—United States. | Motion pictures—Political aspects—United States.
Classification: LCC PN1993.5.U6 L84 222 | DDC
791.430973/09043—dc23/eng/20220707
LC record available at https://lccn.loc.gov/2022025792

ISBN: HB: 978-1-4408-7713-1
PB: 979-8-7651-6621-5
ePDF: 978-1-4408-7714-8
eBook: 979-8-2160-9185-1

Series: Contemporary World Issues

To find out more about our authors and books visit www.bloomsbury.com
and sign up for our newsletters.

Contents

Series Foreword	vii
Preface	ix
Acknowledgments	xiii
Introduction	xv
Chronology	xxvii
1. *Gabriel over the White House* (1933)	1
2. *My Man Godfrey* (1936)	13
3. *Black Legion* (1937)	27
4. *The Grapes of Wrath* (1940)	41
5. *The Night of the Hunter* (1955)	53
6. *They Shoot Horses, Don't They?* (1969)	67
7. *Sounder* (1972)	79
8. *Paper Moon* (1973) and *The Sting* (1973)	95
9. *Chinatown* (1974)	109
10. *Bound for Glory* (1976)	121
11. *The Lindbergh Kidnapping Case* (1976)	135

12. *Kansas City* (1996)	151
13. *Cinderella Man* (2005)	167
Bibliography	183
Index	189

Series Foreword

Just exactly how accurate are Hollywood's film and television portrayals of American history? What do these portrayals of history tell us, not only about the events they depict but also the time in which they were made? Each volume in this unique reference series is devoted to a single topic or key theme in American history, examining 10–12 major motion pictures or television productions. Substantial essays summarize each film, provide historical background of the event or period it depicts, and explain how accurate the film's depiction is, while also analyzing the cultural context in which the film was made. A final resources section provides a comprehensive annotated bibliography of print and electronic sources to aid students and teachers in further research.

The subjects of these Hollywood History volumes were chosen based on both curriculum relevance and inherent interest. Readers will find a wide array of subject choices, including American Slavery on Film, the Civil War on Film, the American West on Film, Vietnam on Film, and the 1960s on Film. Ideal for school assignments and student research, the length, format, and subject areas are designed to meet educators' needs and students' interests.

Preface

The Great Depression (1929–1941) left a deep impression on the imagination of every American who lived through it and continues to cast a shadow a century later. Unlike America's armed conflicts since the Civil War, fought primarily on distant shores, the Great Depression was a daily struggle for most people in the country. It remains the economic downturn by which all others are measured. In 2008, the subprime mortgage crisis that caused the stock market to plummet was called the Great Recession in an anxious backward glance at an earlier crisis triggered on Wall Street.

The children of Depression-era Americans usually heard firsthand stories from their parents, embroidered or not by the vagaries of memory. My mother's earliest memories include the sheriff evicting her family from their home. Periods of temporary layoff for my grandfather, a skilled mechanic at a steelworks, led to at least one summer of migrant farm work picking sugar beets. As the world enters the third decade of the 21st century, the generation that grew up in the Great Depression has fallen silent. Although the period's history has been documented, written, and rewritten from many perspectives, no medium has the power to stamp a uniform impression on the imagination of large numbers of people like film. Nowadays life during the Great Depression is largely recalled by motion pictures, many of them made long after the economic recovery fostered by America's entry into World War II.

Along with radio, movies were the most pervasive form of entertainment during the Great Depression and the word "entertainment" suggests that audiences sought diversion in the cinema. "What movies lacked in realism they supplied in fantasy—escapist fantasies with fairy-tale endings as well as more darkly etched fables that enabled people to tap into their fears and work them through" (Dickstein 2009, 312). Some films caught a fleeting glimpse of actual conditions, as in the opening scenes of hunger on the New York streets in *King Kong* (1933). Others, such as *The Public Enemy* (1931), reflected on the crime wave triggered by Prohibition and the sense that the social order was being undermined. Many Hollywood movies presented a world of affluent sophistication that, while beyond the reach of most viewers, gave rise to dreams of a different way of life.

One of the titles included in *The Great Depression on Film* is characteristic of Hollywood's glib accommodation of contemporary reality. *My Man Godfrey* (1936) is a comedy about a society woman who wants to assist a particular unemployed man by rescuing him from a "Hooverville" encampment of the unemployed. However, it "cheats on the initial titillation of class conflict" by making the protagonist "a Boston Brahmin down on his luck rather than an authentic representation of the masses" (Sarris 1998, 92).

This book examines only two other films produced during the 1930s, both highly unusual. Released only weeks after Franklin D. Roosevelt's inauguration, *Gabriel over the White House* (1933) is a bizarre story of a newly elected U.S. president who, under supernatural guidance, becomes a benign but brutally effective dictator who lifts America out of the crisis. *Black Legion* (1937) is a rare effort by Hollywood to deal frankly with violent xenophobic organizations whose numbers increased under the economic and social uncertainty of the Depression. With 1940 came the classic adaptation of John Steinbeck's bestselling novel, *The Grapes of Wrath*, giving a sympathetic depiction of the rural refugees fleeing the devastation of the Dust Bowl for an unwelcoming California.

Afterward, Hollywood trained its cameras on World War II and then on contemporary settings and westerns. Few films set in the 1930s were released in the 1950s. Based on the novel by Davis Grubb, *The Night of the Hunter* (1955) was exceptional in many ways as a kind of Brothers Grimm fairytale set during the Great Depression.

By the late 1960s, enough time had passed for nostalgia to envelop the memories of the 1930s. The book's remaining films are drawn from a cross section of Depression-related topics addressed by Hollywood since that time.

They Shoot Horses, Don't They (1969) dramatizes the desperation of penniless Americans who earned money by participating in grueling, physically dangerous dance marathons. *Sounder* (1972) examines the poverty and injustice endured by Black sharecroppers in the South. *Paper Moon* (1973) is a touching drama-comedy about a conman and a young girl traveling the heartland during the Depression. *The Sting* (1973) is a period comedy about big-time con artists. *Chinatown* (1974) delves into the political and economic corruption endemic to Los Angeles in the 1930s. The era's political activism is represented in *Bound for Glory* (1976), a biographical picture on the emergence of folk singer Woody Guthrie. *The Lindbergh Kidnapping*

Case (1976) is unusual for its largely accurate, almost documentary dramatization of actual events.

The highwater mark for Hollywood productions with stories set during the Great Depression began in 1967 with *Bonnie and Clyde* (not examined in this book) and persisted through the mid-1970s. However, the Depression era has continued to inspire screenwriters and directors. *Kansas City* (1996) is set against racial and class divisions in a politically corrupt but musically rich city. *Cinderella Man* (2005) is based on the true story of a former contender forced back into the boxing ring to feed his family in the 1930s.

The Great Depression on Film seeks to sort facts from fiction in the 14 motion pictures it assesses. "Memory, as the ultimate in private property, is a vestige of a vanished century," wrote film essayist Geoffrey O'Brien. Especially since the advent of home video, "instead of memory, there is a culture of permanent playback" with the likelihood of fantasy eclipsing reality (O'Brien 1993, 218, 219). History matters and our understanding of the past is often based more on movies than documents or eyewitness accounts. The lessons of the Great Depression remain contentious and the reinvention of the past by agenda-driven actors in the present has often proven dangerous. Perhaps one of the moral imperatives of our time is the willingness to draw distinctions between things that are made up and things that are true.

FURTHER READING

Dickstein, Morris. 2009. *Dancing in the Dark: A Cultural History of the Great Depression*. New York: Oxford University Press.

O'Brien, Geoffrey. 1993. *The Phantom Empire*. New York: W.W. Norton.

Sarris, Andrew. 1998. *"You Ain't Heard Nothin' Yet: The American Talking Film History and Memory, 1927–1949*. New York: Oxford University Press.

Acknowledgments

Most of *The Great Depression on Film* was written during the COVID-19 pandemic, a time when libraries in my hometown were closed to the public (even as bars and liquor stores remained open). Given this lack of access to major libraries with significant holdings on film and American history, completion of the book would have been impossible without help. I would like to thank the librarians who went to work during the public health crisis, especially Bruce Cole of Marquette University's Raynor Memorial Libraries for his curbside delivery, handing books to me through the open passenger window of my car.

I must also extend appreciation to the anonymous workers at the Milwaukee Public Library's Central Library Ready Reference Desk. They took my check-out requests by phone, pulled the books from the stacks (including volumes in deep storage), and readied them for pick-up at the Central Library's drive-through window. At one point, COVID spread into the Central Library even though it was closed to the public, temporarily shuttering the drive-through service.

Appreciation also goes to Paul McComas for an enlightening and lively discussion of *The Grapes of Wrath* and Jamie Lee Rake for his thoughts on folk and country music for my chapter on *Bound for Glory*.

The Great Depression on Film is my fifth book for ABC-CLIO and my third in the publisher's Hollywood History series. I would like to express gratitude to the various editors and copyeditors I've had the pleasure to work with on Hollywood History including Kevin Downing, Robin Tutt, Patrick Hall, Michael Millman, Michelle Scott, Nicole Azze, and Kousalya Krishnamoorthy. My hope is that this interesting series will continue to explore how the past is remembered or misremembered on film.

Finally, I would like to thank Mary Manion for watching many of this book's films with me and reading my manuscript with a moviegoer's appreciation for cinematic storytelling and a copyeditor's eye for typos.

Introduction

For many who lived through those years, the Great Depression was the long hangover after the Roaring Twenties. The urban upper-middle class remembered the 1920s for "flappers," as women in scandalously short skirts were called, dancing to jazz bands and sharing the illicit thrill of alcohol with their partners. For them it was a party that ended in pain, but millions of Americans were never invited. Some historians have minimized the patchy distribution of privilege, such as conservative scholar Paul Johnson who held that during the 1920s "the USA enjoyed a general prosperity which was historically unique in its experience" with millions of Americans of the middle and working classes buying stock for the first time, confidently depositing their money in banks, and purchasing their first homes (Johnson 1991, 222).

He was correct in identifying a real estate boom that survives in the older neighborhoods of many cities as block after block of bungalows on narrow lots. Confidence in banks had grown but the notion that stock ownership was common is a legend with little support. Brokerage firms reported a total of 1,548,707 customers in 1929, representing around 2 percent of the population (Kennedy 1999, 41).

The standard of living varied greatly among the remaining 98 percent. The flow of immigrants had diminished to a trickle under the strict quotas mandated by the Immigration Act of 1924, but many first- and second-generation immigrants were "huddled on the margins of American life," making do with "low-skill jobs in heavy industry, the garment trades or construction" (Kennedy 1999, 15). By 1930, 45 percent of Americans still lived in rural settings. For many of them, their way of life was largely unchanged from peasant life at the dawn of civilization. Lacking electricity or indoor plumbing, they carried water from wells, chopped wood for heat and cooking, and went to sleep when night fell. When prices for crops plunged after World War I, farm debt and foreclosures increased through the 1920s and many freeholders became tenants.

The country's rural Black population endured life under the cruel feudalism of sharecropping. The Great Migration that began during World War I drew more than a million Black people from the South to industrial jobs in the North. Conditions remained impoverished for many. By 1930, Black infant mortality was nearly double that of whites and Black life expectancy was 15 years shorter than that of whites (Kennedy 1999, 19).

The automobile industry was a prominent engine of prosperity in the 1920s and had an enormous social impact. Mass-produced according to principles laid down by Henry Ford's inexpensive Model T, cars became a common sight on city streets and even on rural roads. Unable to afford them outright, most Americans purchased cars through loans. The availability of motor cars granted unprecedented freedom of movement to the working class and spurred the expansion of suburbs as farmlands gave way to homes.

The Prohibition of alcohol, imposed by the Eighteenth Amendment to the U.S. Constitution (1920), was roundly ignored by most Americans including politicians and police officers. Bribery was a source of income for many state and local officials and the fortunes made by bootleggers and rum runners solidified the grip of organized crime over wide sectors of American life. After Prohibition was repealed by the Twenty-First Amendment (1933), criminal syndicates invested their profits in gambling and prostitution. Many of the thousands of illegal Prohibition-era bars, called "speakeasies," provided venues for a new music that originated in New Orleans and traveled north along the riverboat and railroad lines. The Roaring Twenties was also known as the Jazz Age.

Not everyone was optimistic that economic growth would continue into the 1930s. Said to have had a hunch that bad times were ahead, the taciturn Calvin Coolidge (1872–1933) refused to seek another term of office and left the Republican nomination for the presidency in the 1928 election to his commerce secretary, Herbert Hoover (1874–1964) (Johnson 1991, 229). Hoover entered the race as one of America's most widely admired figures but ended his presidency as the country's most despised man. A self-made millionaire who earned his fortune working as an engineer for international mining concerns, Hoover rose to public prominence for organizing a non-governmental food program that kept the citizens of German-occupied Belgium from starving during World War I. His program continued to feed parts of Europe, including the famine zone of Soviet Russia, into the 1920s. After the Great Mississippi Flood (1927), Hoover forced the reluctant Coolidge to take federal initiatives to provide relief for millions of residents who had lost their homes. According to a recent biographer, "If Jimmy Carter was the twentieth century's most useful former president, Herbert Hoover was the most useful chief executive in the years before he became president" (Jeansonne 2012, 1).

The start date for the Great Depression is often given as October 24, 1929, called "Black Thursday," when the Wall Street market lost 11 percent of its value at the opening bell. The alarm caused major investors to prop up the market through stock purchases but on October 28, "Black Monday," the market slid again with a record loss of 12.82 percent. The downward trend was propelled by anxieties that included the September crash of the London Stock Exchange which weakened American optimism in overseas investments. The Wall Street market was already vulnerable to reckless and unregulated speculation involving margin trades on borrowed funds. Stocks were selling at prices that had no relation to the profitability of the companies they represented, much like the dot-com bubble of 2001 but with more disastrous results in a market that resembled an omnibus careening around curves without breaks.

Many underlying factors contributed to the instability. "The basic unsoundness of much of the foreign loan market was one of the principal elements in the collapse of confidence and the spread of the recession to Europe," as U.S. banks lent money to European governments to pay back war loans and reparations and gambled on investments in uncertain Latin American economies (Johnson 1991, 234).

Through much of the 20th century, Hoover continued to be misrepresented as inert in the face of crisis or as having taken steps that worsened the economy (Cantor 1997, 259). Hoover was falsely associated with the cold Darwinian view that only the fit should survive the economic collapse, a doctrine preached by his Treasury Secretary Andrew Mellon (1855–1937). Unlike some members of his own party, Hoover was no stranger to massive undertakings for the public good and believed that government sometimes must step in where private enterprise fears to go. In the initiatives Hoover launched to shore up the economy, the sketchy outline of his successor's New Deal can be discerned. "The package represented a major step in greater involvement in the economy by the federal government, a legislative program that dwarfed the domestic agenda of any previous administration" (Jeansonne 2012, 219).

At first his plans appeared to stop the descent. Hoover prodded corporate leaders not to cut wages, doubled federal public works expenditures, opened lines of credit, and received little criticism when, on May 1, 1930, he told the U.S. Chamber of Commerce, "I am convinced we have passed the worst and with continued effort we shall rapidly recover" (Hoover 1952, 58). Events overtook his optimism. Perhaps Hoover's greatest error was to sign a bill he opposed, the Smoot-Hawley Tariff Act (June 1930), which raised America's already steep tariffs. The new duties it imposed "were devastating blows struck at world commerce" (Johnson 1991, 232). By damaging many foreign economies, Smoot-Hawley further diminished finance and industry in the United States.

By the end of 1930, there were 26,355 businesses that had failed and gross national product fell 12.6 percent from the previous year. Production slumped in many industries. The November elections put control of the House of Representatives in Democratic hands and reduced Republican influence in the Senate. Congressional Democrats bore some responsibility for the ongoing economic decline in their eagerness to "obstruct the president and prepare to reap the political reward in the upcoming presidential election" (Kennedy 1999, 62). Their intransigence contributed to the mounting panic that overtook the banking system. By the end of 1930, there were 1,352 banks that had closed, 600 of them in the final 60 days of the year as mobs of depositors pushed against tellers' windows demanding their money (Kennedy 1999, 65). Banks responded by calling their loans, triggering bankruptcies of businesses and individuals.

Six million were unemployed when 1931 began and their number rose to ten million by January 1932, the start of the presidential election year. The ship of state was sinking despite Hoover's earnest efforts to bail it out with a too-small bucket. Hoover's cautiously innovative policies showed no apparent effect on the economic collapse and his starched-collar, aloof image inspired no confidence. The contrast between Hoover's public impression and that of his Democratic rival in the 1932 election is illustrated by how each of them accepted their party's nomination. Hoover followed tradition by not attending his party's convention and delivered his acceptance speech after it had ended. Franklin D. Roosevelt (1882–1945) broke with tradition by traveling by airplane to accept the Democratic nomination at the Chicago convention. "His nine-hour flight from Albany added urgency and a dash of modernity to his campaign for the White House" (Jeansonne and Luhrssen 2016, 271). In his acceptance speech before cheering delegates, Roosevelt said, "I pledge you, I pledge myself, to a new deal for the American people." It was one of Roosevelt's many well-turned phrases and gave name to the improvisations and achievements of his administration.

The patrician Roosevelt descended from New York's original Dutch settlers. Following the example of his cousin Theodore Roosevelt (1858–1919), he was elected to state offices in New York and became assistant secretary of the navy where he surprised colleagues with the shrewdness he concealed behind his mask of affability. He contracted polio in 1921, after which he could move only with the aid of heavy metal braces hidden under his clothing. His disability, "contrary to later impressions, was never a secret, but it was hardly advertised either" (Alter 2006, 52). In an era when being "crippled" usually meant exclusion from normal social life, Roosevelt's evident vitality caused his handicap to be largely overlooked. He "developed an almost professional acting ability" and "performed a casual verve and ingratiating laugh that left him at once accessible and out of reach" (Alter 2006, 53).

Roosevelt was not especially concerned with the lives of others before he was forced to cope with polio. The affliction brought out traits that proved essential in the 1932 presidential election and his multiple terms in the White House, especially his compassion and "implausible but invigorating hope, where the line between the realistic and the wishful almost didn't matter because he sold it to you either way" (Alter 2006, 65). Roosevelt became governor of New York in 1928, but the example of his cousin continued to guide his aspirations. He wanted to be president and the deepening economic crisis opened the door to the White House.

Chicago was an impoverished backdrop for the Democratic National Convention in June with nearly half its workforce unemployed. The city was bankrupt and its schoolteachers, who had gone unpaid in spring, resorted to loan sharks charging 40 percent interest (Alter 2006, 103). Roosevelt was not seen as the leading contender as the convention began and won the nomination only on the fourth ballot. Hoover remained confident after learning of the Democratic Party's choice, confiding to aides that Roosevelt's infirmity left him unfit to govern (Alter 2006, 120). However, the Great Depression continued as hundreds of thousands of homeless people gathered in shantytowns called "Hoovervilles." In July came another debacle when the "Bonus Army" of protesting World War I veterans and their families was cleared out of Washington, D.C. parks by General Douglas MacArthur using cavalry, tear gas, and tanks. MacArthur's assault violated Hoover's orders. No one was killed but the publicity for the administration was bad. One of the president's friends remarked that Hoover became "the greatest innocent bystander in history" (Wilson 1975, 163).

Roosevelt's campaign thrived on Hoover's failures. His endearing speeches brimmed with sunny personality but avoided specific solutions to the country's problems beyond his insistence, as he told the Commonwealth Club of San Francisco that "every man has a right to life; and this means that he has a right to make a comfortable living." Ironically, given the budget deficits of the New Deal, he criticized the penny-counting Hoover for "reckless and extravagant spending" (Alter 2006, 130). A song originally featured in the 1930 film *Chasing Rainbows*, "Happy Days Are Here Again," became the Roosevelt campaign's theme song.

In his speeches, Hoover counterintuitively insisted that economic recovery was underway. He was "by turns morose and manic," a hapless stump speaker from an earlier epoch. By contrast, Roosevelt's warm tone proved well-suited to the new medium of radio at a time when entire families gathered around their set for news and entertainment. On Election Day, November 8, Roosevelt carried 42 of the 48 states, taking 472 electoral votes to Hoover's 59 and winning 57.4 percent of the popular vote. The incumbent's defeat can be summed up by a telegram Hoover received before the election from a disgruntled citizen: "Vote for Roosevelt and make it unanimous" (Jeansonne and Luhrssen 2016, 285).

Roosevelt has been faulted for refusing to work with Hoover in the final months of the old administration. He "let the outgoing president hang himself—and the American economy—so that he could enter stage left as a hero." As president-elect he had no power, but "understood that the lower Hoover and the country slid, the better he would look upon assuming office" (Alter 2006, 139). Roosevelt told aides that the measures he would take were less important than restoring public confidence, but to help shape his agenda, he followed the example of cousin Theodore and assembled a "Brain Trust" of unofficial advisors. They included senators to point him through the thicket of Capitol Hill politics and respected academics. Columbia University economist Rexford Tugwell (1891–1979) advocated state planning in a "concert of interest" with government, labor, and business playing together.

Although Roosevelt would be denounced by the right wing as a dangerous leftist, perceptive analysts who grew up under his administration knew better. Columnist Max Lerner recalled that Roosevelt "deflected the potential energies of a sullen working population from more destructive revolutionary channels and became—like the New Deal—an essentially conservative force" (Lerner 1957, 324–325). During the Great Depression, membership in the Kremlin-directed American Communist Party peaked at two hundred thousand members. On the far right, organizations such as the Silver Shirts adapted fascism for American consumption. More dangerous were demagogues such as the populist, anti-Semitic "Radio Priest," Father Charles Coughlin (1891–1979), and Huey Long (1893–1935), an ambitious politician who ruled Louisiana like a dictator and had designs on the White House until his assassination cut short his career. Roosevelt had no firm ideological moorings but was determined to preserve the outlines of America's constitutional and economic system while broadening opportunities for many of the nation's citizens.

The radio audience for Roosevelt's inaugural address (March 4, 1933) numbered in the millions as Americans hung onto the words of their new leader. "This is a day of national consecration," he began, and continued in biblical cadences by condemning Wall Street traders as "money changers" who "have fled from their high seats in the temple of our civilization." He did not have a specific agenda to propose but insisted, "This nation is asking for action, and action now. We must act. We must act quickly." One phrase, inspired by Henry David Thoreau, resonated loudly in the coming months: "The only thing we have to fear is fear itself."

True to his word about acting quickly, Roosevelt wasted no time, pushing a series of bills through the Democratic-controlled Congress in a dizzying four-month period called "the Hundred Days." The new president "showed a joyous confidence in the task he had set himself." Unafraid to exercise his authority, he overcame the objections of moss-bound politicians because his measures "made sense in a time of chaos and gave some hope in a desperate era" (Lerner 1959, 407).

However, many of the measures taken were improvised and temporary; most of the New Deal's long-range changes to American life waited until the ship of state had steadied. Although banks in 34 states closed during the final weeks of his administration, Hoover had toyed with the idea of a national "moratorium" on banking. Roosevelt seized the idea but gave it a more cheerful name, calling it a "bank holiday." Roosevelt cut government spending in some areas during the Hundred Days, including salaries of himself and other politicians, but raised it in others to provide relief for the unemployed. Beer was legalized in March (complete repeal of Prohibition followed at year's end). Social critic Studs Terkel later recalled the moment he drank his first legal beer. "In the midst of the Depression it was a note of hope that something would get better" (Alter 2006, 277).

During the Hundred Days, Congress authorized spending on the construction of schools, dams, airports, and hospitals. Roosevelt established the Civilian Conservation Corps, which eventually employed three million young men in manual labor on flood control and other outdoor projects. The Tennessee Valley Authority was chartered to control flooding, build dams, and bring electricity to seven Southern states. Roosevelt took the dollar off the gold standard, but for the average American, the most enduring accomplishment of the Hundred Days was the Federal Deposit Insurance Corporation, which allowed the safe deposit of money by insuring bank deposits against loss.

Roosevelt was a master communicator, spreading his message of optimism through the newspapers and directly to the public via radio. The president usually gave two press conferences each week at the White House and made the Washington press corps feel like colleagues in a campaign to make America better. He set the ground rules and they were adhered to. Roosevelt's remarks at those conferences were never quoted, but their meaning was implied by the press coverage. Although he was unable to stand or walk without aid, the extent of his limitations went unmentioned, "which left the American people under the wrong impression that he had mostly conquered his disability" (Alter 2006, 256).

Roosevelt's mellifluous, crisply enunciated speech reached American ears directly through radio in a series of "Fireside Chats." In contrast to Hoover's dreary monotone, which made him sound like an unfriendly bank loan officer, Roosevelt came across as the benevolent aristocrat concerned for the well-being of his manor and the friendly headmaster who never talked down to his pupils. He timed every pause and inflection like an actor, a movie actor in close-up, not a stage actor or an old-fashioned political orator shouting to be heard in the last row. Like a Hollywood star, he projected warmth. His first Fireside Chat (March 12, 1933) explained how banking works and he assured listeners, "We have provided the machinery to restore our financial system." He added that the restoration of confidence was the shared responsibility of all Americans. "It is up to you to make it work. It is your problem no less than it is mine. Together we cannot fail."

The impact of his reassuring message was swift. The following day, long lines of Americans filed into bank lobbies to deposit the money they had hidden in sock drawers and under their beds. The New York Stock Exchange rose on the news.

At the end of the Hundred Days, Roosevelt signed the law establishing the National Relief Administration (NRA), one of the most prominent agencies of the New Deal. The NRA's blue-eagle symbol was seen everywhere from storefront windows to the credits of Hollywood films. Like many of Roosevelt's programs, it "was created virtually as an afterthought" (Kennedy 1999, 177). The NRA's agenda was defined largely by its colorful chief, Hugh S. Johnson, an army-general-turned-businessman who agreed with Tugwell's "concert of interest" and sought government-sponsored agreements to set production quotas, wages, and working conditions.

Johnson pointed to the textile industry where fierce competition triggered overproduction and price gauging, which led to lower wages and an impoverished workforce. Cotton mills were mostly situated in the South where entire families, including children as young as seven, toiled long hours. They "saw their lives go from unspeakably bad to unimaginatively worse as the Depression deepened." Wages fell and many workers were laid-off and turned out of their cheerless company town shanties (Kennedy 1999, 181). Johnson berated corporate leaders who tried to thwart his efforts. "Away slight men!" he shouted at a meeting of Atlanta businessmen. "You may have been Captains of Industry once, but you are Corporals of Disaster now" (Kennedy 1999, 182).

The NRA may have been a symbol of hope and recovery during its short run, but it faced evasion by industry, lack of enforcement powers, erratic leadership under Johnson, and legal challenges. It was ruled as an unconstitutional extension of federal and executive power by the U.S. Supreme Court in *Schechter Poultry Corp. vs. United States* (1935). However, its provisions on behalf of workers resurfaced in the National Labor Relations Act (1935), which solidified the role of organized labor in American life. The Supreme Court frustrated Roosevelt often with its conservative perspective on the role of government. He proposed a judicial reform allowing him to appoint one new justice for each sitting member who declined to retire at age seventy, but the plan was roundly condemned and never enacted.

Roosevelt was opposed to the creation of what would later be called the "welfare state," calling indefinite relief payments "fundamentally destructive to the national fibre." What he wanted instead was to establish federally funded jobs in useful occupations with the goal of eventually moving many of the people so employed into the private sector. One of the most innovative job programs, the Works Progress Administration (WPA), was formed in 1935. The WPA employed artists to teach their crafts in schools, paint murals in public buildings, and sculpt statues for public places. It sponsored orchestras and jazz combos, folk singers, and theater, including an all-Black production of *Macbeth*. The WPA also hired writers to produce guidebooks for cities and states across the United States. Many of those programs were abolished in 1939 under pressure from right-wing Congressmen who charged that they "spread pro-New Deal propaganda and that it scandalously encouraged black and white mixing in its stage productions" (Kennedy 1999, 255). Although cut short, the WPA set a precedent for federal funding of the arts.

Perhaps the most enduring and pervasive legacy of the New Deal was the Social Security Act (1935), which initiated America's first nationwide system of old-age pensions. Aside from military veterans and civil servants, few Americans enjoyed old-age insurance of any kind before Social Security. "Most elderly laborers worked until they dropped or were fired, then threw themselves either on the mercy of their families or on the decidedly less tender mercies of a local welfare agency" (Kennedy 1999, 261). Given the Supreme Court's hostility to ambitious New Deal programs, and the disinclination of many Southern Congressmen toward anything that suggested welfare, Roosevelt worried that any bill to provide for the elderly would be tabled in the Senate or struck down by the Court. He devised the method still employed today by which employees contribute to their own insurance through payroll deductions. Nevertheless, the president's original vision of covering all Americans was compromised in the early years by provisions that excluded farmer laborers, domestic servants, and employees of small businesses from Social Security benefits. Roosevelt originally intended to include health care for the elderly but, being politically untenable in 1935, the health of seniors would wait until the passage of Medicare in 1966. As Roosevelt's labor secretary Frances Perkins (1880–1965) recalled, the original Social Security Act was "the only plan we could have put through Congress" (Perkins 1946, 284).

As America's first female cabinet secretary, Perkins had to endure the dismay of some of her male colleagues but not of Roosevelt, who accommodated himself to the first wave of feminism, flush with its recent success in gaining women's suffrage. A graduate of the exclusive Mount Holyoke women's college, Perkins was an activist with progressive views who encouraged Roosevelt to weave a social safety net that would outlast the Great Depression. Her cabinet appointment was recommended by the president's wife, Eleanor Roosevelt (1884–1962), whose role as First Lady went beyond the hostess responsibilities of her predecessors. Eleanor came from the same social background as her husband; she was the niece of his cousin Theodore, who gave her away at their wedding. Eleanor was the first First Lady to hold press conferences and became a member of the press as a syndicated columnist known for promoting social reform. She advocated legal equality for Black Americans, but while her husband enjoyed watching her put burrs under the saddles of conservative Southern Democrats, he needed their support in Congress to pass legislation. Roosevelt enrolled Blacks in the Civilian Conservation Corps but kept them in segregated barracks. He never vigorously pursued federal antilynching legislation or challenged Jim Crow.

Roosevelt was raised with the widely held idea that America was a white Anglo-Saxon Protestant nation. However, from early in his political career, Roosevelt worked with Roman Catholics who were part of the Democratic coalition in Northern cities and grew more sympathetic to the perspectives of others as his career progressed. As president, he appointed more Roman Catholics to the federal bench than his Republican predecessors. Although anti-Semitism was almost inevitable in early-20th-century America, Roosevelt appointed Henry Morgenthau (1891–1967) as treasury secretary, only the second Jewish cabinet member in U.S. history, and Felix Frankfurter (1882–1965) to the Supreme Court, the third Jew to serve on America's highest bench. With barely any public enthusiasm outside the Jewish community to open America to refugees from Hitler's Germany, Roosevelt did little in response to the persecution but prioritized opposition to Hitler and fought against America's tendency toward isolationism and xenophobia, represented by the powerful America First Committee headed by Colonel Charles Lindbergh (1902–1974).

Roosevelt initiated an "Indian New Deal," appointing the reform-minded John Collier (1884–1968) as commissioner of Indian affairs. Collier sought to document and preserve Native languages and culture and was opposed to policies of total assimilation. Under the Indian Reorganization Act (1934), schools were established on reservations and elected councils gave tribes a democratic form of self-government. On immigration, Roosevelt's hands were tied by the racist Immigration Act (1924) restricting the flow of immigrants from beyond Northern Europe. On the southern border, many Mexican migrants returned home voluntarily during the work slowdowns of the Great Depression but others were packed into box cars by immigration agents and sent south.

In 1936, Roosevelt easily defeated his Republican challenger, Kansas governor Alf Landon (1887–1987), by inspiring a large turnout on Election Day. "In the immigrant wards of the great industrial cities, where many people had never bothered to cast a vote before the Depression," voters turned out for Roosevelt whose success "flowed from his rhetorical blasts at the right and from gratitude for unemployment relief and the prospective benefits of Social Security." Union members turned out in support of the New Deal and "where they could vote, African-Americans, too, registered their political gratitude not only for WPA jobs but for the highly publicized solicitude of Eleanor Roosevelt" (Kennedy 1999, 285).

The 25 percent unemployment of 1933 was cut to 14.3 percent in May 1937 and production, profits, and wages regained their late-1920s levels.

The progress was reversed by the onset of a recession within the Great Depression. Profits fell, work slowed, and unemployment jumped to 19 percent. The recession was triggered by tax hikes and spending cuts in an effort to balance the federal budget. By the fall of 1938, Roosevelt changed course and injected billions more dollars into the economy. The Great Depression continued but employment and productivity returned to their early 1937 numbers.

According to some historians, the New Deal "petered out" before Roosevelt's 1939 State of the Union address, in which the president proposed no new social or economic programs but insisted only on maintaining the reforms of the previous five-and-a-half years (Kennedy 1999, 363). Increasingly preoccupied by foreign affairs, Roosevelt called out the threat posed by aggressor nations in Europe and Asia. He was hampered by the Neutrality Acts (1935, 1937) that limited his ability to support nations threatened by war but worked to ease restrictions on arms sales and began providing support to Great Britain in March 1941 under the Lend-Lease Act. The 1940 election, with Roosevelt breaking tradition by seeking a third term, was fought over foreign policy. Republican contender Wendell Wilkie (1892–1944) argued against American involvement in another European war but poll numbers indicated that the majority of Americans already believed that war was inevitable and preferred the reliable voice of Roosevelt in a time of crisis.

Although the benefits were distributed unevenly, most Americans were uplifted or at least sustained by the New Deal. Roosevelt's first two terms were the most crowded period of institutional change in the United States until the Great Society of the 1960s. Many of America's wealthiest citizens complained angrily about his "socialist" policies despite Roosevelt's success in upholding the fundamentals of an economic system from which they continued to benefit. The upper class wasn't diminished by the New Deal, but Roosevelt's support for organized labor and Social Security enlarged the middle class even if it failed to end the Great Depression. The economic crisis that began in 1929 concluded only in the aftermath of the Japanese attack on Pearl Harbor (December 7, 1941). Pulled into a world war with Japan and its German and Italian allies, America finally shook off the Great Depression through the total mobilization of its economy and people by a massive infusion of federal money.

FURTHER READING

Alter, Jonathan. 2006. *The Defining Moment: FDR's Hundred Days and the Triumph of Hope.* New York: Simon & Schuster.

Cantor, Norman F. 1997. *The American Century: Varieties of Culture in Modern Times.* New York: HarperCollins.

Hoover, Herbert. 1952. *The Memoirs of Herbert Hoover: The Great Depression, 1929–1941.* New York: Macmillan.

Jeansonne, Glen. 2012. *The Life of Herbert Hoover: Fighting Quaker 1928–1933*. New York: Palgrave Macmillan.
Jeansonne, Glen, with David Luhrssen. 2016. *Herbert Hoover: A Biography*. New York: New American Library.
Johnson, Paul. 1991. *Modern Times: From the Twenties to the Nineties*. New York: HarperCollins.
Kennedy, David M. 1999. *Freedom from Fear: The American People in Depression and War, 1929–1945*. New York: Oxford University Press.
Lerner, Max. 1957. *America as a Civilization: Life and Thought in the United States Today*. New York: Simon & Schuster.
Lerner, Max. 1959. *The Unfinished Country: A Book of American Symbols*. New York: Simon & Schuster.
Perkins, Frances. 1946. *The Roosevelt I Knew*. New York: Viking.
Wilson, Joan. 1975. *Herbert Hoover: Forgotten Progressive*. Boston: Little, Brown.

Chronology

October 24, 1929	On Black Thursday, billions of dollars are lost in Wall Street trading, ruining many investors.
October 28, 1929	On Black Monday, steep declines in stock market continue.
June 17, 1930	President Herbert Hoover signs Smoot-Hawley Tariff Act, worsening the world economic crisis by imposing high duties on imported raw materials.
May 1, 1931	World's tallest building, the Empire State Building, opens in New York.
February 2, 1932	Reconstruction Finance Corporation is established to release frozen assets of failing financial institutions.
March 1, 1932	The kidnapping of the infant son of Charles Lindbergh became one of the year's top news stories.
June 17, 1932	Bonus Army, made up of veterans, protests outside the Capitol.
July 28, 1932	U.S. troops drive the Bonus Army out of Washington.
November 8, 1932	Franklin D. Roosevelt defeats Hoover and is elected president.
January 30, 1933	Adolf Hitler is appointed chancellor of Germany.

February 14, 1933	All banks in Michigan are ordered closed as crisis mounts.
March 2, 1933	*King Kong* premieres in New York.
March 4, 1933	Roosevelt is inaugurated as president.
March 6, 1933	Roosevelt closes banks for four days and bans export of gold.
March 9, 1933	Congress approves Roosevelt's actions and authorizes federal takeover of insolvent banks.
March 12, 1933	Roosevelt gives his first "Fireside Chat" on coast-to-coast radio broadcast.
March 15, 1933	Economy Act cuts government salaries.
March 31, 1933	*Gabriel over the White House* is released to cinemas.
April 5, 1933	Civilian Conservation Corps is established to provide work for unemployed men.
May 12, 1933	Agricultural Adjustment Act allows federal government to purchase livestock and pay farmers for not planting crops.
May 18, 1933	Tennessee Valley Authority Act is created to provide electric power and flood control in seven Southern states.
May 27, 1933	Securities Act imposes federal regulation on the stock market.
June 16, 1933	Farm Credit Act authorizes Farm Credit Administration to centralize all agricultural credit.
June 16, 1933	Federal Deposit Insurance Corporation is established to guarantee bank deposits.
June 16, 1933	Glass-Steagall Act separates commercial banking from investment banking.
June 20, 1933	National Recovery Administration is established to set prices, wages, and fair practices.
December 5, 1933	Ratification of the Twenty-First Amendment repealing the Eighteenth (Prohibition) Amendment.
January 31, 1934	Farm Mortgage Refinancing Act is approved to help refinance farm debt.

February 23, 1934	Crop Loan Act permits federal loans to farmers for harvesting crops.
April 21, 1934	Cotton Control Act implements cotton production quotas.
May 9, 1934	Jones-Costigan Sugar Act supports sugar beet and sugarcane harvests.
June 13, 1934	Production Code Administration is established to enforce censorship of Hollywood films.
June 28, 1934	Frazier-Lemke Farm Bankruptcy Act facilitates agreements between farmers and creditors.
June 28, 1934	Tobacco Control Act implements tobacco production quotas.
February 13, 1935	Accused Lindbergh kidnapper is convicted and sentenced to death.
May 6, 1935	Works Progress Administration is created to provide employment in public works projects.
May 27, 1935	National Recovery Administration is declared unconstitutional by U.S. Supreme Court.
June 19, 1935	Federal Communications Commission is established to regulate interstate telegraph, telephone, cable, and radio.
July 6, 1935	National Labor Relations Act solidifies the role of organized labor in American economic life.
August 9, 1935	Motor Carrier Act places interstate bus and truck lines under federal regulation.
August 14, 1935	Social Security Act provides support for the elderly.
August 26, 1935	Public Utility Holding Company Act imposes federal regulations on electric companies.
August 31, 1935	Neutrality Act imposes arms embargo on all nations at war.
September 10, 1935	U.S. senator Huey Long is assassinated in Louisiana.
September 30, 1935	*Porgy and Bess* debuts in Boston.
November 23, 1935	Robert Johnson records classic blues songs in San Antonio.

January 6, 1936	U.S. Supreme Court declares Agricultural Adjustment Act unconstitutional.
March 1, 1936	Boulder Dam (later renamed the Hoover Dam) is dedicated by Roosevelt.
April 14, 1936	Orson Welles stages an all-Black production of *Macbeth*.
August 30, 1936	Wealth Tax Act increases taxes on high incomes to diminish the "unjust concentration of wealth and economic power."
September 6, 1936	*My Man Godfrey* opens in cinemas.
November 3, 1936	Roosevelt defeats GOP candidate Alfred M. Landon in the presidential election.
January 17, 1937	*Black Legion* opens in cinemas.
January 20, 1937	Roosevelt is inaugurated for a second term as president.
February 5, 1937	Roosevelt suggests "packing" federal courts with new appointees. Congress eventually denies approval of the idea.
April 26, 1937	Guffey-Vinson Act brings federal regulation to the coal market.
May 6, 1937	German airship Hindenburg explodes while landing in New Jersey.
May 27, 1937	Golden Gate Bridge opens to traffic.
July 2, 1937	Aviator Amelia Earhart disappears while on a flight across the Pacific Ocean.
September 2, 1937	Wagner-Steagall Act provides federal funds to help the housing shortage.
October 24, 1938	Wages and Hours Act sets minimum wages and maximum hours for industries engaged in interstate commerce.
October 30, 1938	Orson Welles' broadcast of "War of the Worlds" startles radio listeners with its realism.
December 23, 1938	Spirituals to Swing concert brings vernacular American music to Carnegie Hall.

April 14, 1939	John Steinbeck's novel *The Grapes of Wrath* is published.
April 20, 1939	Billie Holiday records anti-lynching song "Strange Fruit."
April 30, 1939	Roosevelt becomes the first president to speak on the new medium of television.
April 30, 1939	World's Fair opens in Queens, New York.
August 25, 1939	*The Wizard of Oz* opens in cinemas.
September 1, 1939	World War II begins in Europe with Germany's invasion of Poland.
September 5, 1939	United States proclaims neutrality after World War II begins in Europe.
December 15, 1939	*Gone with the Wind* premieres in Atlanta.
January 20, 1940	Roosevelt is inaugurated for his third term as president.
January 24, 1940	*The Grapes of Wrath* opens in cinemas.
February 27, 1940	Japan signs defense pact with Germany and Italy.
May 9, 1940	Winston Churchill becomes Great Britain's prime minister.
June 22, 1940	France signs armistice with Nazi Germany.
September 4, 1940	America First Committee founded to keep the United States out of World War II.
September 16, 1940	First peacetime draft in U.S. history is established.
October 27, 1940	New York World's Fair closes.
November 5, 1940	Roosevelt elected to an unprecedented third term as president.
December 29, 1940	Roosevelt proclaims the United States as "the Arsenal of Democracy."
March 11, 1941	Lend-Lease Act allows Roosevelt to send aid to the Allies.
May 27, 1941	Roosevelt declares a State of Emergency in response to the Nazi threat.

July 8, 1941	U.S. forces occupy Iceland to deny its use by Nazis as a base.
July 26, 1941	Roosevelt freezes Japanese assets in the United States.
August 1, 1941	Roosevelt declares an oil embargo against Japan.
October 31, 1941	U.S. destroyer Reuben James is sunk by U-boat.
December 7, 1941	Japanese bomb Pearl Harbor and the United States enters World War II.

Chapter 1

Gabriel over the White House (1933)

Gabriel over the White House was released by Metro-Goldwyn-Mayer Studios (MGM) on March 31, 1933, just 27 days after the inauguration of Franklin D. Roosevelt (1882–1945) as president of the United States. The film was produced with the intention of encouraging Roosevelt to assume dictatorial powers to manage the Great Depression and other social problems. The film was produced by Walter Wanger (1894–1968), newly hired at MGM but a long-time associate of the man who pushed for the film's production, William Randolph Hearst (1863–1951). A media giant who owned a chain of newspapers and a fleet of magazines, Hearst also held a stake in MGM and exerted influence over the movie industry through his powerful gossip columnists and much-read film reviewers. *Gabriel over the White House*'s director, Gregory La Cava (1892–1952), had worked for Hearst's International Film Service, transforming editorial cartoons into animated-short subjects before establishing himself as a successful silent movie director (Pizzitola 2002, 122).

Gabriel over the White House was adapted from a novel that had been published early in 1933 and written by "Anonymous." The author was actually Thomas Frederick Tweed (1891–1940), chief of staff for British prime minister David Lloyd George (1863–1945). Lloyd George wrote opinion pieces for the Hearst syndicate and was on friendly terms with the media mogul. The British statesman may have alerted Hearst to the novel before its publication, enabling him to purchase film rights for a story that promised to be a hot topic (Pizzitola 2002, 294). Because of its timeliness, the project was fast-tracked at MGM and produced in under two weeks at the behest of Hearst, who took a hand in shaping the screenplay and sent it to the president elect for his comments (Alter 2006, 184). "Roosevelt liked the movie script so much that he found time to put some finishing touches on it," including changing one setting from a battleship to a yacht and another from Washington, D.C. to Baltimore. He also cut a scene in which an assassin tries to take the president's life (Alter 2006, 185).

The film retained the novel's narrative structure but underwent many changes in the course of its production. The novel was set in the future but screenwriter Carey Wilson (1889–1962) moved it to the present and added several scenes, including a dramatic car crash. Hearst added material on social programs that echoed editorials from his newspaper. The censors from the Hays Office, responsible for maintaining standards in Hollywood movies, insisted on watering down criticism of Congress and foreign governments and toning down the threat of revolution (Bernstein 1994, 83–84). Another major change involved deleting a character called Peale Lindsey. In the novel, Lindsey owns newspapers, a public relations firm, and a Hollywood studio and becomes the new president's propaganda chief. Hearst may have found the depiction too close to the role he hoped to play in the Roosevelt administration (Pizzitola 2002, 298–299).

Gabriel over the White House stars Walter Huston (1884–1950)—acclaimed for his lead role in the 1930 film *Abraham Lincoln*—as the newly elected president, Judd Hammond. As carelessly corrupt as Warren G. Harding (1865–1923), Hammond is also as hapless in the face of the Great Depression as Herbert Hoover (1874–1964). The new president is a bachelor who appoints his mistress, Pendie Molloy (Karen Morley, 1909–2003), as assistant to his private secretary, Harley Beekman (Franchot Tone, 1905–1968). His reckless disregard is evident as he tops 98 mph in his motorcar, racing ahead of his escort. When one of his tires is punctured, Hammond careens off the road. The concussion to his brain leaves him in a coma with physicians privately confessing that he's "beyond any human help." His advisors remain silent about his condition, which 1933 audiences recognized as a comment on how the public was kept in the dark about Woodrow Wilson (1856–1924) after he suffered a stroke.

As curtains stir from unseen hands and celestial trumpets intone, a miracle occurs. Hammond is on his feet again, physically fit but, as one of his advisors says, "he's not the John Hammond we once knew." He acts as if possessed, his personality displaced by a higher power.

Hammond suddenly takes interest in a growing protest movement he had previously ignored—the Army of the Unemployed, camping in public parks and marching toward Washington. Organizer John Bronson (David Landau, 1879–1935) is a man of integrity who refuses to cut a deal with the crime kingpin Nick Diamond (C. Henry Gordon, 1883–1940), even when the mobster promises to feed the unemployed. Bronson pays for his honesty with his life at the hands of Diamond's hitmen. Hammond steps in, meeting the Army of the Unemployed and Bronson's daughter, Alice (Jean Parker, 1915–2005), in a public park. He pledges to organize an Army of Construction to provide the unemployed with public works jobs.

In his next move, Hammond addresses a joint session of Congress demanding that they adjourn after approving a massive appropriation of money to "restore prosperity" along with a declaration of national emergency. When Congress balks, he declares martial law and seizes power. Speaking to the nation by radio, he lays out a reasonable agenda that includes forbidding foreclosures, federal insurance for bank deposits, aid to farmers, and repeal of the Eighteenth (Prohibition) Amendment.

Hammond proclaims a federal monopoly on the distribution of alcoholic beverages, and when his government liquor stores are attacked by Diamond's gangsters, the president hits back. His newly established, militarized Federal Police launch an assault on the mob. Diamond and his associates are brought before a military court and swiftly sentenced to die. The execution by firing squad is carried out with the Statue of Liberty looming in the background.

With his domestic agenda achieved, Hammond moves onto the international front. He gathers foreign diplomats on his yacht and demands that their nations pay their debts to the United States instead of spending money on an arms race. To display American resolve, he orders his aircraft to sink a pair of battleships in a demonstration modelled after the 1921 bombing run conducted on naval targets by Brigadier General Billy Mitchell (1879–1936). Hammond tells his startled guests that in the next war, armies and navies will be destroyed from the air "with inconceivably deadly explosives." Afterward, as world leaders assemble at the White House to sign the "Washington Covenant" to reduce armaments, he collapses and dies. His mission has been accomplished.

At the time of its release, critics on the left identified *Gabriel over the White House* as an effort "to convert innocent American movie audiences to a policy of Fascist dictatorship in this country" (Birdwell 2000, 15). The *New York Times* spoke for the mainstream in calling it "a curious, somewhat fantastic and often melodramatic story" about a "conscientious President, who tackles the problems of unemployment, crime and the foreign debts something after the fashion of a Lincoln" (Hall 1934). In *Hearst Over Hollywood: Power, Passion, and Propaganda in the Movies*, Louis Pizzitola relates, "Reviewers at the time called *Gabriel* the first important political film of the sound era and hailed it as the first Hollywood production to acknowledge the Depression openly" (2002, 293).

Although it did well at box offices and turned a profit of $200,000 for MGM, *Gabriel over the White House* was quickly forgotten, overtaken not only by the rush of events but the development of new genres and technology in Hollywood. In recent years, the film has been rediscovered and reevaluated in light of America's reaction to 9/11, the Great Recession, and the election of Donald Trump. Writing in the *New Yorker*, film critic Richard Brody called it "visionary," "extraordinary," and a "chilling topical drama," comparing Hammond's climactic speech to Charlie Chaplin's Hitlerian oration in *The Great Dictator* (1940). He added that it would be hard "to imagine any modern-day liberal exulting" in the film's message, which reflected "the incommensurable depth of the crisis faced in the Depression" (Brody 2013). More recently, Emmy Award-winning television journalist Jeff Greenfield wrote that *Gabriel over the White House* shows how "the impulse toward strongman rule is fed, more often than not, by a legitimate sense of grievance against the 'powers that be'" and "offers us significant insights into what tempts countries to travel down an authoritarian road" (Greenfield 2018).

HISTORICAL BACKGROUND

As the 1930s began, there were many reasons to believe that the world was heading into an age of dictators, not democracy. Economic woes and the bitterness of nations defeated in World War I or disadvantaged at the peace table encouraged authoritarianism in many nations. The concentration of power in the hands of industrialists and financiers bred resentment, especially during the economic downturn, and a willingness to turn toward new systems that promised to uplift the masses.

Many Americans from all walks of life and political persuasions, as they considered the future in the shadow of the Great Depression, were moved to ponder dictatorial alternatives to political gridlock. The status quo appeared to have failed, the can-do optimism of Wall Street and Main Street had a hollow ring as families faced eviction and the homeless gathered in Hoovervilles. The unregulated speculation of 1920s capitalism had driven the lives of millions into the abyss and great fortunes had evaporated like frost in the light of day.

Americans were not alone in their dismay at politics as usual. Parallel to the 1932 American presidential election was the rise of the German National Socialist (Nazi) Party. The once-marginal group took 37.2 percent of the vote in Germany's parliamentary election that year. Roosevelt's inauguration in 1933 coincided with Hitler's appointment as chancellor, but at that moment, no one, not even the conservatives who lifted him into power, imagined what was to come in Germany. As Roosevelt prepared to take office, Hitler was irrelevant. Two long-running dictatorships served as the models in the United States and across the world, the Soviet Union under Josef Stalin (1878–1953) and Fascist Italy under Benito Mussolini (1883–1945).

As historian Paul Johnson aptly observed, the founders of the Bolshevik and Fascist parties, Vladimir Lenin (1870–1924) and Benito Mussolini

HERBERT HOOVER (1874–1964)

Herbert Hoover began his political career as one of America's most respected leaders and ended it, with his defeat in the 1932 presidential election, as the country's most unpopular public servant.

Hoover was a millionaire, an engineer by training who earned his fortune running mining operations in Australia, China, and Russia for a British corporation. He gained renown as "the Great Humanitarian" during World War I by establishing an organization to feed the starving Belgians under German occupation. When the United States entered the war in 1917, he became food administrator under Woodrow Wilson. Through conservation, victory gardens, and massive mobilization of the country's agriculture, Hoover fed the Allies and, after the war, much of Europe and the Soviet Union.

In 1920, Hoover became commerce secretary and did outstanding work providing relief for victims of the catastrophic 1927 Mississippi flood. As the Republican candidate for president, he easily won the 1928 election at a time of prosperity and faith in Wall Street.

His popularity and reputation fell after the 1929 stock market crash. Although he instituted measures that foresaw aspects of the New Deal, he was unable to halt the rapid economic decline that came with the onset of the Great Depression. Unlike his opponent in the 1932 election, Franklin D. Roosevelt, he was unable to project optimism and confidence. Hoover lost the election in a landslide but survived as an elder statesman of American conservatism.

(1883–1945), were both "Marxist heretics and violent revolutionary activists" (Johnson 1991, 58). While Bolshevik Communism and Fascism became mortal enemies by the 1920s, in the years before World War I Lenin praised Mussolini's decisive actions within Italy's far left on the pages of *Pravda* (Johnson 1991, 57). Lenin's heresies included the speed at which he endeavored to transform Russia and the world into a Communist utopia rather than allow the inevitable to unfold under Marx's "laws of history." In Marx's view, Russia was highly unsuitable for the development of Communism and he might have blanched at the wholesale murderousness of Lenin's regime. Marx would have had an even harder time recognizing his ideas in the Mussolini who emerged after World War I as a fervent Italian nationalist but one who never entirely lost sight of his original vision of building a new society. If Mussolini had remained in the Marxist camp, his grandiose ego would have made him an impossible underling in the international Communist movement radiating out of Moscow. He would have gone his own way.

Nowadays Fascist Italy may seem an unlikely model for the nations of the world, especially in light of Mussolini's later reputation as Hitler's clown-sidekick. However, il Duce, as he liked to be called, was der Fuhrer's role model and was taken seriously as a world leader until his megalomania and growing desire to keep up with Hitler led him to disaster. "From the end of 1922 to the mid-1930s, he appeared to everyone as a formidable piece on the European chessboard" (Johnson 1991, 100). He was legendary for "making the trains run on time" but could claim many other accomplishments including draining Italy's malarial swamps in massive public works projects. Government direction of industry fostered developments in many sectors, including an aviation industry that was the envy of the world. After one of his top advisors, Aviation Minister Italo Balbo (1896–1940), flew a squadron from Rome to Chicago's Century of Progress world's fair in 1933, Roosevelt invited him to lunch at the White House (Alter 2006, 186). Along with improvements in postal and phone services, Mussolini encouraged social and recreational benefits including summer camps for urban children, greater access to performing arts, and the construction of Europe's largest film studio. His much-publicized crusade against the mafia failed to destroy organized crime but resulted in thousands of arrests and drove the criminal enterprise underground (Gilmour 2011, 307, 317).

Mussolini employed brutality in his ascent but once ensconced in power, his persecution of political dissidents usually involved internal exile rather than death or prison. He delivered on some of his promises to modernize Italy with vigorous, dramatic flair, and yet was a politician willing to compromise with existing institutions. He preserved the monarchy and established good relations between the Italian government and the previously hostile Roman Catholic Church. "Mussolini's way of dealing with this problem [of apparent contradictions] was to insist that fascism was both modern and traditional, conservative and revolutionary, a movement that drew from the past yet looked to the future" (Gilmour 2011, 304).

For anyone outside of Italy imagining how their own country's moribund system could be shaken but not destroyed, Mussolini seemed to provide an example. Winston Churchill hailed him as "the greatest living legislator" (Payne 1995, 218). The respected American journalist Lowell Thomas narrated a 1933 documentary newsreel, *Mussolini Speaks*, whose advertisement claimed that the dictator's approach "might be the answer to America's needs" (Alter 2006, 186).

Mussolini was even celebrated on Broadway in the original 1934 version of Cole Porter's hit "You're the Top," which contained the couplet:

You're the top!
You are Mussolini! (Payne 1995, 218)

Aside from his carefully sculpted image of virile competence and a portfolio of actual accomplishments, Mussolini offered an economic model for other countries. His "corporatism" descended from his years at the cutting edge of the far left, where he encountered anarcho-syndicalists who theorized about social organization once the state had been destroyed. In the version he implemented in 1930, a network of syndicates represented management and labor from an array of professional and economic groups; their representatives met with government and party leaders in a corporate assembly to implement economic plans and workplace initiatives (Payne 1995, 213).

The tension between the employers and the employees, the conservative necessities of Mussolini's regime and its revolutionary tendencies, was never resolved. Nevertheless, versions of corporatism were officially adapted by several nations, including the Spain of Francisco Franco (1892–1975), Portugal under António de Oliveira Salazar (1889–1970), and Brazil during the Estado Novo period (1937–1945). Some of Roosevelt's New Deal advisors travelled on a parallel train of thought, leading to the establishment of the National Recovery Administration (NRA).

Mussolini's reputation fell as a result of his belligerent foreign policy, beginning with Italy's invasion of Ethiopia (1935) and his increasing dependence on Adolf Hitler, which led to his adaptation of anti-Semitic and other policies resembling the Nazi regime.

On the other hand, Josef Stalin (1878–1953) was able to maintain a favorable reputation among influential elements in the West until after World War II. With the death of Lenin in 1924, he inherited the Soviet regime that had clamped its hold across most of the former Russian Empire by the early 1920s. Even before Stalin, the Soviet Union was a brutal police state that imposed its will on a reluctant citizenry through a network of informers and military power. After the withdrawal of the American, European, and Japanese forces that had haphazardly intervened against the Bolsheviks in the Russian Civil War (1917–1922), the commercial opportunities in the enormous Soviet market overwhelmed Western objections to dealing with the Communist state. Even before Lenin's death, Great Britain signed a trade pact with the Soviets and some American business interests urged the United States to normalize relations with the Union of Soviet Socialist Republics (USSR). As secretary of commerce in the 1920s, Herbert Hoover "reasoned that the Bolsheviks could not be trusted" but welcomed news "that American businesses were signing independent deals with the Soviet government" at their own risk (Service 2012, 319).

The Soviets proved masterful at manipulation, and in the tradition of the Potemkin villages—the nonexistent towns established in the 18th century to promote the appearance of progress—they conducted foreign visitors through model projects and false fronts whose favorable impression was out of sync with reality. As early as 1921, U.S. senator Joseph I. France (1873–1939) returned from Moscow praising Soviet leaders as "statesmanlike" and calling for an alliance with Lenin. The senator may have been a fool, but he was encouraged by duplicitous supporters of the Soviet system in high places. Most notable was Armand Hammer (1898–1990) of Allied Drug and Chemical Corporation who signed a deal in 1921 for an asbestos concession in Russia. Hammer made a fortune from his commercial relations with the Soviets while also "carrying out secret political errands for the Kremlin and virtually becoming its intelligence agent" (Service 2012, 322–323). Hammer's success in the Soviet Union convinced businessmen and others that the USSR was governed by reasonable men.

Although the famine and utter economic ruin throughout the former Russian Empire forced Lenin to make pragmatic decisions that permitted a measure of free enterprise and small land ownership, his successor, Stalin, forcefully reversed course. His policy of centralized state control over all aspects of economic life was implemented by a series of Five-Year Plans, the first one covering 1928–1932. State regulation of planning was extended over every aspect of industrial production and distribution; agriculture was "collectivized" into vast government-run farms. Stalin was impatient for massive growth in the production of oil, coal, finished goods, and grain and eventually demanded that the first Five-Year Plan be completed three years early. His bureaucracy manufactured impressively rising statistics to overcome any doubt of his success. To many outside observers, Stalin's program of rapid industrialization and mammoth public works represented the transformation of a backward land into a modern state through the rational if forceful application of sound principles.

The reality was far less favorable than the glowing reports flowing from the Kremlin. Hundreds of thousands of small landowning peasants were expelled from their property and deported to Siberia. Many died en route or were brutally crushed in uprisings. The resulting destruction of agriculture resulted in widespread starvation. Estimates for the number of deaths resulting from the first Five-Year Plan run as high as 15.2 million (Heller and Nekrich 1986, 222–242). In Ukraine, the famine took on genocidal dimensions as Stalin's confiscatory policies seemed to deliberately punish a population with national aspirations. The Holodomor, as Ukrainians call the catastrophe, took 3.9 million lives.

While America's press barons were resolutely anti-Communist, the Soviet regime's careful monitoring of the Moscow press corps, augmented by favorable stories by foreign visitors on chaperoned tours, helped to not only muffle the agony of Stalin's brutality and failure but also to present it as a shining model for emulation. "Why should the Russians have all the fun of remaking a world?" economist Stuart Chase asked in his book, *A New Deal*, whose title Roosevelt borrowed for his program of reform (Chase 1932, 252). Favorable appraisals of Stalin's Five-Year Plan resulted in a spate of books published in 1932, including Joseph Freeman's *The Soviet Worker*, Waldo Frank's *Dawn in Russia*, William Z. Foster's *Towards Soviet America*, Kirby Page's *A New Economic Order*, Harry Laidler's *Socialist Planning*, and Sherwood Eddy's *Russia Today: What We Can Learn from It?* Even humorist Will Rogers joined the chorus, remarking about America's high unemployment rate, "Those rascals in Russia, along with their cuckoo stuff have got some mighty good ideas . . . Just think of everybody in a country going to work" (Johnson 1991, 260).

The outstanding figure in misrepresenting the Soviet Union to the outside world was British writer Walter Duranty (1884–1957), whose reporting from Moscow for the *New York Times* won a Pulitzer Prize in 1932. Among other falsehoods, Duranty claimed there was no famine in Ukraine, admitting only to sporadic hunger, and lavished the Soviet leader with praise. "Stalin didn't look upon himself as a dictator but as a 'guardian of a sacred flame' that he called Stalinism for lack of a better name," he insisted (Duranty 1934, 238).

In a childhood story recounted by the Cambridge-educated writer, Duranty's strict Presbyterian grandmother held his finger to a hot fire grate after catching him in a lie and told him, "Liars go to hell and in hell it burns like this forever" (Duranty 1935, 11). The incident set Duranty against Christendom and may have inspired him to embrace lies as a pathway to higher forms of truth. Duranty's early life gives no indication of any sympathy for the materialist philosophy at the bottom of Bolshevism. He was an intimate of occultist Aleister Crowley and took part in magical rituals whose sexual dimension would have shocked Lenin (Sutin 2000, 217, 236, 238).

Duranty's initial reporting from Eastern Europe was anti-Communist; he later recanted any stories that spread bad rumors about the Bolsheviks and, as early as 1920, began to ingratiate himself with Soviet leaders (Taylor 1990, 94–98). He inched toward easy acceptance of Soviet falsehoods and was fortunate that his reporting tended to favor Stalin over the dictator's rival for Communist Party leadership, Leon Trotsky (1879–1940). Duranty achieved distinction when he was granted an interview with Stalin, the first foreign journalist to receive that honor who was not a Communist Party hack. Whether from a residual memory of journalistic ethics or for delight in biting any hand that fed him, Duranty occasionally reported on problems in the Soviet Union but, on the whole, painted an impossibly rosy picture of events (Taylor 1990, 168). Within days of the Wall Street crash of 1929, Duranty filed reports praising Stalin's Five-Year Plan (Taylor 1990, 155).

Duranty's dispatches were at odds with the *New York Times's* editorial policy on Russia, but his unusual access to the Kremlin made him a valuable correspondent. Duranty also owed his status to trans-Atlantic circles of prominent friends, starting with the old-boys network from Cambridge and extending to New York's Algonquin Round Table. When visiting Gotham, Duranty exchanged quips at the Algonquin Hotel with the likes of writers such as Dorothy Parker (1893–1967), Alexander Woollcott (1887–1943), and *New Yorker* editor Harold Ross (1892–1951).

Respect for Duranty only grew when the Pulitzer Prize committee praised his reporting on the Five-Year Plan as "marked by scholarship, profundity, impartiality, sound judgment and exceptional clarity." In his acceptance speech, Duranty played politics both ways while favoring the Soviet position. He called the Bolsheviks "sincere enthusiasts, trying to regenerate a people that had been shockingly misgoverned" but added that their line was "unsuitable for the United States and Western Europe" (Taylor 1990, 182–183).

Duranty's reputation was such that as a presidential candidate in 1932, Roosevelt summoned him for a discussion on Russia; despite this, the writer complained that FDR's main concern was whether the Soviets would be able to pay their debts in gold if U.S. trade were to be fully opened following a restoration of diplomatic recognition (Taylor 1990, 184). That recognition followed on November 16, 1933, and while Roosevelt's interests were mainly economic, Duranty's favorable reporting was seen as a factor behind his decision to send an ambassador to Stalin.

DEPICTION AND CULTURAL CONTEXT

The Democratic politician and onetime Roosevelt mentor, Al Smith (1873–1944), reminded his audience that in World War I, President Woodrow Wilson "took our Constitution, wrapped it up and laid it on the shelf and left it there until it was over." The Republican governor of Kansas declared that "even the iron hand of a national dictator is in preference to a paralytic stroke." Influential nationally read columnist Walter Lippmann (1889–1974), visiting Roosevelt in January, told the president-elect that the situation was so critical, "You may have no alternative but to assume dictatorial power" (Kennedy 1999, 111).

As Roosevelt prepared to take office, prestigious magazines such as *The Atlantic*, *Scribner's*, and *Harper's* debated the possibility of a revolution. The liberal Roman Catholic journal *Commonweal* opined that Roosevelt should be granted "the powers of a virtual dictatorship to reorganize the government." A widely seen editorial cartoon depicted Uncle Sam presenting Roosevelt with a sword labelled DICTATORIAL POWERS with a caption reading "In Safe Hands!" (Alter 2006, 186–187).

The moment was right for Roosevelt to follow the steps suggested by Hearst in his production of *Gabriel over the White House*. In his inaugural address, the new president castigated the financiers as "a generation of self-seekers" without vision. He spoke of putting people back to work, raising farm prices, and preventing foreclosures and called for "national planning" and "strict supervision of all banking and credits and investments." Roosevelt added that the crisis might call for a "temporary departure from [the] normal balance" of power. First Lady Eleanor Roosevelt found the audience's response "a little terrifying." She explained that the crowd "would do *anything*—if only someone would tell them what to do." The applause was loudest, she recalled, when her husband announced that he would ask

Congress for "broad executive power to wage war against the emergency" (Hickock 1962, 103–104).

In an early draft of the address, Roosevelt toyed with the word "dictatorship" but settled instead on "broad executive power" (Alter 2006, 219). Within days of the inauguration, the *New York Daily News*, the paper with the largest circulation in the United States, ran the headline "The Dictatorship of Roosevelt" over an editorial that stated, "A lot of us have been asking for a dictator. Now we have one. His name is not Mussolini or Stalin or Hitler. His name is Roosevelt." The editorial added, "Dictatorship was ancient Rome's best idea" (Alter 2006, 221).

Roosevelt's well-known tendency of appearing to agree with people's ideas while concealing his reservations may have convinced advocates of drastic measures that the president was of like mind. Among them was William Randolph Hearst, who continually offered advice to the president-elect through phone calls and emissaries (Pizzitola 2002, 292). He later turned on Roosevelt when he realized that the president wasn't following his lead. Unlike the dictators mentioned in the *Daily News*, Roosevelt had no fixed ideas about revolutionizing the world but sought only to reform the society he inherited, even if by means his harshest critics would describe as authoritarian. "At the heart of the New Deal was not a philosophy but a temperament" (Hofstadter 1948, 316). That temperament included the willingness to entertain a profusion of contradictory ideas in service to the overall goal of economic recovery and, in the end, winning a global war.

FURTHER READING

Alter, Jonathan. 2006. *The Defining Moment: FDR's Hundred Days and the Triumph of Hope*. New York: Simon & Schuster.

Bernstein, Matthew. 1994. *Walter Wanger: Hollywood Independent*. Berkeley: University of California Press.

Birdwell, Michael E. 2000. *Celluloid Soldiers: The Warner Bros. Campaign against Nazism*. New York: New York University Press.

Brody, Richard. 2013. "The Hollywood Movie Made for F.D.R.'s Inauguration." *The New Yorker*, January 21, 2013.

Chase, Stuart. 1932. *A New Deal*. New York: The Macmillan Company.

Duranty, Walter. 1934. *Duranty Reports Russia*. New York: Viking Press.

Duranty, Walter. 1935. *I Write as I Please*. New York: Simon & Schuster.

Gilmour, David. 2011. *The Pursuit of Italy: A History of a Land, Its Regions, and Their Peoples*. New York: Farrar, Strauss and Giroux.

Greenfield, Jeff. 2018. "The Hollywood Hit Movie That Urged FDR to Become a Fascist." *POLITICO Magazine*, March 25, 2018. https://www.politico.com/magazine/story/2018/03/25/gabriel-over-the-white-house-fdr-inauguration-217349

Hall, Mordaunt. 1934. "Walter Huston as a President of the United States Who Proclaims Himself a Dictator." *New York Times*, April 1, 1934. https://www

.nytimes.com/1933/04/01/archives/walter-huston-as-a-president-of-the-united-states-who-proclaims.html

Heller, Mikhail, and Aleksandr M. Nekrich. 1986. *Utopia in Power: The History of the Soviet Union 1917 to the Present.* New York: Summit Books.

Hickcock, Lorena. 1962. *Reluctant First Lady.* New York: Dodd, Mead.

Hofstadter, Richard. 1948. *The American Political Tradition.* New York: Alfred A. Knopf.

Johnson, Paul. 1991. *Modern Times: From the Twenties to the Nineties.* New York: HarperCollins.

Kennedy, David M. 1999. *Freedom from Fear: The American People in Depression and War, 1929–1945.* New York: Oxford University Press.

Payne, Stanley G. 1995. *A History of Fascism 1914–1945.* Madison: University of Wisconsin Press.

Pizzitola, Louis. 2002. *Hearst over Hollywood: Power, Passion, and Propaganda in the Movies.* New York: Columbia University Press.

Service, Robert. 2012. *Spies and Commissars: The Early Years of the Russian Revolution.* New York: Public Affairs.

Sutin, Lawrence. 2000. *Do What Thou Wilt: A Life of Aleister Crowley.* New York: St. Martin's Press.

Taylor, S. J. 1990. *Stalin's Apologist: Walter Duranty, The New York Times's Man in Moscow.* New York: Oxford University Press.

Chapter 2

My Man Godfrey (1936)

My Man Godfrey was released on September 6, 1936 by Universal Pictures. The film was produced by the studio's vice president of productions, Charles R. Rogers (1892–1957). The director, Gregory La Cava (1892–1952), was a Hollywood veteran who had directed the Great Depression–themed film *Gabriel over the White House* three years earlier. *My Man Godfrey* was based on a 1935 novella by Eric S. Hatch (1901–1973), originally serialized in *Liberty*, a popular weekly magazine, under the title *1011 Fifth Avenue*. Hatch adapted his story for the screen along with Broadway writer Morrie Ryskind (1895–1985). Playwright and screenwriter Zoe Byrd Akins (1886–1958) may have contributed to the final script.

Hatch's social satire is smoothed and polished by its stars, William Powell (1892–1954) and Carole Lombard (1908–1942). Powell was well known to audiences for the sophisticated nonchalance of the upper-class detective he played in *The Thin Man* (1934) and Lombard had starred in one of the films credited with birthing the genre known as "screwball comedy," *Twentieth Century* (1934). *My Man Godfrey* was among the most popular screwball comedies, whose characteristics included the "teaming of a male star and a female star as both love interest and comic center of the spectacle" (Sarris 1998, 89). The genre tended toward comedies of courtship, with laughter rising as its protagonists fumbled over the accepted conventions of behavior. Film historian Andrew Sarris identifies the inception of screwball comedies with the tightening censorship of the Hollywood Production Code (1934) (Sarris 1998, 95). With the censors removing "sex from the sex comedies," the courtship expressed itself through a fast-paced dialogue of wisecracks and double entendres. Critics during that period related screwball comedy to the psychological disruption caused by the Great Depression. "The loss of credibility in former values, the breakdown of the smugness and self-confidence of the jazz era, the growing bewilderment and dissatisfaction in a 'crazy' world that does not make sense" was thought to find reflection in the fun house mirror of those films (Jacobs 1939, 535).

The combustible chemistry between *My Man Godfrey*'s protagonists, Godfrey Parke (Powell) and Irene Bullock (Lombard), may have been enhanced by the stars' real-life relationship as this was one of the few films in which a divorced couple played the romantic leads. Powell's insistence on bringing his ex-wife into the project was "merely pragmatic: he sensed that she could bring to the picture the quality of personality it needed for hitting the comedy bull's eye" (Swindell 1975, 185). However, the secondary characters are at least as memorably enacted as the leads. As in many of the best Hollywood movies from the 1930s and 1940s, those secondary players "brought an indelible character with them from film to film," recognized immediately by audiences of that time (Lazar 2020, xii).

In the film's opening scene, Irene meets Godfrey when a pack of socialites and playboys descend on a garbage dump where men left unemployed by the Great Depression shelter in shacks. Irene's sister Cornelia (Gail Patrick, 1911–1980) offers to give Godfrey five dollars if he accompanies them to a charity "scavenger hunt" at one of New York's grand hotels. Rather than one of the rusty bicycles or pieces of broken furniture brought to the charity auction by other wealthy patrons, Cornelia and her companions think they can fetch one of the "forgotten men" to the affair. Audiences of 1936 would have understood the reference to a musical number called "Remember My Forgotten Man" from the hit movie *Gold Diggers of 1933* that evoked the gritty atmosphere of Depression-era poverty.

Angered by her patronizing tone, Godfrey pushes Cornelia into an ash heap and a confrontation ensues. Irene is undaunted and continues to engage Godfrey in conversation. The movie's zany tone is set by Irene's first rambling monologue. "A scavenger hunt is just like a treasure hunt, except in a treasure hunt you find something you want and in a scavenger hunt you find things you don't want and the one who wins gets a prize, only there really isn't any prize, it's just the honor of winning, because all the money goes to charity if there's any money left over, but there never is." Irene seems on the verge of recognizing that the society she inhabits is a sham.

Mollified by her scatterbrained-yet-not-unkind attitude, Godfrey accompanies her to the scavenger hunt event at the hotel. He provides a shabby contrast at a catered affair whose invited guests wear evening gowns and black ties and tails. The following morning, he begins work as a butler in the Bullock's Park Avenue mansion.

Irene and Cornelia live in the grand and spacious dwelling with their stockbroker father, Alexander (Eugene Pallette, 1889–1954), and eccentric mother, Angelica (Alice Brady, 1892–1939). The sleeping arrangements for Angelica's "protégé," Carlo (Mischa Auer, 1905–1967), are unclear. Carlo is a European aesthete who provides Angelica with the culture and amusement apparently missing in her marriage. Alexander's tolerance for him is ill-humored. With the assistance of a wisecracking maid, Molly (Jean Dixon, 1893–1981), Godfrey navigates the peculiarities of the household, ducking Cornelia's spite and dodging Irene's affections until the final scene. Irene is madly in love with her "forgotten man," unaware that Godfrey is actually the Harvard-educated scion of an old Boston family living in the squatters' camp to forget a failed love affair. At the story's conclusion, Godfrey's financial skills save the Bullocks from bankruptcy and with the profits from his transactions, he bulldozes the camp where he once lived, turning the site into a swanky nightclub employing the "forgotten men" who befriended him.

Although not one of the year's top movies at box offices, *My Man Godfrey* was popular with the public and critics alike. The *New York Times* named it "the daffiest comedy of the year" (Nugent 1936). Reviewing the film before its release, the entertainment industry trade paper *Variety* wrote that Powell and Lombard were "pleasantly teamed" in a "splendidly produced comedy" and went on to call the storyline "balmy, but not too much so" (*Variety* 1935). In a 1936 review for one of Britain's most distinguished magazines, *The Spectator*, novelist Graham Greene praised *My Man Godfrey* as "acutely funny" but added, perceptively, that its "social conscience" was "a little confused" (Greene 1995, 144).

My Man Godfrey received six nominations at the 1937 Academy Awards, including Best Director (La Cava), Best Actor (Powell), Best Actress (Lombard), Best Supporting Actor (Auer), Best Supporting Actress (Brady), and Best Screenplay (Hatch, Ryskind). However, it took home no trophies on Oscar night.

The film has endured as one of the most popular movies of its era. The American Film Institute ranked it among the 100 funniest Hollywood comedies and *Premiere* magazine named it No. 7 in its "50 Greatest Comedies of All Times" roster (*Premiere* 2013). Film historian David Thomson called *My Man Godfrey* "one of the most amusing screwball comedies ever, in which the poor behave decently and quietly and the rich are demented monkeys" (Thomson 2008, 588). *My Man Godfrey* has also been embraced by feminist film historians. Princeton University's Maria DiBattista praised Lombard's performance as "the fast talk of a child who breathlessly wants to get her words out before she is cut off" and Irene as a character deeply connected with "the American ideal of fellowship, a fellow-feeling that survives fluctuations in the economy and changes of class fortune" (DiBattista 2001, 109, 111–112).

In 1999, the Library of Congress deemed *My Man Godfrey* as "culturally significant" and added it to the National Film Registry.

HISTORICAL BACKGROUND

Although most Americans owned no stock in 1929, few escaped the consequences of the market crash. The sharp decline on Wall Street set off a chain of events that reverberated on every street. Unemployment grew rapidly in a shrinking economy, leading to eviction and poverty. In *The Great Depression: America in the 1930s*, T. H. Watkins notes, "When neighbors you had known all your life were found one morning with all their furniture on the sidewalk, nowhere to go, no hope in sight, it did not take much imagination to see yourself standing there with them" (1993, 55–56).

"Most of the rich remained quite comfortable, although the extent of their deprivation was hinted at by the findings of a WPA research project that the most common previous occupations of people on urban relief rolls in 1934 were servant and chauffeur," writes historian Robert S. McElvaine (1983, 17). Despite legends of ruined investors hurling themselves from high-rise windows, most suicides occurred among unemployed workers who had lost hope. "People were sullen rather than bitter, despairing rather than violent" (Schlesinger 1957, 168). The suicide rate rose from 14 per 100,000 in 1929 to 17.4 per 100,000 in 1932 (McElvaine 1983, 17–18).

Average weekly wages in manufacturing fell from $24.76 in 1929 to $16.65 in 1933 and didn't recover to their pre-Depression levels until 1940. However, millions of Americans earned less-than-average wages or no wages at all as economic panic spread (McElvaine 1983, 17). When the Soviet Union advertised in New York for 6,000 skilled workers to aid in building that country's industrial base, more than 100,000 applications were received.

Even Washington, D.C., where 33 percent of workers were employed by the federal government, wasn't spared. Many federal employees were furloughed without pay. As happened elsewhere in America, banks and businesses closed and property foreclosures rose in number. The district's commissioners asked the army to deliver hundreds of cots and mattresses to the Salvation Army and other rescue missions. "The bodies of men and women, often nameless and homeless, arrived from the city's streets and alleys at the city's single, antiquated morgue" (Lewis 2015, 327).

Once the Depression was underway, President Herbert Hoover famously remarked that "no one is actually starving" (Smith and Walch 2004). The statement was probably intended to be hopeful but was interpreted as callous disregard. Hoover was comparing conditions in the early months of the Great Depression to the starvation in German-occupied Belgium during World War I that he had helped alleviate as head of an international relief committee. After the war, as chairman of the American Relief Administration, he had saved former enemies from hunger in the defeated German, Austrian, and Turkish empires and fought the effects of famine in the Soviet Union (Jeansonne and Luhrssen 2017, 94–149). While conditions in the United States in 1931 were considerably less dire than they had been in Soviet Russia, where agriculture had failed due to civil war and harsh Communist farm policies, 95 cases of starvation were reported that year in New York City. Sickness increased due to malnourishment and illness among the unemployed was 66 percent higher than in families with one full-time worker. In cities, people picked through garbage dumps for food and fights broke out in alleys behind restaurants over scraps (McElwaine 1983, 18).

Private philanthropy and enterprise tried to help. In the fall of 1930, the International Apple Shippers Association began selling apples to the unemployed on credit for $1.75 a crate. The buyers resold the apples on street corners for a nickel a piece, and if they sold the entire crate, they could earn $1.85. At a time when bread sold for 7 cents a loaf and a dozen eggs for 29 cents, an unemployed person could eat from the profits. By November 1930, some 6,000 apple sellers were working the streets of New York. Apples were also hawked on streets of other big cities, and oranges were hawked in New Orleans. However, as the Depression worsened, fewer customers were able to purchase the fruit and sales dwindled. Larger interventions were needed to keep the country clothed and fed.

Some of the dispossessed went on the road, usually jumping onto slow-moving freight trains to get from town to town. They were known as hobos and the freight cars they rode were derisively called "Hoover Pullmans" (Leuchtenberg 2009, 113). The Southern Pacific Railroad, whose tracks covered the western states, estimated that its security guards threw 683,000 transients from its box cars during a single year of the Great Depression. At least one-third were adolescents from broken families. Most were male but females were counted among them, usually joining hobo gangs formed for mutual protection. They begged for money on the streets of the towns they stopped in and knocked on the back doors of homes and restaurants asking for food. They were chased by police and, when caught, could spend time in jail for vagrancy (Watkins 1993, 60).

"Those homeless who did not drift—and there were thousands in every city of any size at all—slept in lice-ridden and rat-infested flophouses" if they could scrape together a few pennies (Watkins 1993). Some slept on park benches or under bridges. "The more ambitious among them contrived fragile shelters from scraps of wood and cardboard, old beer signs and fence posts, anything they could find . . . They built them anywhere they could, but most of the time on the outskirts of cities and towns big enough to have outskirts, where villages began to coalesce like ramshackle suburbs. Everyone called them Hoovervilles" (Watkins 1993, 61).

Although some said that the derisive word was coined by Charles Michelson, publicity chief for the Democratic National Committee, the public needed little encouragement to blame the ramshackle encampments on the sitting president (Kaltenborn 1956, 88). Hundreds of them sprang up across the country. Not all of Hoovervilles' residents were homeless men. Entire families were sometimes camped out in shacks, sustained by nearby food kitchens, charity, and begging on city streets. One Hooverville was established in New York's Central Park on the site of the recently drained reservoir that later became the park's Great Lawn. The New York City parks department dubbed it "Hoover Valley" and although residents were periodically arrested, the makeshift village grew. Several of the hovels were built of brick and boasted tin roofs. According to press reports at the time, most were furnished with chairs and beds and were kept tidy (Gray 1993).

In cities such as St. Louis, a large Hooverville encompassed many acres of previously vacant land. Seattle, on the other hand, had eight smaller Hoovervilles. America's most notorious Hooverville was thrown up in Washington, D.C. in the summer of 1932 when the Bonus Army marched into the capital. The Bonus Army was a movement of tens of thousands of World War I veterans who demanded that Congress grant them the bonus they had been promised. The law pledged payment in 1945 but the veterans, suffering like almost everyone in the early years of the Depression, insisted on being paid immediately. Congress debated the issue but legislation authorizing the bonus stalled in a House committee. If paid in full, each veteran would have received a bonus of around $1,000, an impressive sum at a time when a hamburger could be purchased for 12 cents.

In May 1932, a jobless ex-sergeant, Walter W. Waters (1898–1959), stood up at a veterans' meeting in Portland, arguing that every veteran should go to Washington, hopping freight trains with the hobos, if necessary, to force Congress to act on their behalf. Veterans across the country began to mobilize around the idea while public response to his call was divided. "Some people saw them simply as men of the Great Depression, homeless, hopeless, and looking for cash. But for many who had fought in the war, these were their comrades" (Dickson and Allen 2004, 5).

Passage of the "Bonus Bill," as the proposed legislation for paying the veterans was called, was led by Congressman Wright Patman (1893–1976), a Democrat from Texas and a war veteran, but it had many prominent opponents. The archconservative leadership of the American Legion denounced the bonus, as did many business leaders. Although Hoover's policies toward veterans had been relatively generous, he noted that the "demand for relief was infinite, and the supply [of money] was finite," adding that instant payment of the promised money would bankrupt the treasury and "consume a disproportionate amount of the entire federal budget for a small segment of the population, not all of whom were poor or unemployed" (Jeansonne 2012, 292).

The charismatic Waters set forth on a freight train from Portland with a few hundred followers. Their journey drew attention from newspapers and radio and their movement snowballed. They were given handouts along the way by fellow veterans and donations of food and money from well-wishers. Waters organized that part of the Bonus Army over which he could keep control along military lines, dividing his contingents into companies with buglers, medics, and officers elected by their men. He formed a police squad to enforce his rules, which included "no drinking, no panhandling, no antigovernment talk" (Dickson and Allen 2004, 64). As the weeks went on, groups of veterans as well as individuals converged in Washington from across the United States under the Bonus Army banner. By June, 45,000 had descended on the city, including entire families.

Washington's police superintendent, Brigadier General Pelham D. Glassford (1883–1959), had commanded troops in France during World War I and was sympathetic to the overall goals of the protesting veterans. He arranged for many of them to encamp on the Anacostia Flats, across the Anacostia River from the Washington Navy Yard and only a few blocks from the Capitol. Glassford obtained lumber and tar paper, enough to allow some veterans to put up shelters. The Bonus marchers "washed themselves in the river, washed their travel-stained clothes, and hung them on the riverside trees" (Lewis 2015). Many spent their first night sleeping on the wet ground. "Next day, they went to dumps to salvage materials" and brought them back to Anacostia. Photographs document a sprawling, tumble-down shanty town spread across the Flats but with a few buildings that look almost professionally constructed as if by military engineers. Waters organized the encampment into blocks along demarcated streets, established a city square with a speakers' platform, dug latrines, and authorized a camp newspaper and lending library. His most trusted men formed a police brigade that enforced his orders (Lewis 2015, 329).

The War Department refused the requests to provision the camp, but Glassford did his best to provide food donations from private sources. Fearing revolution and responding like a wealthy character from one of the era's screwball comedies, socialite Evalyn Walsh McLean (1886–1947) helped Anacostia's residents by purchasing a thousand sandwiches and a thousand cups of coffee from the startled owner of a nearby diner and used her connections with local charities for assistance. She became concerned after seeing "the unshaven, tired faces" of veterans marching past her mansion on Embassy Row with walking sticks that seemed "less canes than cudgels." She worried that the mansions of her district gave the marchers "a kind of challenge" (McLean and Sparkes 1936, 305).

Most of the Bonus marchers harbored no designs to overthrow the government or overturn capitalism, but the Communist Party saw potential and sought to infiltrate their ranks and transform them into a revolutionary movement. Members of a Communist front group, the Workers' Ex-Servicemen's League under ex-Marine John T. Pace, arrived in the capital and sought to mix in with the Bonus Army even as Waters was determined to keep the Communists out (Dickson and Allen 2004, 82–83). Likewise, the U.S. military and elements of the Hoover administration interpreted the Bonus Army as the vanguard of revolution and infiltrated its encampments. Colonel Edmund W. Starling, chief of the Secret Service's presidential security detail, sent his agents into Waters' ranks. "Generally speaking there were few Communists," he recalled. "The veterans were Americans, down on their luck" (Starling and Sugruve 1946, 296).

Also mingling with the veterans were agents of the Washington Metropolitan Police, the Military Intelligence Division, and the Bureau of Investigation (forerunner of the FBI) whose informants took special note of the large numbers of Blacks and people of Jewish appearance in the Bonus Army. Jews were viewed as susceptible to Communism and the startling presence of Black veterans, encamped alongside whites in defiance of segregation, was deemed especially problematic. "Unlike the rest of Washington, the encampment was a fully integrated city" (Lewis 2015, 329). The U.S. military was more alarmed than the Secret Service or the police. Chief of staff General Douglas MacArthur (1880–1964) and his deputy, Major General George Van Horn Moseley (1874–1960), were receiving alarming secret reports from military commanders across the nation of Communist agitation and plots to seize power. The army began to quietly prepare for implementing Plan White, an operation to defend Washington during an uprising.

Although the U.S. House of Representatives passed the Bonus Bill on June 15, two days later the Senate tabled the measure without bringing it to the floor for a vote. Most Washingtonians expected the disappointed Bonus Army to march home after hearing the news. Some did leave but many were determined to stay for years, if necessary, until their demands were met. Waters called the Senate's inaction a "temporary setback" and sent representatives to major cities to recruit reinforcements from among the nation's unemployed. During this time the rough and ready democracy of the Bonus Army's early weeks dissolved into something that looked like an American version of fascism. At a mass meeting of veterans, Waters demanded and received "complete dictatorial powers." Officers of the Bonus units were no longer elected but appointed by Waters, who took to wearing a khaki uniform with cavalry boots and prepared to establish a corps of "shock troops." His ambitions no longer seemed limited to leading a protest or running the nation's largest Hooverville. "To hell with civil law and General Glassford. I'm going to have my orders carried out!" he bellowed (Dickson and Allen 2004, 134–135).

Despite Waters' direct challenge to his authority, Glassford continued to help feed the encampments, often spending his own money when he failed to find donors. His efforts prevented starvation but not hunger or discomfort. Although a Washington dairy donated 40 quarts of milk each day, which Waters' khaki-clad officers doled out to children in the Hoovervilles, it wasn't enough to provide all of the children with a steady ration of milk. Life in the encampments became increasingly uncomfortable. Washington's rainy summer of 1932 reduced the Flats to a muddy field that reminded observers of the frontlines in France during World War I. "The mud and body lice, along with the general worsening of sanitary conditions and the dwindling supply of food, began to wear heavily on the men, women, and children of Anacostia" (Dickson and Allen 2004, 137).

The Bonus Army also occupied 26 smaller Hoovervilles in Washington. Only three blocks from Capitol Hill and half a mile from the White House, more than 2,000 veterans and their families lived in a set of half-demolished Civil War–era government buildings and in shacks and tents in adjacent lots. In late May, Glassford commandeered those buildings for the veterans with Hoover's quiet consent. In late July, the police tried to clear out one of the buildings after the fire department declared it hazardous, but the veterans refused to budge. While newspapers focused on the larger Anacostia Flats, the Hooverville on Pennsylvania Avenue was a greater irritant to the federal government for its visibility in the heart of Washington. Furthermore, the occupation was impeding a major public works project, the construction of the Federal Triangle complex of government offices.

During July, Communists from the Workers' Ex-Servicemen's League caused trouble in the streets and tried to storm the White House even as the overall number of Bonus marchers in Washington fell to around 12,000. By the end of the month, the federally appointed District Commissioners who ran the city decided to give the Bonus Army a final eviction notice. Glassford dropped leaflets on the Anacostia Flats from a plane, warning them to leave. Waters remained defiant. "I, as your commander in chief need only to raise my hand above my head and my following of 12,000 men will either fight or frolic, according to my wishes," he proclaimed (Dickson and Allen 2004, 158).

Waters dreamed of establishing a semipermanent community called Camp Bartlett on the sole piece of private property whose owner, former New Hampshire governor and Washington insider John Henry Bartlett (1869–1952), welcomed the Bonus Army. Thirty families were housed on the site in tents and had access to kitchens and electricity. As the threat of forced eviction from government property became more serious, Waters hoped to move all remaining marchers to Camp Bartlett and claimed he had secured lumber to build permanent barracks. However, he did not have the time to make his next move.

On July 28, the Washington police and U.S. Treasury agents began forcing veterans out of the Hooverville on Pennsylvania Avenue. Violence erupted. Several police officers were injured and two veterans died in the melee. After the shooting, the District Commissioners asked for federal troops and Secretary of War Patrick J. Hurley (1883–1963) gave MacArthur the go-ahead. Plan White was initiated.

With MacArthur giving the orders, infantry companies with fixed bayonets and squadrons of cavalry with drawn sabers, supported by a handful of tanks, moved against the Hoovervilles. Responding to bricks and stones, the troops fired tear gas and jabbed civilians with bayonets and sabers. The assault on the Bonus Army began in broad daylight and had many prominent witnesses. A tear gas grenade exploded at the feet of U.S. senator Hiram Bingham (1875–1956). A member of the Federal Trade Commission,

A. Everette McIntyre (1901–1997), recalled that "flames were coming up, where the soldiers had set fire to the buildings to drive these people out" (Terkel 1970, 17–18). Their belongings were consumed by fire. "Be careful men, don't burn any flags," an officer told his troops. But this proved impossible since the Stars and Stripes flew above many shanties. According to a press report, one woman pleaded to be allowed into her hovel to claim one suitcase with all her children's clothes. "Get out of here, lady, before you get hurt," a soldier said before setting her place on fire (Dickson and Allen 2004, 175–176).

As night fell, MacArthur sent his forces against the encampment at Anacostia Flats, ignoring Hoover's order to wait. The beam of a searchlight revealed panic-struck scenes of mothers gathering their children, men desperately starting their jalopies, and a surging crowd of terrified people fleeing on foot from the advancing troops. The huts where they had lived for many weeks were torched.

At a midnight press conference, convened with his usual flair for drama, MacArthur claimed that most of the Bonus Army's members were not veterans but "insurrectionists" who "severely threatened" the seat of government (Dickson and Allen 2004, 181–182). As he spoke, hundreds of people driven from the Flats by his troops fled into the surrounding neighborhood where many were given shelter. One resident recalled eight children laying in a doorway, coughing from tear gas, and their mother applying wet cloths over their stinging eyes. The great mass fleeing Anacostia found the bridges into Virginia blocked by troops and Maryland roads closed by state troopers. At 4:00 a.m. on July 29, Maryland's governor allowed them to pass on the condition that they travel out of his state as quickly as possible. "The dispersed were supposed to return to their homes, which most of them did not have" (Dickson and Allen 2004, 185).

With MacArthur's action, America's most infamous Hoovervilles went up in flames, but armed force didn't eliminate the unemployment and poverty that had caused the shanty towns to be built. Elsewhere in the United States, some Hoovervilles endured through 1940 or 1941, when unemployment fell with conscription and the transformation of American industry into—as President Roosevelt put it—the "Arsenal of Democracy." America's preparation for World War finally brought the Great Depression to its final chapter.

DEPICTION AND CULTURAL CONTEXT

In his 1926 short story "The Rich Boy," F. Scott Fitzgerald famously wrote, "Let me tell you about the very rich. They are different from you and me." Like the Bullocks of *My Man Godfrey* and similar characters from numerous other Hollywood movies from the 1930s, the very rich saw themselves as "high society," living apart from the common folk, insulated from economic anxiety, and waited on by servants. They dressed and spoke differently from everyone else and those distinctions were magnified in the movies. "When high-society dames consort with the lower or under classes, they risk appearing out of place or glad to be away from home, depending on whether they are condescending or slumming" (DiBattista 2001, 138).

The very rich depicted by Hollywood, such as the Bullocks, often belonged to the New York elite descended from the landed aristocracy of Dutch colonial times and entrepreneurs who had exploited the resources of the young republic on a grand scale in the 19th century. They traveled between Manhattan townhouses and country estates. They played polo and sailed on yachts. Mrs. Bullock wasn't alone in looking to Europeans for cultural guidance. At least among the older generation of the very rich, America was still a backwater. The wealthy elite enjoyed the freedom of movement money could buy and the average moviegoer gaped at "the mobility that had been denied them during hard times" (Dickstein 2009, 362).

The proliferation of syndicated gossip columns fed the public's curiosity about what went on beneath the decorum and elaborate set of social manners cultivated by the upper class. Screwball comedies such as *My Man Godfrey* played to that interest as did a proliferation of "madcap heiress comedies" (DiBattista 2001, 23). The idea of romance across class lines was a popular theme in pulp fiction and movies, even if less common in real life.

ELEANOR ROOSEVELT (1884–1962)

Before Eleanor Roosevelt, America's first ladies acted as hostesses at state dinners but had no other role. As first lady, Eleanor set standards for activism that none of her successors could match; but she also set an example for future first ladies who became advocates for particular projects.

She was born into American aristocracy. Eleanor was the niece of President Theodore Roosevelt and fifth cousin to her husband, Franklin D. Roosevelt (FDR). Their marriage was troubled but she worked with him throughout his political career. With a strong sense of noblesse oblige, she took interest in the lives of working-class Americans. Her concerned image was so pronounced that women from many backgrounds wrote to her, asking her to intervene with the president on their behalf to alleviate their problems during the Great Depression.

Unafraid to court controversy, she championed causes that FDR supported privately but was unwilling to assist in public due to concern over political backlash. She made African Americans a priority and famously arranged for Black opera singer Marian Anderson to perform at the Lincoln Memorial (1939) after she was banned at other Washington venues. After FDR's death, Eleanor served as a delegate to the United Nations (1945–1952) and oversaw the drafting of the UN's Universal Declaration of Human Rights. She continued to speak on behalf of progressive causes till the end of her life.

While poverty was sometimes acknowledged by Hollywood, few films aside from *My Man Godfrey* included a Hooverville among their settings. The tumble-down appearance of Godfrey's Hooverville conforms to reality, and given its riverbank location, it may have been inspired by the Hooverville that occupied New York City's Riverside Park in those years. *My Man Godfrey*'s plot device of high society treating shanty towns as a tourist attraction was borne out by reality. During the Great Depression, an unemployed bricklayer living in the Central Park Hooverville reported that he received nearly $50 in tips from no less than 3,000 curious visitors over a period of many weeks (Gray 1993).

FURTHER READING

American Film Institute. n.d. "AFI's 100 Years . . . 100 Laughs." Accessed November 24, 2020. https://www.afi.com/afis-100-years-100-laughs/

DiBattista, Maria. 2001. *Fast Talking Dames*. New Haven: Yale University Press.

Dickson, Paul, and Thomas B. Allen. 2004. *The Bonus Army: An American Epic*. New York: Walker & Company.

Dickstein, Morris. 2009. *Dancing in the Dark: A Cultural History of the Great Depression*. New York: W. W. Norton.

Gray, Christopher. 1993. "Streetscapes: Central Park's 'Hooverville'—Life Along 'Depression Street.'" *New York Times*, August 29, 1993. https://www.nytimes.com/1993/08/29/realestate/streetscapes-central-park-s-hooverville-life-along-depression-street.html

Greene, Graham. 1995. *The Graham Greene Film Reader: Reviews, Essays & Film Stories*. Edited by David Parkinson. New York: Applause Books.

Jacobs, Lewis. 1939. *The Rise of the American Film*. New York: Harcourt Brace.

Jeansonne, Glen. 2012. *The Life of Herbert Hoover: Fighting Quaker 1928–1933*. New York: Palgrave Macmillan.

Jeansonne, Glen, with David Luhrssen. 2017. *Herbert Hoover: A Life*. New York: New American Library.

Kaltenborn, Hans. 1956. *It Seems Like Yesterday*. New York: Putnam.

Lazar, David. 2000. *Celeste Holm Syndrome: On Character Actors from Hollywood's Golden Age*. Lincoln: University of Nebraska Press.

Leuchtenberg, William E. 2009. *Herbert Hoover*. New York: Times Books.

Lewis, Tom. 2015. *Washington: A History of Our National City*. New York: Basic Books.

McElvaine, Robert S., ed. 1983. *Down & Out in the Great Depression: Letters from the Forgotten Man*. Chapel Hill: University of North Carolina Press.

McLean, Evalyn Walsh, and Boyden Sparkes. 1936. *Father Struck It Rich*. Boston: Little, Brown.

Nugent, Frank S. 1936. "The Screen: 'My Man Godfrey.'" *New York Times*, September 18, 1936. https://www.nytimes.com/1936/09/18/archives/the-screen-my-man-godfrey.html

Premiere. 2013. "50 Greatest Comedies of All Time." September 17, 2013. https://www.imdb.com/list/ls053819173/

Sarris, Andrew. 1998. *"You Ain't Heard Nothin' Yet": The American Talking Film History and Memory, 1927–1949.* New York: Oxford University Press.

Schlesinger, Arthur M., Jr. 1957. *The Age of Roosevelt: Crisis of the Old Order 1919–1933.* Boston: Houghton Mifflin.

Smith, Richard Norton, and Timothy Walsh. 2004. "The Ordeal of Herbert Hoover, Part 2." *Prologue Magazine,* Summer 2004. https://www.archives.gov/publication/prologue/2004/summer/hoover-2.html

Starling, Edmund W., and Thomas Sugruve. 1946. *Starling of the White House: The Story of the Man Whose Secret Service Guarded Five Presidents from Woodrow Wilson to Franklin D. Roosevelt.* New York: Simon & Schuster.

Swindell, Larry. 1975. *Screwball: The Life of Carole Lombard.* New York: William Morrow.

Terkel, Studs. 1970. *Hard Times: An Oral History of the Great Depression.* New York: Pantheon Books.

Thomson, David. 2008. *"Have you Seen...?": A Personal Introduction to 1,000 Films.* New York: Alfred A. Knopf.

Variety, unsigned review. 1935. "My Man Godfrey." December 31, 1935. https://variety.com/1935/film/reviews/my-man-godfrey-1200411202/

Watkins, T. H. 1993. *The Great Depression: America in the 1930s.* Boston: Little, Brown.

Chapter 3

Black Legion (1937)

Black Legion was released by Warner Brothers on January 17, 1937. The film was produced by Academy Award–winning screenwriter Robert Lord (1900–1976), whose original story was adapted for the film by Warner Brothers' contract writer Abem Finkel (1889–1948) and novelist William Wister Haines (1908–1989). Archie Mayo (1891–1968), whose Hollywood career began in the silent era, directed the film.

Black Legion was the second movie based on the notorious organization by that name and was preceded by *Legion of Terror* (1936). Mayo, who had previously worked with Humphrey Bogart (1899–1957) on the crime drama *The Petrified Forest* (1936), cast the as yet little-known actor in the starring role because the studio wanted a writer who wasn't "ethnic" in appearance (Sperber 1997, 76–77). Bogart plays Frank Taylor, an amiable drill press operator in a Midwest factory town. He dreams of the new car and vacuum cleaner for his wife, Ruth (Broadway actress Erin O'Brien-Moore, 1902–1979), which he plans to purchase when he receives an expected promotion. His face sinks when he learns that the job will go instead to a Polish immigrant, Joe Dombrowski, played by character actor Henry Brandon (1912–1990).

Frank begins to listen to an anti-immigrant radio broadcaster who condemns "hordes of grasping, pushing foreigners who are stealing jobs from American workmen and bread from American homes." The broadcaster's rallying cry is "America for Americans!" Frank's resentment is encouraged by a coworker, Cliff Moore (Joseph Sawyer, 1906–1982), who introduces him to the secretive Black Legion whose black-hooded members gather in nocturnal meetings to lash out against anyone deemed insufficiently American.

After Frank joins, his wife Ruth becomes suspicious of his newly purchased gun and his late nights, but he explains that the gun is to protect the family from crime and his nights are spent in a fraternal lodge. Frank participates as the Black Legion ransacks the farm where Joe Dombrowski lives with his father and in a series of night raids on immigrants and immigrant-owned businesses. When Frank recruits a coworker for the Black Legion during work hours, in violation of policies against conducting outside business on company time, he is demoted in favor of an Irishman, Mike Grogan (Clifford Soubier, 1891–1984). Mike is severely beaten in revenge. In one of her final roles before rising to stardom, Ann Sheridan (1915–1967) plays Mike's wife Betty.

Wrestling with guilt and the secrets he keeps from his wife, Frank turns to alcohol and another woman, Pearl Danvers, played by an actress familiar to audiences at the time for several "loose woman" roles, Helen Flint (1898–1967). When Frank's neighbor and friend, Ed Jackson (Dick Foran, 1910–1979) discovers him with Helen, Frank breaks down and confesses to participating in Black Legion violence. Worried afterward that Ed might tell the police, Frank incites the Black Legion to attack Ed. In the ensuing assault, Frank ends up killing his friend and cries out, "I didn't mean to shoot!"

Frank is arrested and despite the Black Legion's threats to harm his wife and son, he denounces the group in court and identifies its members. The judge sentences all of them to life in prison. The film ends as Frank exchanges a regretful stare with Ruth.

For Bogart, *Black Legion* marked a turning point from his earlier roles as gangsters and shady characters as he inched his way toward his characteristic persona as a tough but sympathetic leading man. The role was prominent and emotionally diverse enough to show the studio his star potential. Bogart "realized this was his shot" (Mueller 2020). The notices at the time of the film's release were favorable. According to the reviewer for New York's *Morning Telegram*, "his powerful performance establishes Humphrey Bogart as a star" (Sperber 1997, 79); and *the New York Post* predicted "No more B pix for Bogart!" (Thomson 2009, 21). Those reviewers recognized Bogart's emerging talent, but it took Warner Brothers several more years before *High Sierra* (1941) finally assured his stardom.

The *New York Times* praised *Black Legion* as "editorial cinema at its best" (Nugent 1937). Novelist Graham Greene, in a 1937 review for the upscale British magazine *Night and Day*, echoed the thoughts already expressed by most American critics, calling *Black Legion* "an intelligent and exciting, if rather earnest film." Greene understood the production as a warning against the rising tide of authoritarian populism, writing that its writers and director "know where the real horror lies . . . not in the black robe and skull emblems, but in the knowledge that these hide the weak and commonplace faces you have met over the [store] counter and minding the next machine [in workplaces]" (Greene 1995, 202).

Black Legion generated almost universally favorable publicity and was considered one of the year's important films for its fictionalized dramatization of recent headlines, what the *New York Times* called its "quasi-documentary record" (Nugent 1937). The screenplay was nominated for an Academy Award but lost to *A Star Is Born*. The National Board of Review named it the film of the year and Bogart as actor of the year. *Black Legion* earned a profit for Warner Brothers but was not a hit when compared to such top films of 1937 as *Stella Dallas* and *The Good Earth*.

HISTORICAL BACKGROUND

Xenophobic organizations have existed and sometimes thrived in the United States since the first large influx of new immigrants in the 1850s, and since the Civil War, white supremacist groups have sprung up whenever unquestioned white dominance was threatened by "outsiders" or activism among Black people. Xenophobic and white supremacist groups cannot always be neatly separated because their aims and ideologies have often overlapped.

WILLIAM DUDLEY PELLEY (1890–1965)

The Great Depression encouraged radicalism on both sides of the political spectrum. The American Communist Party grew during the 1930s as did nationalist white supremacist groups. The largest far right militia, the Silver Shirts (emulating Hitler's Brown Shirts), enrolled 15,000 uniformed fighters at its peak in 1935 and had many more followers. Members were entirely of Northern European heritage. The Silver Shirts was led by its "Beloved Chief," William Dudley Pelley.

Pelley was dubbed America's leader among the "star-spangled fascists" and found mention in Sinclair Lewis's bestselling novel about an impending right-wing dictatorship in the United States, *It Can't Happen Here* (1935). Pelley was a prolific and prize-winning author who had worked as a Hollywood screenwriter in the 1920s. He called out the industry's Jewish producers—the intensity of his anti-Semitism may have resulted from a search for scapegoats after the failure of his Hollywood career.

Pelley claimed contact with disembodied spirits and was guided by their voices. He attended Germany's Anti-Comintern Congress (1938), which brought together far-right leaders from around the world. Pelley's agenda for America included confining Jews to ghettos and exploiting Blacks as laborers. He was arrested for sedition in 1942 and released from prison in 1950. He was considered a "martyr" by the far right.

The persistence of xenophobia and white supremacy, whether on the margins or in the mainstream of American life, is bound up with the contentious issue of American identity. The question of who gets to be American and accorded the full rights of citizenship was already on the minds of the men who authored the U.S. Constitution. The issue of slavery was left to the states but "those bound to Service for a Term of Years," as slaves were euphemistically called, were counted as three-fifths of a person for the purpose of Congressional representation. While the morality of slavery was already being questioned at the Constitutional Convention (1787), the science of the era was reinforcing the idea of racial hierarchy by proposing that certain races were better suited and adaptable than others to a wider variety of environments. Many American Christians embraced the notion that Black people were an accursed branch of the children of Adam that bore "the mark of Cain" as punishment for murdering his brother Abel (Gates 2019, 57–58).

Although Americans proudly consider themselves as a nation of immigrants, there have always been Americans eager to lock the door behind them once they establish themselves in the New World. In the 19th century, the push to restrict immigration was compounded by the prevailing ideal of American identity, which remained staunchly white Anglo-Saxon Protestant. While Jews and Roman Catholics had lived in the United States since before the Revolution, their numbers were few in most places and they enjoyed the official tolerance of a Constitution that banned a state-established church. Their presence became problematic to organized groups of American Protestants only when their numbers swelled.

In 1830, only 1 percent of the white population was foreign-born. By 1860, that number had risen to 15 percent (Luhrssen 2015, 21). Some of the new arrivals were German-speaking political refugees escaping failed revolutions in Central Europe, but most were Irish who poured into the country after 1850 to flee the ravages of poverty and a potato famine in their homeland. Their adherence to Roman Catholicism was seen as a threat by the Protestant supremacy for introducing alien ideas into the United States. "The deepest and most widespread antipathy [to immigrants] was reserved for the Irish," deemed by many Americans as dirty, unruly, criminal-minded, and incapable of assimilation (Green 2010, 18).

In response to the perceived threats posed by immigrants, the first significant xenophobic movement in the United States emerged. The secret society called the Order of the Star Spangled Banner was popularly known as the "Know Nothings," a name supposedly given it by the hostile editorial writers of the *New York Tribune*. Members of the Order were sworn to secrecy and pledged to "know nothing" when questioned about their activities. Their agenda focused on restricting immigration through legislation by electing its members and supporters to public office (Anbinder 1992, 20–21).

The attitudes underlying the Know Nothings were widespread and espoused by some of the country's leading men. The pioneer of telegraphy,

Samuel Morse (1791–1872), claimed that the Roman Catholic Church conspired with European monarchies to send hordes of immigrants to the United States to undermine the republic's foundation. Despite the separation of church and state, Protestant prayers were imposed on students in many American public schools and anti-Catholic references were included in textbooks. During the 1850s, as Irish immigrants grew in number anti-Catholic riots broke out in several cities and Catholic churches were burned (Anbinder 1992, 9–10, 12).

While membership in the Know Nothings probably peaked at 50,000 by 1854, the organization achieved wider influence for several years through a front group, the American Party. Benefitting from resentment against the two major parties, the American Party sent 48 members to the U.S. Congress, captured legislatures in eight states, and elected mayors in Boston and Philadelphia in the 1854 and 1855 elections (Green 2010, 19–20). Their candidates ran on a platform of antislavery and antiliquor as well as anti-immigration under a slogan condemning "Rum, Romanism and Slavery."

The noisy rise and rapid fall of the Know Nothings and the American Party set precedents in America that continue to play out in the 21st century. Although it remains one of the most successful third parties in U.S. history, the American Party collapsed from infighting and an inability to maintain well-funded local organizations. The Know Nothings "represented a paranoid strain" in American politics whose nativist distrust of foreigners was coupled to a reformist impulse rooted in Puritan ethics (Luhrssen 2015, 26). Before the Know Nothings, Protestant clergy had generally kept aloof from politics, but many ministers avidly championed the American Party, making evangelical Christianity a distinct political force for the first time.

Irish Catholics, the primary target of the Know Nothings and the prejudices they embodied, often fought back on their way to assimilation in American society. In Pennsylvania, an Irish secret society called the Molly Maguires was active in coal country and was accused of assassinating brutal police officers and mining supervisors and sabotaging mining company property. The organization disappeared after 20 alleged members were sentenced by Pennsylvania courts and executed in 1877 and 1878 (Luhrssen 2015, 32–33, 38–39).

Although the Ku Klux Klan has correctly been associated with blocking the advancement of Black people through intimidation and murder, the Klan also "stood for white Anglo-Saxon Protestant dominance over the United States and promoted social issues such as Prohibition" and, like white supremacists of the 21st century, "the Klan believed that America, conceived as a nostalgic ideal, was under assault from powerful, malign forces whose designs must be thwarted" (Luhrssen 2015, 61).

The history of the Ku Klux Klan can be divided into three periods. Its first incarnation (1865–1871) began shortly after the Civil War ended. A band of former Confederate officers, opposed to the emancipation of their slaves and the occupation of the defeated Southern states by the U.S. military during the period known as the Reconstruction, sought to frighten Black people into submission through night raids by hooded horsemen. They tried to drape their terrorism with an "aura of the uncanny" (Luhrssen 2015, 61). In 1867, representatives of the secret organization convened in Nashville to draw up a more formal structure for the *Kuklos*, the Greek word for circle. The Invisible Empire, as they called their realm of terror, claimed to be a chivalric order dedicated to protecting the weak and defenseless—from which they excluded all ethnic and religious minorities. Nathan Bedford Forest (1821–1877), a Confederate general famed for his hit-and-run tactics, was elected to rule the Empire with the title of Grand Wizard.

The Ku Klux Klan was the most infamous of several Southern terrorist groups whose primary purpose was to prevent the former slaves from securing the benefits of their newly won freedom; to drive out Northern "carpetbaggers" who came south seeking jobs and opportunities under the federally administered Reconstruction; to harass "scalawags," Southerners deemed as traitors for collaborating with the North; and to fight a guerilla war against pro-U.S. forces in the South. Lynch law and "rough justice" were familiar sights in many corners of 19th-century America and the Klan's assaults were accepted by many white Southerners fearful of crime and the rising influence of former slaves.

As an organization, the Klan was never tightly disciplined with local leaders often acting on their own initiative in defiance of the Wizards, Dragons, and panoply of ranking Klansmen. Forest ordered the Klan disbanded, probably as part of the campaign by Southern leaders to ingratiate themselves with the North and reintegrate their states into the Union, but his decree was disobeyed. The original Klan was finally stamped out by federal troops under martial law, yet in the end their objectives were met. "A combination of violence, fraud, the aftershocks of the [economic] Panic of 1873, and dissipating will and a shift of priorities in the North" allowed the "Democrats (then the 'white man's party') to take back control of the various state governments in the South" (Gates 2019, 29). Although slavery could not be reestablished, the South substituted laws mandating racial segregation and discrimination along with a sharecropper-based economic system.

The years following the end of Reconstruction saw a flowering of nostalgia for the "lost cause" of Southern independence and the struggle against federal authority following the Civil War. In this context, the novel by Thomas Dixon (1864–1946), *The Clansman: An Historical Romance of the Ku Klux Klan* (1905), became a bestseller. Dixon "provided the Klan and its violence with its most enduring romantic mythology . . . and neatly framed the story of the rise of heroic vigilantism in the South" (Blight 2001, 111). As one Southern woman put it in 1914, "No brighter chapter in all her [the South's] history, no fairer page, will ever be read than that which tells of that illustrious and glorious organization called the Ku Klux Klan" (Jackson 1967, 25).

The Clansman's enduring importance was achieved with its adaptation into a popular film by director D. W. Griffith (1875–1948), *The Birth of a Nation* (1915). Griffith's epic production was cinematically innovative and helped establish the grammar of filmmaking with dramatic, tension-heightening crosscuts between settings. In one infamous scene, the camera cut back and forth as Klansmen rode to the rescue of a white woman besieged by sex-crazed Black men. *The Birth of a Nation* had the additional influence of inspiring the revival of the Ku Klux Klan and the birth of the Klan's second period (1915–1944). Taking its cue from Dixon's novel, the film includes a nighttime cross-burning, an act never committed by the original Klan but that became the new Klan's signature.

That "second Klan" was established by an avid fan of the movie, Atlanta physician William Joseph Simmons (1880–1945), but his leadership as Imperial Wizard was inept and at first attracted only a few hundred followers. The Klan grew with the support and direction from an Atlanta-based public relations agency headed by Elizabeth Tyler (1881–1924) and Edward Young Clarke (1877–?). Contracting with Simmons for 80 percent of the Klan's revenue from the sale of robes and memorabilia, they were driven to promote the organization nationally through press releases and prominently placed interviews. Simmons was pushed aside as Imperial Wizard in 1922 by an Alabama-born dentist, Hiram Wesley Evans (1881–1966).

The second Klan "differed significantly from its parent" and "was stronger in the North than in the South" (Gordon 2017, 2). The true number of Klansmen during the organization's peak years of the 1920s is impossible to determine but numbered in the millions, although many who joined soon left, uneasy with the group's leadership or its penchant for violence. During those years, the Klan owned or controlled 150 magazines and newspapers, two colleges, and a small movie studio (Rice 1972, 367). "Most important, the 1920s Klan's program was embraced by millions who were not members, possibly even a majority of Americans" (Gordon 2017, 3).

The Klan's popularity brought attention to the ongoing argument over who was truly American. Reflecting views widely held by many of the country's white Anglo-Saxon Protestants, the Klan declared Jews, Italians, Irish, Greeks, and Slavs as insufficiently white. Hispanics, Asians, and African Americans were beyond the pale and Roman Catholicism was denounced. The Klan organized boycotts of Jewish businesses, even though a Jewish-owned firm manufactured its robes (Chalmers 1965, 39–40). The Klan also "built a politics of resentment" against elites and denounced the immorality of big cities and modern life (Gordon 2017, 3–4). Many klaverns, as local Klan lodges were called, boasted Protestant ministers as chaplains. Violence increased as the Klan attacked anyone it deemed as un-American or immoral, including bootleggers, abortionists, adulterers, trade unionists, socialists, and attorneys representing clients opposed to their agenda. Some of the Klan's victims were murdered; many more were flogged or tarred and feathered. In Dallas, "KKK" was burned on a Black bellhop's forehead.

At its peak, the organization wielded great power in many parts of the United States. In Texas, Klansmen were elected to the U.S. Senate and as sheriffs, mayors, and police chiefs. In Oklahoma, where 1 person in 20 was said to be a Klansman, the vice president of the state university was the organization's Grand Dragon. Indiana's governor was a Klansman and Arkansas sent Klansmen to Congress. In Oregon, the Klan dominated local elections and police departments. Some of the heaviest concentrations of Klan membership in the 1920s were in the Midwest states of Indiana, Ohio, and Illinois. They flaunted their numbers and power. In 1925, over 40,000 Klansmen, robed but with faces exposed, marched down Pennsylvania Avenue in Washington, D.C. at the organization's national convocation (Luhrssen 2015, 64–65).

Although the U.S. Justice Department deemed the Klan's crimes as a state rather than a federal matter, the U.S. House of Representatives held hearings and state and local authorities in many parts of the country began to take action in the face of mounting violence and bad publicity. In Oklahoma the governor, who had once belonged to the Klan, declared martial law and went to war against them. By the end of the 1920s, newspaper accounts of the personal lives of Klan leaders—which included rape, kidnapping, and murder within their own circles as well as embezzlement of funds—caused membership to fall "almost as rapidly as it had risen" as power struggles splintered the shrinking Klan into rival factions (Gordon 2017, 191–193).

By the dawn of the Great Depression, the Klan had largely retreated into the Deep South, where it fought against union organizers and committed acts of terror against Black people. In 1944, when the Internal Revenue Service filed a lien against the Klan for back taxes, Imperial Wizard James Colescott (1897–1950) dissolved the organization. However, many klaverns continued to operate in the Southern countryside.

The Ku Klux Klan's third period (1954–Present) began in reaction to the U.S. Supreme Court's *Brown vs. Board of Education* decision outlawing segregated public schools and unleashed a wave of terrorism against Southern Blacks and civil rights activists. Various organizations claiming the Klan's name and history remain active in the 21st century and continue their legacy of violence.

DEPICTION AND CULTURAL CONTEXT

Black Legion was among the few Hollywood movies of the 1930s to boldly confront a problem in American society in a story "ripped from the headlines" and undisguised except to change the names of individual perpetrators. The events that inspired the film grew out of the May 1936 murder of Charles Poole (1914–1936) by members of a secret society called the Black Legion. During the ensuing and much publicized trial, one of the defendants, Dayton Dean, moved by guilt, gave a confession that led to criminal charges against 50 members of the organization. The trial effectively ended the Black Legion, an organization "more sinister and violent than the Ku Klux Klan" (Jackson 1967, 143).

The connections were numerous between the white-robed Ku Klux Klan and the Black Legion, whose members, as shown in the film, wore black robes emblazoned with skulls and crossed bones. The Black Legion was founded by Billy Stanton, a physician in Bellaire, Ohio, following his expulsion from the Klan after one of the Invisible Empire's continual struggles between rival factions. By 1929, control of the Legion fell to another former Klansman, Virgil "Bert" Effinger, an electrician from Lima, Ohio, who gave himself the title of major-general. Although the Legion had chapters, called regiments, in eastern Ohio, western Pennsylvania, and West Virginia, they grew powerful only around the city where *Black Legion* was set, Detroit (Stanton 2016, 28).

Detroit became a boom town with the success of the Model T and a mecca for industrial labor as home to Ford, Chrysler, Dodge, Hudson, and other automakers. Between 1919 and 1930, the population tripled, making Detroit the fourth largest city in the United States with 1.5 million residents in 1930. The Black population skyrocketed from 40,000 in 1920 to 125,000 a decade later. Along with the migration of Southern Blacks and whites escaping rural poverty came immigrants from Poland, Yugoslavia, Hungary, and Italy, before the Immigration Act of 1924 sharply curtailed the entry of immigrants from beyond Northern Europe. Few among the new arrivals from overseas were Protestant, most were Roman Catholic, and their presence in large numbers outraged white Anglo-Saxon Protestant extremists (Jackson 1967, 127–128). "As a result, Detroit became the unquestioned center of Klan strength in Michigan" with more than 30,000 members in the Wolverine State during its peak years in the 1920s (Jackson 1967, 129). The Klan took an active role in local politics and supported several successful candidates for public office. After the discredited Klan retreated to the deep South and disappeared from the Upper Midwest, many disgruntled former Klansmen remained committed to the violent enforcement of white supremacy, anti-Semitism, and anti-Catholicism. The Great Depression, which resulted in job loss, only exacerbated the tension between ethnic and religious groups.

Humphrey Bogart's character, Frank Taylor, was inspired but not strictly based on a Legionnaire named Dayton Dean. Like Frank, Dean was a blue-collar laborer recruited at his workplace; he lived in "a plain, nameless, working-class" neighborhood and dreamed of a better life. However, Dean's back story is more troubling and less sympathetic than Frank's. He had a history of explicit racism. During the 1919 race riots in Washington, D.C., as a member of the U.S. Navy Shore Patrol, he obeyed orders and opened fire on Black men and women. "We shot them down. Quite a few of them," he recalled. He was more of an eager joiner than Frank and had belonged to the Orangemen, a Protestant fraternal society, as well as the Ku Klux Klan. In the film, Frank is married with a son. Dean's home arrangements were more complicated and included a common-law wife, Margaret O'Rourke, her two adolescent daughters, and two children from his first marriage (Stanton 2016, 11–12). Depiction of Dean's personal life was out of bounds under the Hollywood Production Code that determined what could be seen on screen.

The overall size of the Black Legion's membership is not shown in the film, which focuses on the activities of a single squad within one of the four regiments active in the Detroit area. From the early through the mid-1930s, the Legion was able to assemble 3,000 or more members for its two- or three-day "general musters," held a few times each year on farms in the Michigan countryside (Stanton 2016, 22). The film identifies and focuses on the Black Legion's animosity toward white ethnic minorities; Black people are omitted from the screenplay in keeping with Hollywood studios' aversion to offending Southern audiences, censors, or cinema owners with anything that could be construed as favoring civil rights.

The larger context of the Black Legion's activities and their backdrop in Detroit is left off camera, although many moviegoers in 1937 understood the political and social milieu from their own experience or from having followed events in the newspapers. Detroit was a place of great unrest during the Great Depression. In 1932, when thousands of demonstrators took part in a protest against low wages, the Ford Hunger March, Detroit police and Ford Motor Company security opened fire on the crowd, killing four. The funeral march for the victims attracted tens of thousands of protestors. The Communist Party was active, trying to gain union leadership and publishing a Michigan edition of its *Daily Worker* newspaper.

The Black Legion responded in several ways. A Legionnaire named Isaac "Peg-Leg" White, an ex-Detroit policeman, became an investigator for the city's auto companies, supplying names of local radicals for blacklisting (Stanton 2016, 27–28). The Legion produced inflammatory literature falsely ascribed to the Communist Party, calling on workers to "kill the aggressors of the common people" and calling on Black people to "rise against your white oppressors" (Stanton 2016, 111). Members of the Legion infiltrated leftist organizations but easily crossed the line from keeping tabs to intimidation and murder. The fact that many within the police departments of Detroit and the Motor City's suburbs were members of the Legion helped matters, providing cover for the Legion's reign of terror. When Auto Workers Union organizer George Marchuk was murdered by the Legion, police refused to follow leads and publicly blamed the killing on rival leftists.

The Legion plotted but failed to assassinate the publisher of the *Highland Parker* newspaper, Art Kingsley, and his editor, Curtis Swanwick. Legionnaires blew up the home of Bill Voisine, the Roman Catholic mayor of Ecorse, a steel town near Detroit, and burned down a Communist Party camp in Farmington Hills. Their arson squad, armed with dynamite and firebombs, attacked "black and tan" nightclubs where races mixed as well as houses of prostitution, businesses the Legion deemed equally immoral. They went after bookshops and Communist Party offices (Stanton 2016, 184–185). Malcolm X believed that his father, a preacher dedicated to improving conditions for his race, was murdered by the Black Legion while the family lived in Lansing (X and Hailey 1965, 5).

For fear of offending religious sensibilities, the *Black Legion* film didn't show that one of the Legion's central meeting places in Detroit, the headquarters where Dean received his orders, was a dilapidated Protestant church called the Little Stone Chapel. The Legion also met in other rooms under a variety of false fronts, including the Wolverine Republican League, the United Brotherhood of America, and the Malekta Club (Stanton 2016, 38, 54, 224). Members of the Legion infiltrated the Wayne County Rifle and Pistol Club, which received free ammunition for defense preparedness from the U.S. War Department (Morris 1936, 8).

Also unseen in the film is the Black Legion's bid for political power. Their ultimate goal, as Effinger told his followers, was to overthrow President Franklin D. Roosevelt and establish a new government (Stanton 2016, 106). Although never able to seize power in Washington, they achieved success at the ballot box in the Detroit area. They exercised significant authority over the suburb of Highland Park, where they elected Mayor N. Ray Markland and at least one council member. After losing his bid for reelection in 1934, Markland became an investigator for Wayne County Prosecutor Duncan McCrea, a fellow Legionnaire who, ironically, would play the lead role in prosecuting the Legion two years later. Detroit's police commissioner Heinrich Pickert was a supporter and possibly a member (Stanton 2016, 38, 238–239, 242). Members of the Legion assumed positions as state and local employment directors and hired Legionnaires to fill public jobs (Morris 1936, 9).

The *Black Legion* film accurately reflects the group's rituals and rhetoric as well as the fear that kept some members bound to the organization. Prospective members were asked if they were native-born Americans, white, and Protestant. The initiation took place at night amid black-robed men in woods or dark basements with a gun pointed at the head of the prospective member. The initiate took an oath "in the name of God and the devil" and pledged to dedicate "my heart, my brain, my body and my limbs . . . to devote my life to the obedience of my superiors" lest his soul "be given unto torment through all eternity" (Morris 1936, 5). A prospect also swore to "take an order and go to your death if necessary to carry it out" and was told that he "might be required to perform some duty on a higher plane than the routine night riding" and sign a pact in his own blood (Stanton 2016, 13–14). Like Frank in the movie, if the new member didn't already own a gun, he was required to obtain one. As in the film, more of the Legion's victims were brutally flogged than murdered, though the number of murders committed by the Legion can never be fully tallied. According to Michigan

State Police Captain Ira H. Marmon, one of the leaders in the investigation that broke the Black Legion, the secret society may have been behind at least 50 suspicious "suicides" in the state (Morris 1936, 4).

The political verbiage heard in the screenplay echoes remarks such as those by the Black Legion's Michigan commander, Arthur Lupp. "I have preached the doctrine of Americanism, the doctrine of the Flag," he said. "We believe first, last, and always in pro-Americanism and support the Red, White, and Blue" (Stanton 2016, 26). The film shows the Black Legion as a profitable racket for ringleaders. While the Ku Klux Klan was notorious as a moneymaking enterprise for its chiefs, less is known about the Black Legion's finances. However, it was a source of revenue for its leaders and Effinger received 10 cents each month from each member's dues (Janowitz 1952, 308).

In an early scene, Frank listens to a radio orator who decries immigrants as "grasping foreigners" stealing American jobs. While it's not impossible that the Black Legion covertly sponsored radio programs in Detroit, the obvious reference was to the broadcasts of Father Charles Coughlin (1891–1979), Detroit's notorious "radio priest" before the archdiocese silenced him. The Legion and Coughlin's National Social Justice Union despised each other for religious reasons but their messages sometimes overlapped.

Unlike Frank who stumbled naively toward homicide, Dean was involved in several murders and murder conspiracies including an unsuccessful bid to assassinate labor organizer Maurice Sugar (1891–1974) and the killing of a Black man, Silas Coleman, apparently for fun. The crime for which he and his associates were caught, which led to the unraveling of the Black Legion, was the May 1936 murder of Charles Poole, a worker for the Works Progress Administration (WPA), a New Deal public works agency (Morris 1936, 3). The film mirrors the rough code of "chivalry" the Legion sporadically sought to impose. Although he denied their accusations, Poole was executed for beating his wife, Rebecca, a relative by marriage to a Legionnaire.

Although the police cared little about the Legion's previous murders of Blacks and political activists, the killing of a white, apolitical victim spurred the authorities into action. Clues were uncovered, suspects were arrested, and raids carried out, uncovering weapons, robes, political literature, and a network of terror even more extensive than most of its members had suspected. At first the suspects refused to answer police questions for fear of harm to themselves and their families from vengeful Legionnaires—until Dean began to confess. Although he was one of 13 shackled prisoners on trial, he became the public face of America's most sensational criminal case since the Lindbergh kidnapping (1932).

The case generated sensational headlines across the nation with references to a "Masked Army," "Secret Militia," "Terrorists," and even a "ritual slaying" (Janowitz 1952, 306). The *New York Times* and other major daily newspapers as well as *Time*, *The New Republic*, *The Nation*, and other nationally circulated magazines sent correspondents to cover the proceedings. The courtroom was crowded with photographers and newsreel cameras. The Hearst syndicate got the scoop on their competition when they discovered Prosecutor Duncan McCrea's membership card in the Black Legion. He denied being a member but admitted that the "signature certainly looks like mine. It might be a tracing or I might have signed it. I don't know" (Stanton 2016, 245).

As if to disavow any ties to the Legion, McCrea pursued the case with vigor as the investigation spread across Michigan. Detroit's mayor suspended city employees shown to be Legionnaires, including several policemen. He obtained the convictions of 27 Legionnaires who were sentenced to prison, albeit not the life sentences handed down in the film's climax. The Legion shriveled under the heat of publicity, its rapid demise "reflective of an organization in which loyalty was exacted only partly by common consent and more by violence" (Janowitz 1952). However, some members "reappeared in other similar organizations, which were already active or which sprang up in the areas where the Black Legion operated" (Janowitz 1952, 308).

With the enormous publicity generated by the trial of Dean and his confederates, the Black Legion became a hot subject for popular culture. *Black Legion* was preceded in November 1936 by a less successful and more heavily fictionalized Hollywood film, *Legion of Terror*. The organization inspired pulp fiction and several radio dramas, including an episode of Orson Welles' *The Shadow*. None captured the essence of the society and its methods as accurately as *Black Legion*. Although largely forgotten save for occasional airings on TCM, the film has drawn commentary in recent years. Paul Batters notes in his review of the film, "What is particularly scary about *Black Legion* is that it *still* hits close to the bone, particularly in this era, as strong as it ever did. The rising ugliness of populism openly espousing racism, bigotry and sexism has become more than evident in the world today, dividing people and polarising (sic) society" (Batters 2018).

FURTHER READING

Anbinder, Tyler. 1992. *Nativism and Slavery: The Northern Know Nothings and the Politics of the 1850s*. New York: Oxford University Press.

Batters, Paul. "The Black Legion (1937): A Warning against Fascism and Bigotry." Silver Screen Classics blog, June 30, 2018. https://silverscreenclassicsblog.wordpress.com/2018/06/30/the-black-legion-1937-a-warning-against-fascism-and-bigotry/

Blight, Thomas. 2001. *Race and Reunion: The Civil War in American Memory*. Cambridge, MA: Harvard University Press.

Chalmers, David M. 1965. *Hooded Americanism: The First Century of the Ku Klux Klan*. Garden City, NY: Doubleday.

Gates, Henry Louis, Jr. 2019. *Stony the Road: Reconstruction, White Supremacy, and the Rise of Jim Crow*. New York: Penguin Press.

Gordon, Linda. 2017. *The Second Coming of the KKK: The Ku Klux Klan of the 1920s and the American Political Tradition*. New York: Liveright Publishing.

Green, Donald J. 2010. *Third-Party Matters: Politics, Presidents, and Third Parties in American History*. Santa Barbara, CA: Praeger.

Greene, Graham. 1995. *The Graham Greene Film Reader: Reviews, Essays, Interviews & Film Stories*. Edited by David Parkinson. New York: Applause Books.

Jackson, Kenneth T. 1967. *The Ku Klux Klan in the City, 1915–1939*. Chicago: Ivan R. Dee.

Janowitz, Morris. 1952. "Black Legions on the March." In *America in Crisis*, edited by Daniel Aaron. New York: Alfred A. Knopf.

Luhrssen, David. 2015. *Secret Societies and Clubs in American History*. Santa Barbara, CA: ABC-CLIO.

Malcolm X, with Alex Hailey. 1965. *The Autobiography of Malcolm X*. New York: Grove Press.

Morris, George. 1936. *The Black Legion Rides*. New York: Workers Library Publishing.

Mueller, Eddy von. 2020. "How Bogart Became a Star." TCM. https://www.youtube.com/watch?v=eU8fnoC2o6U

Nugent, Frank. 1937. "The Stand's 'Black Legion' Is an Eloquent Editorial on Americanism." *New York Times*, January 18, 1937. https://www.nytimes.com/1937/01/18/archives/the-screen-the-strands-black-legion-is-an-eloquent-editorial-on.html

Rice, Arnold S. 1972. *The Ku Klux Klan in American Politics*. New York: Haskell House.

Sperber, A. M. 1997. *Bogart*. New York: William Morrow and Company.

Stanton, Tom. 2016. *Terror in the City of Champions: Murder, Baseball, and the Secret Society That Shocked Depression-Era Detroit*. Guilford, CT: LP.

Thomson, David. 2009. *Humphrey Bogart*. New York: Faber and Faber.

Chapter 4

The Grapes of Wrath (1940)

The Grapes of Wrath was released on January 24, 1940 by 20th Century Fox. The film was produced by Darryl F. Zanuck (1902–1979), the studio's cofounder and executive, and Nunnally Johnson (1897–1977), a screenwriter and producer for 20th Century Fox. It was based on the novel by John Steinbeck (1902–1968) and adapted for the screen by Johnson.

The project was given to a man who had worked in Hollywood since the movie town began, John Ford (1895–1973). Ford was a director best known for westerns but whose resume included movies of many genres. By the late 1930s, he was one of Hollywood's premiere filmmakers, following his Best Director Academy Award for *The Informer* (1935) and his box-office success with *Stagecoach* (1939).

The Grapes of Wrath's message of social justice and working-class solidarity may have struck a sour note for Hollywood's politically conservative studio heads, but a Steinbeck novel was considered a hot product. United Artists had scored a commercial and critical hit with its adaptation of Steinbeck's previous novel, *Of Mice and Men* (1939), and *The Grapes of Wrath*, one of 1939's bestselling works of fiction, had earned a National Book Award and a Pulitzer Prize. The book had also generated a great deal of publicity and controversy; it had been "debated in public forums, banned, burned, denounced from pulpits, attacked in pamphlets" for its allegedly "Red" sympathies (Lisca 1978, 88). Zanuck's enthusiasm for the project can be judged by key production dates. The novel was published in April 1939. Johnson's screenplay was completed by July 13 and Ford started filming on October 4 (Thomson 2008, 342). Zanuck promised that *The Grapes of Wrath* would be strictly nonpolitical and adhere faithfully to the novel. He knew this was a contradictory pledge, made to assuage the concerns of Fox's board of directors. An apolitical adaptation of Steinbeck's novel "would have been like making a film about the New York Yankees and not mentioning baseball" (Malham 2013, 114).

The film version was as true to its source as allowed by the censorship of the Production Code Administration and the expectations of the era's movie audience. Johnson retained Steinbeck's dialogue as much as possible and maintained the emotional complexity of the main characters. Many scenes were trimmed or cut altogether to fit the film's running time, long by the standards of 1940 at 2 hours and 15 minutes. The most significant change was in omitting the novel's final chapters, which left the Joads, the family at the story's heart, in desperate straits. The film concludes at an earlier point in Steinbeck's story, allowing for a more hopeful note in the final scene. The sexual transgressions of the former preacher Jim Casy, played in the film with brooding derangement by John Carradine (1906–1988), are toned down, leaving him as a mysterious figure of spiritual longing and vacancy.

The film stars Henry Fonda (1905–1983) as Tom Joad. Fonda had worked with Ford on the movie that solidified his image as a star, *The Young Mr. Lincoln* (1939). He brought inner strength and quiet resolve to a role that might have seemed unsympathetic in lesser hands. As *The Grapes of Wrath* begins, Tom is on his way home after serving four years for manslaughter. He has been paroled for good behavior yet is testy with the truck driver who gives him a lift, defensive about the drunken brawl that ended in homicide. Ford brilliantly condensed Tom's back story in only a few minutes of screen time.

Because of the environmental catastrophe known as the Dust Bowl, the Oklahoma countryside where Tom grew up has changed dramatically since his sentencing. A harsh wind blows continually, carrying away the topsoil and dimming the sunlight. The deserted Joad house is now the hiding place of his neighbor, Muley (John Qualen, 1899–1987). Visualized in flashbacks, Muley tells Tom how the great caterpillar tractors demolished houses and barns and pushed the farmers off the land they had worked for three generations. Shooting the tractor drivers or the agents of the Shawnee Land and Title Company would have been futile. They were cogs in a vast machine and would be replaced the next day. One of the land company agents explained that aside from the windstorms that blew the topsoil away, a single man on a tractor could do the work of an entire farm family.

Tom finds his family sheltering in the shack of Uncle John (Frank Darien, 1876–1955), where they find hope in a handbill promising plentiful jobs picking crops in California. The multigenerational family also includes Ma (Jane Darwell, 1879–1967), Pa (Russell Simpson, 1880–1959), Grandma (Zeffie Tilbury, 1863–1950), Grandpa (Charley Grapewin, 1869–1956), and Tom's younger siblings, Al (O. Z. Whitehead, 1911–1998), Winfield (Darryl Hickman, 1931–Present), Ruthie (Shirley Mills, 1926–2010), Noah (Frank Sully, 1908–1975) and his pregnant sister, Rosasharn (Dorris Bowdon, 1914–2005). Rosasharn is married to Connie (Eddie Quillan, 1907–1990).

Each actor plays a fully credible individual who is also representative of their class and circumstance.

The entire clan, plus Casy, pack their meager belongings onto a sagging old truck and begin a cross-country odyssey on Route 66 to the promised land of California. It's a hard journey. Grandma and Grandpa die on the way. Noah and Connie desert the family. Once they arrive in California, they find that wages are low and diminishing with the arrival of more migrants willing to work for pennies. Casy becomes a labor agitator and calls for the farm laborers to strike for higher pay. He is murdered by vigilantes and in the struggle, Tom kills one of them. The Joads find their way to a U.S. Department of Agriculture camp run by a benign superintendent (Grant Mitchell, 1874–1957). Conditions are good in the camp, but Tom flees when he learns that the police are seeking him for the killing of the vigilante. Before departing, he tells his mother, "I'll be all around in the dark. I'll be everywhere. Wherever you can look, wherever there's a fight, so hungry people can eat, I'll be there. Wherever there's a cop beatin' up a guy, I'll be there."

Afterward, the remaining Joads drive to Fresno where they are promised 20 days of work at good pay. The film ends on a rousing populist note as Ma Joad tells her husband, "Rich fellas come up and they die, and their kids ain't no good and they die out, but we keep a-coming. We're the people that live. They can't wipe us out, they can't lick us. We'll go on forever, Pa, cos we're the people."

The Grapes of Wrath was well received by critics. *The New York Times* called it "one of cinema's masterworks" and said it was "destined to be recalled not merely at the end of this particular year but whenever great motion pictures are mentioned" (Nugent 1940). According to the *New Yorker*, "With a majesty never before so constantly sustained on any screen, the film never for an instant falters" (Mosher 1940). *Time* magazine's editor Whittaker Chambers (1901–1961) called it a great movie and "possibly the best picture ever made from a so-so book" by preserving the novel's best elements and discarding the rest (Chambers 1940).

However, the American political right took *The Grapes of Wrath* to task. In 1941, a U.S. Senate hearing investigated Hollywood for insinuating "propaganda" into its products to sway the American public. At that hearing Martin Quigley (1890–1964), coauthor of the Hollywood Production Code that guided film censorship, denounced the movie as a "demagogic preachment" (Sbardellati 2012, 39). Pearl Harbor distracted the Senate from its critique of Hollywood films, but the campaign against cinematic subversion resumed after the war ended. Under pressure from the House UnAmerican Activities Committee, Motion Picture Association of America president Eric Johnston (1896–1963) promised, "We'll have no more *Grapes of Wrath* ... we'll have no more films that deal with the seamy side of American life" (Sbardellati 2012, 126).

Despite the denunciations, *The Grapes of Wrath* was nominated for seven Academy Awards, including Best Picture, but won only for Ford as Best Director and Darwell as Best Supporting Actress. It was one of 1940's most successful films at the box office and became part of American folklore thanks to singer Woody Guthrie's recording, "The Ballad of Tom Joad" (1940). In a 1940 column for the leftist *People's World* newspaper, Guthrie called the film "the best cussed pitcher I ever seen" (Guthrie 1975, 133).

Influential film historian Andrew Sarris gave *The Grapes of Wrath* a mixed assessment, calling it "overrated in its time as a social testament" but honoring Fonda's "gritty incarnation of Tom Joad" as standing "up to every test of time" (Sarris 1998, 192). His dismissal of the movie is a minority view. According to critic Roger Ebert, the film's message "is boldly displayed, but told with characters of such sympathy and images of such beauty that audiences leave the theater feeling more pity than anger or resolve. It's a message movie, but not a recruiting poster" (Ebert 2002). Historian David Thomson wrote that *The Grapes of Wrath* "still looks like an earnest and touching attempt by the film industry to honor years of national hardship and sacrifice" and called Ford's Joad "timeless and true and a key warning of how society may make outlaws out of its best material" (Thomson 2008, 342). Bruce Springsteen's song "The Ghost of Tom Joad" (1995) carried the outlaw legend to new generations.

HISTORICAL BACKGROUND

Encompassing more than 100 million acres, the Southern Plains are spread across the boundaries of Oklahoma, Kansas, Colorado, New Mexico, and Texas. In the 1930s, the plains were the site of the Dust Bowl, called "one of the three worst ecological disasters in history" (Borgstrom 1973, 203). The catastrophe wasn't the result of climate change or centuries of human mistakes but occurred after only 50 years of reckless exploitation, "sod busting" by farmers with little understanding or concern for long-term consequences. Some observers were dismayed that the Great Depression and the Dust Bowl should coincide in the same decade. Others saw both events as linked, facets of an American crisis of market-driven overexpansion and overconfidence (Worster 1979, 9).

The Southern Plains had been a grassland roamed by buffalo and deer and inhabited by Native Americans who hunted the game. Warnings of drawbacks to settling the region were heard years before the flatlands were transformed from wild grass to agriculture. In 1806, Lieutenant Zebulon Pike (1779–1813), dispatched by President Thomas Jefferson (1743–1826) to explore the west, called the plains the "Great American Desert" and thought they formed a necessary barrier to American overexpansion (Jackson 1966, 2:28). However, the westward march of the United States continued and overspilled all barriers. After the Civil War, the Plains Indians were forcibly subjugated and confined to reservations and buffalo were slaughtered for their pelts. Ranchers occupied wide swaths of the plains—the land was good for pasture.

The cattle boom, celebrated in countless Hollywood westerns depicting cowboys driving their herds across the plains, became the "Beef Bust" of the 1880s after several severe winters reduced herds and prompted ranchers to abandon sections of the Southern Plains. They began to be replaced by farmers abetted by federal homestead grants and encouraged by false advertising from real estate speculators. Settlers were sold cheap—but abundant—acreage and the promise of prosperity in a countryside of thin topsoil where no more than 20 inches of rain fell in any given year. Most settlers had no idea how vulnerable was the land they worked. "As farms spread across the region, more sod was broken and more soil was exposed to oxidation and wind erosion" (Hurt 1981, 20).

The settlers in the Plains states, including Oklahoma, which gained statehood only in 1907, were migrants from many places, including Southern sharecroppers looking to own their own land and European immigrants seeking opportunity in the New World. The pace of settlement quickened in the 1910s, when relatively high rainfall led some to think the climate was growing more favorable for farming. Real estate syndicates purchased abandoned ranches and subdivided them into farms. When the United States entered World War I (1917), the federal government, under the slogan "Wheat Will Win the War," encouraged additional settlement by paying farmers more than $2 a bushel, twice as much as the prewar rate (Hurt 1981, 23). In the five-year period beginning in 1917, more than 11 million virgin acres were plowed for the first time, turning an area the size of New Jersey from native grassland into wheat fields. "No one seemed immune from the optimism filling the air. It was part of the oxygen everyone breathed" (Duncan and Burns 2012, 25).

The opportunities were tempting. A Missouri farmer with 40 acres could sell his land and buy 160 acres in Oklahoma. A young girl in the early 1930s, Pauline Arnett Hodges, recalled that her parents "plowed up every piece of land they could get ahold of . . . And the more wheat they raised, the more land they plowed up." Her family was able to buy a car, build a larger house and live well by growing and selling wheat (Duncan and Burns 2012, 28). Along with farm families new to the region came investors, dubbed "suitcase farmers," who bought acreage and hired workers to plant the crop and bring in the harvest. Although agricultural prices were depressed in many parts of the United States during the 1920s, the wheat boom continued, and even after Wall Street crashed in 1929, the farmers of the Southern Plains prospered. "No Slump for Us Yet" boasted the headline of a Kansas newspaper as 1929 saw the richest harvest yet (Duncan and Burns 2012, 34). However, the following year, wheat prices began to slide along with the rest of the American economy. In response, many farmers planted every plot of ground they owned, trying to make up for their losses by increasing production.

Although drought was spreading through much of the South and Midwest, 1931 brought a bumper crop on the Southern Plains and a glut on the wheat market that caused prices to fall below the cost of production. The region's farmers were in precarious economic straits when the Dust Bowl finally hit.

High winds and dust storms were familiar to the earliest homesteaders on the Plains. However, the rapid expansion of agriculture coupled with lack of conservation left the region increasingly vulnerable to nature. "Continued plowing and overgrazing made the soil almost immediately subject to wind erosion during a drought. Sandy soil could be completely blown away within a few days" (Hurt 1981, 29). Some have assigned January 21, 1932 as the day that the massive wind erosion of the Dust Bowl began. On that date, a dust cloud appeared outside Amarillo, Texas, with dirt carried 10,000 feet into the air by 60 mph winds. Robert "Boots" McCoy, five years old at the time, recalled, "When it hit, in thirty minutes it's just like midnight. Middle of the day was just like midnight with no stars." He added, "And it choked you and choked you with the dust" (Duncan and Burns 2012, 42).

The hardship caused by the dust storms was compounded by intense heatwaves and the ongoing drought, which brought a poor wheat harvest in the summer of 1932. Come fall, the farmers planted again. "You didn't try something different; you just tried harder, the same thing that didn't work," said Oklahoma farmer Wayne Lewis (Duncan and Burns 2012, 46). Some western states endured an additional plague in the form of clouds of grasshoppers that "ate what little remained of many farmers' wheat and corn—along with their fenceposts and the washing on their clotheslines" (Worster 1979, 12). Unable to meet their payments, many families lost their farms to foreclosure. Failure in the wheat fields rippled through nearby communities. Towns and counties were on the verge of bankruptcy as property taxes went unpaid. Some school districts paid teachers with vouchers rather than cash. In Boise City, Oklahoma, the Cimarron County sheriff placed sacks of sugar confiscated from bootleggers on the courthouse steps for the indigent to take and left "road kill" on the steps to feed starving families (Duncan and Burns 2012, 47).

The dust only worsened. In 1932, the Southern Plains were visited by 14 dust storms categorized as severe. In 1933 there were 38 severe storms, some lasting several days. The wind carried sharp points of gravel as well as soil. "It was just like knives cutting into you," recalled Virginia Kerns Frantz, a child during the Dust Bowl in Beaver County, Oklahoma (Duncan and Burns 2012, 50). The conditions gave rise to "dust pneumonia," sickening or killing vulnerable residents of the Plains states.

In May 1934, the environmental cataclysm of the Dust Bowl enveloped most of the nation. On May 9, brown earth from Montana and Wyoming was brought up into the sky by extreme winds and blown eastward, sucking up more dust along the way until 350 tons of dirt was in the air. The storm swept through the Midwest, dropping 12 tons of dust on Chicago. By midday on May 10, the sky over Buffalo was black and on May 11, the dust descended on Boston, New York, Washington, D.C., and Atlanta before blowing out into the Atlantic. "The storms were mainly the result of stripping the landscape of its natural vegetation to such an extent that there was no defense against the dry winds, no sod to hold the sandy or powdery dirt" (Worster 1979, 13).

Following the unusual phenomena of May 1934, the nation was seldom inundated by debris carried by high-altitude air currents, what the New York press dubbed as "Kansas dirt." The worst storms were confined to the Southern Plains, which continued to be buffeted by paralyzing "black blizzards" and "sand blows" that piled sandy soil into dunes (Worster 1979, 14–156). The dirt blown by the wind came in many colors, from the expected brown and black to surprising shades of yellow, ash gray, or red. "And each color had its own peculiar aroma, from a sharp peppery smell that burned the nostrils to a heavy greasiness that nauseated" (Worster 1979, 15). After June 1937, "scattered rainfall reduced the number of dust storms," and although they continued through 1940, "only a few dust storms were serious enough to be classified as severe" in most sections of the plains (Hurt 1981, 43).

As the weather changed, so did farming. The Dust Bowl "made plainsmen acutely aware that they had to change dramatically their agricultural methods" (Hurt 1981, 67). Organized under New Deal legislation, new agencies such as the Civilian Conservation Corps and the Soil Erosion Service (later renamed the Soil Conservation Service) demonstrated new farming methods and signed many farmers to five-year contracts to implement conservation. Some farmers resisted the new ways, but others embraced them, motivated by access to federal loans and funding. Since the federal government didn't believe it had constitutional authority over private land use, states such as Kansas, Oklahoma, and Colorado were encouraged to adopt model legislation that mandated soil conservation. Among the conservation methods employed were crop and pasture rotation, terraced fields, "contour plowing" that allowed the soil to retain more moisture, and "strip cropping" by planting aisles of grass and feed crops in between rows of wheat (Hurt 1981, 69–79). By the end of 1937, the amount of badly eroded farmland had been reduced by more than half through the example and encouragement of federal agencies.

On July 11, 1938, Franklin D. Roosevelt's train pulled into Amarillo, Texas, the largest city in the Dust Bowl and the place where the first storm had been sighted. He was greeted by a 3,000-strong marching band and spoke to an audience estimated at 200,000, four times the population of the city. In his address, he condemned "people who are ignorant and people who think only in terms of the moment." He declared, "We seek permanently to establish this part of the nation as a fine and safe place," not a desert but a region "where a large number of Americans can call home." Members of the audience recalled that as he spoke of the "water that falls from the heavens," it began to rain (Duncan and Burns 2012, 204–206).

Dust storms continued into 1939 but rainfall increased and crop yields rose. The mayor of Hooker, Oklahoma, wasn't the only local official that fall who called on local businesses to allow their employees to help in the fields with the harvest. So many farmers had left in the previous years that farm labor was scarce (Duncan and Burns 2012, 199). Prosperity returned to the Southern Plains in 1942 as the United States entered World War II and the federal government purchased wheat once again for the war effort. However, most of the farm families that fled the Dust Bowl never returned.

DEPICTION AND CULTURAL CONTEXT

The film version of *The Grapes of Wrath* hewed as closely as possible to the novel, whose realism was enhanced by "Steinbeck's intimate knowledge of the materials" (Lisca 1978, 88). The author had worked on California farms as a boy and wrote a series of nonfiction essays on migrant workers. However, the story he told, etched in memory by the film, closely represented the experience of only one segment of the Southern Plains' population. Some were not as poor to begin with as the Joads and the majority of farmers in the region did not journey to California.

JOHN STEINBECK (1902–1968)

By the time John Steinbeck won the Nobel Prize for Literature in 1962, his most enduring work was already several years behind him. Steinbeck grew up in the small towns of California and viewed the people and the land with curiosity and sympathy. His debut novel, *Cup of Gold* (1929), was historical fiction. He hit his stride with *Tortilla Flat* (1935), the first in a cycle of California novels that included *Of Mice and Men* (1937), *The Grapes of Wrath* (1939), *Cannery Row* (1945), and *East of Eden* (1955).

The Grapes of Wrath was derived from his nonfiction essays, a series he wrote for the *San Francisco News* in 1936 on the desperate conditions of Dust Bowl refugees in California. His descriptions of migrant camps, the habits and dialect of the refugees and their hopes in coming to California became the material from which he shaped *The Grapes of Wrath*. Steinbeck's bestselling novels were popular in Hollywood. During Steinbeck's lifetime, 11 of his novels were adapted into feature films by the studios. A man of heroism as well as words, he was wounded at the frontlines covering World War II for a New York newspaper.

The reaction of critics to his Nobel Prize was harsh. He was derided as old-fashioned and out-of-touch. A year before his death, he reported from Vietnam for *Newsday* magazine, praising the U.S. war effort.

The Joads would have been on the lower end of the rural economy before the Dust Bowl began. They were tenants, as were over 60 percent of farmers in Oklahoma and upward of 40 percent in neighboring states. The Joads lived in a wooden shack with few possessions and no modern conveniences and seemed to lack even mechanized farm equipment or an automobile. They were forced to sell their belongings to buy the broken-down truck that carried them to California.

The archetype of the Joads and their neighbors, while firmly grounded in reality, stood in contrast to a middle class of farmers. Before the Dust Bowl, some farmers took loans on crops not yet planted to pay for a new tractor or a Chevrolet roadster. They had enlarged their homesteads, buying larger tracts of land during the wheat boom; a few had jobs in town and hired workers to tend the fields. Others made enough money to build homes with a full basement, an indoor bathroom, and even a telephone (Duncan and Burns 2012, 33, 36). However, the Joad children's unfamiliarity with flush toilets, encountered for the first time in the federal camp in California, reflected reality for a large percentage of farm families. As late as 1940, only one farm in four had electric lights; even fewer had vacuum cleaners, washing machines, or telephones. The electrical grid was thin in many regions. Cooking was done with bottled gas, coal, or wood. Only half of America's farmers had running water. The rest drew their water in buckets from wells (Worster 1979, 129).

Even some of the more prosperous farmers, ruined by the Dust Bowl, "simply loaded what they could into a car and drove off in the night, telling no one, least of all their creditors, where they were going" (Worster 1979, 121). Like the Joads, moving to the nearest town was seldom an option. There were few jobs and little industry in the region aside from Texas, where displaced farmers found work in the gas and oil industry. "Some kind of agricultural employment elsewhere was what most hoped for" (Hurt 1981, 49). The population in many rural counties dropped by as much as 30–40 percent. Altogether, some 3.5 million people left their homes in the plains during the 1930s.

But despite steep population declines in some areas, "the vast majority of the people remained in the Dust Bowl" (Hurt 1981, 54–55). Some farmers were stubborn or trusted in God; others realized that federal subsidies and loans introduced by New Deal programs enabled them to "endure the menaces of drought, dust, and hard times until the rains returned" (Hurt 1981, 55). But by 1935, repeated crop failures and ongoing dust storms forced some valiant holdouts to leave. "Where can you go when you're penniless?" recalled Clarence Beck, the child of Oklahoma farmers, when asked why they stayed so long. "At least where you are, you have the feel-at-homeness." Discouraged by poverty, his mother and aunt abruptly left the family for Kansas; his father finally gave up when his tractor was repossessed (Duncan and Burns 2012, 132).

Unlike the Joads, most of the migrants looked for farm work in neighboring counties or states. However, there was significant westward migration. During the Dust Bowl decade, the Pacific Northwest eventually drew 460,000 migrants and California may have seen the arrival of as many as 300,000. The majority of migrant families consisted of a young couple with a small child—a much smaller kinship group than the Joads. Only 12 percent of Oklahomans and 17 percent of Kansans interviewed at the time claimed crop failure as their primary reason for moving west (Worster 1979, 50). This low number may be attributed to a deeply ingrained sense of shame rather than the truth of their circumstances. Many migrants might have denied their failure to manage the crisis, claiming instead that they came in pursuit of the promised land that California boosters had marketed so astutely for several decades.

Although the multigenerational Joads may have been in the minority, documentary photographs from the Dust Bowl reveal the accuracy of their appearance in *The Grapes of Wrath*. The photos were taken for a New Deal agency, the Farm Security Administration, by Dorothy Lange (1895–1965) and Arthur Rothstein (1915–1985). Some of them show large families looking much like the Joads on the road heading west on U.S. Route 66. In those photos, old trucks like the Joads's vehicle were packed with as many as 10 people, often perched on mattresses laid on the roofs. Some families even found room for a goat or a kitchen table in their truck. The photographs were much publicized in the 1930s and provided director John Ford with visual inspiration.

Regardless of which state they came from, the Dust Bowl refugees arriving in California were given the derogatory name of "Okies." As in the film, they had to pass police inspections, sometimes called "bum blockades." Many Californians were hostile. A sign at a San Joaquin Valley theater defined the antimigrant attitude: "Negroes and Oakies upstairs" (Worster 1979, 52).

Immigration restrictions in the early years of the Great Depression had resulted in the deportation of many of the Mexican migrants who had worked in California's fields. The arrival of thousands of farmhands from the plains was welcomed by growers who sought cheap short-term labor for picking the state's oranges, lemons, asparagus, and lettuce. *The Grapes of Wrath* accurately depicts conditions in the thousands of migrant camps that sprang up during the period. Families were quartered in shacks if they were lucky and tents if less fortunate. A farm family with all its members pitching in could expect to earn $450 for half a year's work, which was half of a subsistence wage in 1930s California. As dramatized in *The Grapes of Wrath*, the growers kept wages low because there were two or three migrants for every available job. Okies who spoke up were jailed by local police or, worse, beaten or shot by vigilantes (Worster 1979, 53). The migrants moved with the harvest like the Joads, traveling hundreds of miles from one corporate farm to another. As shown in the film, contractors went to migrant camps promising decent wages, but the offering price dropped by the time the farmers arrived to begin work (Duncan and Burns 2012, 170).

The Joads found their best accommodations at a U.S. Department of Agriculture camp, which accurately represents the centers operated in California by the Farm Security Administration. In researching his series of nonfiction essays on migrants, Steinbeck became friends with Thomas E. Collins, the director of one of those centers, the Migratory Labor Camp in Kern, California. Collins became the model for the benevolent camp administrator in the novel and the film. Steinbeck dedicated *The Grapes of Wrath* "To Tom who lived it," meaning Collins, not the fictional Tom Joad as many readers assumed (Nealand 2008). Like the administrator in the movie, Collins insisted that the migrants govern their camps through elected committees and maintained high standards.

Tex Pace, a child when he arrived with his parents at a Farm Security Administration camp near Visalia, California, could have been describing scenes from the film when he recalled, "You had a big building in the middle of the cabins with a shower. You had washing machines, you had clotheslines and ironing rooms." Outside the gates, the campers found hostility. Opposition to the camps from growers, local authorities, and many Californians was as real as shown in the film (Duncan and Burns 2012, 178).

Steinbeck's novel and the film that followed erred in transposing the practices of agribusiness to the Southern Plains, implying that the Joads and their neighbors were driven off the land by corporate-owned tractors as much as by dust storms. "In fact, however, there were few farming corporations anywhere in Oklahoma. Agriculture there was organized more primitively than that" (Worster 1979, 58). At the time, some observers found that the problem was less about who owned the land than the heedless commercialization of plains agriculture by tenants and landlords alike. "Their tragedy is part of a greater tragedy—the wasteful and senseless exploitation of a rich domain" (McWilliams 1942, 187). The migrants were environmental refugees, forced off lands ill-tended by their inhabitants.

Steinbeck's novel "taught an entire reading public what to think about the Okies" and the Dust Bowl and Ford's film embedded the "story of the heroic, embattled, tenacious Joads" in popular memory (Worster 1979, 54). *The Grapes of Wrath* is accurate in most of its details and although it depicts the lives of only one subset of Dust Bowl migrants, the film's epic story is deeply rooted in experience.

FURTHER READING

Borgstrom, B. George. 1973. *World Food Resources*. New York: Intext Educational Publishing.

Chambers, Whittaker. 1940. "Cinema: The New Pictures." *Time*, February 12, 1940. https://whittakerchambers.org/articles/reviews/grapes-of-wrath/

Duncan, Dayton, and Ken Burns. 2012. *The Dust Bowl: An Illustrated History*. San Francisco: Chronicle Books.

Ebert, Roger. 2002. "The Grapes of Wrath." rogerebert.com, March 31, 2002. https://www.rogerebert.com/reviews/great-movie-the-grapes-of-wrath-1940

Guthrie, Woody. 1975. *Woody Sez*. New York: Grosset & Dunlap.

Hurt, R. Douglas. 1981. *The Dust Bowl: An Agricultural and Social History*. Chicago: Nelson-Hall.

Jackson, Donald, ed. 1966. *The Journals of Zebulon Pike* (2 vols). Norman: University of Oklahoma Press.

Lisca, Peter. 1978. *John Steinbeck: Nature & Myth*. New York: Thomas Y. Crowel Company.

Malham, Joseph M. 2013. *John Ford: Poet in the Desert*. Chicago: Lake Street Press.

McWilliams, Carey. 1942. *Ill Fares the Land*. Boston: Little, Brown.

Mosher, John. 1940. "The Current Cinema." *The New Yorker*, February 3, 1940. https://archives.newyorker.com/landing

Nealand, Daniel. 2008. "Archival Vintages for the Grapes of Wrath." *Prologue Magazine*, National Archives, Winter 2008. https://www.archives.gov/publications/prologue/2008/winter/grapes.html

Nugent, Frank. 1940. "The Grapes of Wrath." *New York Times*, January 25, 1940. https://www.nytimes.com/reviews/movies?res=9802E7D91E3EE23ABC4D51DFB766838B659EDE

Sarris, Andrew. 1998. *"You Ain't Heard Nothin' Yet": The American Talking Film History and Memory, 1927–1949*. New York: Oxford University Press.

Sbardellati, John. 2012. *J. Edgar Hoover Goes to the Movies: The FBI and the Origins of Hollywood's Cold War*. Ithaca, NY: Cornell University Press.

Thompson, David. 2008. *"Have You Seen…": A Personal Introduction to 1,000 Films*. New York: Alfred A. Knopf.

Worster, Donald. 1979. *Dust Bowl: The Southern Plains in the 1930s*. New York: Oxford University Press.

Chapter 5

The Night of the Hunter (1955)

The Night of the Hunter was released on July 26, 1955 by United Artists. It was the directorial film debut of Charles Laughton (1899–1962), a veteran Oscar-winning British actor acclaimed for his roles in Hollywood pictures such as *Mutiny on the Bounty* (1935) and *The Hunchback of Notre Dame* (1939). The film was produced by Laughton's friend Paul Gregory (1920–2015), a Broadway impresario known for his innovative staging. Gregory discovered *The Night of the Hunter*, a novel by Davis Grubb (1919–1980), and encouraged Laughton to transform the story into a film.

Grubb came from a prominent family in a small West Virginia town whose "fortunes were reduced by the Depression." Like millions of Americans, his family was evicted from their home "and the trauma, no doubt dramatized by Grubb, became in his writing a cry against the powerful and against capitalist society" (Plumley 2014).

His novel, *The Night of the Hunter*, belonged to the emerging Southern gothic genre. Both the book and Laughton's adaptation include signatures of gothic fiction such as a stark "Calvinistic . . . polarity of good and evil," the "use of setting and atmosphere to create a mood and stimulate the imagination," and a "revelation of the blackness in the depths of human nature" (Kerr 1979, 6, 13). With novelist William Faulkner as Southern gothic's progenitor, the genre's sometimes uncanny stories unfolded against the unspoken history of slavery, the defeated Confederacy, unresolved racial and class tension, and the pervasive influence of Protestant fundamentalist sects and itinerant preachers in the region. Christianity in its darker forms was an essential element of the Southern gothic genre from which *The Night of the Hunter* derived. William Faulkner wrote of "the old violent vindictive mysticism" prevalent in the region's "isolated puritan country households" (Faulkner 1936, 82, 93). In a survey of the genre, essayist Margarita Smith commented, "I wonder sometimes if what they call the 'Gothic' school of Southern writing, in which the grotesque is paralleled with the sublime, is not due largely to the cheapness of human life in the South" (Smith 1972, 319).

Many filmmakers avoid the authors of the published stories they are adapting, but Laughton engaged with him to an unusual degree, even asking Grubb, a former art student, to draw sketches of certain scenes (Callow 2000, 29). However, Laughton picked a bankable name in Hollywood to write the screenplay, choosing James Agee (1909–1955), who had received an Oscar nomination for *The African Queen* (1951). Agee was also chosen for the sensibility of his nonfiction account of Southern sharecroppers, *Let Us Now Praise Famous Men* (1941). Although some film historians believe that the final screenplay was almost entirely rewritten by Laughton, the discovery of Agee's first draft shows *The Night of the Hunter* resulted from an active collaboration with Laughton (Strangow 2010, 18). Agee's ideas also influenced the film visually by encouraging Laughton to study the silent cinema of D. W. Griffith for inspiration. "Griffith was the master of heightened, poetic melodrama, and that's what Laughton wanted for *The Night of the Hunter*" (Rafferty 2010, 10).

To play the unforgettable star role of the evil preacher, Reverend Harry Powell, Laughton chose Robert Mitchum (1917–1997). The actor's much-publicized 1948 conviction for marijuana possession had "firmly established him in the public mind as a figure of thoroughly dubious morals" (Callow 2000, 33). As Willa Harper, the widow he marries, Shelley Winters (1920–2006) "is cast ideally to type, as a gullible sexual optimist doomed to perish early" (Rafferty 2010, 11). For Miz Rachel Cooper, the good Christian who protects Willa's children from the preacher, Laughton chose D. W. Griffith's silent star, Lillian Gish (1893–1993), who "invoked the mighty spirits of the elders of cinema" in her quiet but forceful role (Rafferty 2010, 11).

The film's children are at the center of many scenes. The believably mature and responsible John Harper is played by nine-year-old Billy Chapin (1943–2016), already a Broadway star. The role of his younger sister Pearl went to Sally Jane Bruce (1948–).

The film leaves no doubt about Powell's character or motivations. He continually speaks out aloud to God and his first monologue reveals that he's a serial killer who preys on women. Before his arrest at a burlesque show for car theft, the switchblade he plays with while watching the dancers is introduced as a visual motif representing his sexual dysfunction. The audience also sees the tattoo on his fingers, HATE across one hand and LOVE across the other. Powell's ongoing one-way conversations with God establish that he isn't a religious fraud but a sociopathic believer.

The Night of the Hunter's pivotal scene comes early with the arrest of the children's father, Ben (Peter Graves, 1926–2010), for a bank robbery that ended in a double murder. As state troopers descend on the family's home, Ben entrusts the stolen money to John, making him swear that he will hide the cash, tell no one, and look after his sister. The bank notes are concealed inside Pearl's ragdoll. While in prison awaiting sentencing, Powell becomes Ben's cellmate and overhears him talking in his sleep about the hidden money. Ben is sentenced to die but Powell, having served his time, is released and sets out in search of that money.

John is the film's protagonist, and his point of view is prominent. He is immediately suspicious of Powell, though his mother and the small town's adults are captive to the preacher's oily charm and sanctimonious rhetoric. Powell marries Willa and becomes the town's spiritual leader. Despite his rise to prominence, Powell remains focused on finding the stolen money and is convinced that the children know where it is hidden. He murders Willa, hides her body, and tells the townsfolk that she ran off with another man.

Losing patience with John's stubborn denials, Powell lunges at the children, but they escape. After receiving no help from the town's only sympathetic adult, the benign but alcoholically hapless Uncle Birdie (James Gleason, 1882–1959), they set forth on a skiff and drift downriver in a sequence evoking Mark Twain's *Adventures of Huckleberry Finn*. Powell is in pursuit with an almost supernatural ability to follow their trail. John and Pearl are given shelter by Miz Cooper, who runs an informal mission for orphan children on her farm, and when Powell shows up at her door, demanding custody of the siblings, she warns him away at gunpoint, shooting him. He is eventually arrested and sentenced to death for Willa's murder.

The *New York Times* praised *The Night of the Hunter* as a "weird and intriguing endeavor" that did an "exceptionally effective job of catching the ugliness and terror of certain small town types" but criticized its "tangled traffic with both melodramatic and allegorical forms" (Crowther 1955). *Photoplay* praised Mitchum for "a performance of power and depth that nothing in his earlier career has ever approached" and the *New York Herald Tribune* called the film "a somber study of good and evil with characters more complex than the usual Hollywood type" (Callow 2000, 53). Although the reviews were generally sympathetic, *The Night of the Hunter* confused audiences by refusing to conform to 1950s Hollywood genre expectations. It was a horror film unlike other horror films, a Southern melodrama unlike any other, social realism that turned surreal and a thriller that crossed the line into religion, a subject handled cautiously under Hollywood censorship rules. Even so, although the Roman Catholic Legion of Decency didn't forbid the film to the faithful, the watchdog agency labelled *The Night of the Hunter* as "morally objectionable in part." The Protestant Motion Picture Council took a harder line, calling it offensive to religious sensibilities. In 1955, relatively few moviegoers were prepared to remember the Great Depression, an era left behind in America's postwar prosperity. Few tickets were sold. Heartbroken by its failure at the box offices, Laughton never directed another film.

However, by the late 1950s, *The Night of the Hunter* was shown on television and began to find admirers who had never seen it in theaters. During the 1960s, its reputation rose in the emerging network of university film schools, encouraged by favorable nods from influential French critics. The reviewer in *Cahiers du cinema* understood that the story is "shown from the point of view of a child's gaze," adding, "we're in a world of wonders" (Callow 2000, 59). Some measure of the film's enduring power comes from a visual language of impossibly long expressionist shadows and Powell's body language, suggesting a bat or some other nocturnal creature. The direction and cinematography elevate the characters and story to a level that looks slightly larger than life.

By the end of the 20th century, appreciation for *The Night of the Hunter*'s "triumphs of poetic cinematography" as well as the poetry of its screenplay were "well established" and "universal," according to British writer-director Simon Callow (Callow 2000, 62). The *New Yorker*'s Terrence Rafferty ranked it "among the greatest horror movies ever made, and perhaps, of that select company, the most irreducibly American in spirit" (Rafferty 2010, 7). For film historian Dave Thomson, *The Night of the Hunter* "is one of the masterpieces of American cinema"; he adds that Mitchum's performance is "one of the most compelling studies of evil in American cinema" (Thomson 2010, 557, 671).

HISTORICAL BACKGROUND

As recently as 1942, President Franklin D. Roosevelt put America's religious identity bluntly, saying "America is a Protestant country and the Catholics and Jews are here under sufferance." He reflected an attitude deeply rooted in the earliest history of the United States. Christianity came to the original 13 states with the largely Protestant settlers arriving from the British Isles in the 17th century. Some were Anglicans who transplanted the Church of England (Episcopalians) to the New World. Massachusetts was settled by Congregationalists. Pennsylvania granted religious freedom to anyone who believed in God while Maryland granted freedom only to believers in the divinity of Jesus.

In several of the original states, "established churches" were supported by state governments, but those ties were eventually dissolved. The U.S. Constitution (1789) mandated the separation of church and state and guaranteed freedom of religion but not freedom from religious prejudice. As the United States expanded into former Spanish and French colonies such as Florida, Louisiana, Texas, and the Southwest, Roman Catholic populations were absorbed into the growing nation, yet they remained apart and even suspect in the minds of white Anglo-Saxon Protestants. The arrival of Jews, Irish and Italian Catholics and other immigrants in the 19th and early 20th centuries did little at first to alter America's Protestant identity.

American Protestantism began to assume a distinct form and direction even before the nation's independence with the Great Awakening, a series of religious "revivals" that began in New England and New Jersey in 1734 and "rose to intercolonial crescendo in 1740" (Heimert 1966, 2). The revival divided some existing denominations such as the Congregationalists and the Presbyterians into supporters and opponents and spurred the spread of evangelical Presbyterianism in the South. In many places, "the Baptists rose into new prominence as the beneficiaries of the revival" (Heimert 1966, 3). The Awakening's spirit was opposed by members of the educated upper classes. Many of the emerging nation's leaders were steeped in the Enlightenment philosophy that informed the Declaration of Independence and the U.S. Constitution and actively networked in Free Mason lodges while maintaining formal membership in established churches.

In keeping with the spirit that animated much of Protestantism, the "revivalism" of the Great Awakening was meant as a return to the imagined Christianity of the earliest apostles. The Awakening represented the spiritual hunger of the lower classes, the need for certainty which came to be associated with literal readings of the Bible. The Awakening grew in part from the followers of John Calvin (1509–1564), the Swiss theologian who valued faith more than good works and maintained that God chose those whom he wanted to save from hell, a doctrine called "predestination."

The leading figure behind the Awakening, Jonathan Edwards (1703–1758), came from a family of Congregationalist pastors. His sermons in the 1730s are credited with sparking the movement with his call for worshippers to feel the presence of God personally and with fervor. His followers emphasized the emotional aspect of the religious experience, the reception of the Holy Spirit—an evangelical imperative to win over converts and those who oppose the intellectual or rational precepts of older Protestant denominations. Because of the established churches' ties to the Old World, the emerging "evangelical religion embodied a radical and even democratic challenge to the standing order of colonial America" (Heimert 1966, 12). In many ways, the Great Awakening allowed the American Revolution to happen, even though most of the Revolution's prominent leaders were unsympathetic to its doctrines and worship.

The experiential aspect of the Awakening remained foundational to developments in American Protestantism, even as the elitist Calvinist doctrine of predestination fell away in favor of the more democratic idea that salvation is free to anyone who seeks it. Methodists and Baptists gathered white and Black audiences for revival gatherings "full of dramatic preaching, shouting, dancing, fainting, ecstatic trances." Formal instruction wasn't required for conversion, "only inner communion with the Holy Spirit"

(Gates 2021, 40). During this time, Americans of African origin converted to Christianity en masse.

The Second Great Awakening is the loose term applied by historians to the new wave of evangelical and revivalist movements that swept across the United States after the Revolution and in the first half of the 19th century. The denominations most closely associated with the Awakening were the ones that expanded rapidly. "Starting from scratch just prior to the Revolution, Methodism in America grew at a rate that terrified other more established denominations" and "Baptist membership multiplied tenfold in the three decades after the Revolution" (Hatch 1989, 3).

Segregated congregations were organized among enslaved and free Blacks, sometimes under white patronage. The Second Great Awakening "would bring even greater numbers of African Americans to both the Baptist and Methodist churches," with Black preachers—some unable to read or write—relying on memory and oratory to rouse their congregants (Gates 2021, 46). They often delivered messages of liberation encoded in biblical passages, and in Northern states they became essential contributors to the Abolitionist movement.

Abolition wasn't the only political cause associated with the evangelicals. Although such eminent Free Masons as George Washington and Benjamin Franklin became revered, even mythologized, figures in the American imagination, "a fervent anti-Masonic movement gained prominence in the late 1820s and early 1830s, fueled by Protestant church groups and reformers who feared the concentration of power" in the hands of elites (Luhrssen 2015, 5). Building on old prejudices inherited from the first British settlers, anti-Roman Catholic bigotry and hate crimes rose in response to the first wave of Irish Catholic immigration following the potato famine of 1845. White Anglo-Saxon Protestant anxiety coalesced into a secret society called the Order of the Star Spangled Banner, popularly known as the Know Nothings after their members' oath to say nothing about their activities. The Know Nothings were among the early campaigners for the Prohibition of alcohol and successfully supported candidates for public office in the 1850s. Many Protestant ministers "responded avidly to the Know Nothings condemnation of 'Rum, Romanism and Slavery,'" and many Baptist and Methodist clergymen joined the Order of the Star Spangled Banner (Luhrssen 2015, 26).

Even if the political campaigns associated with the Second Great Awakening often fell short, as a religious movement it continued to hurry forward with centrifugal force. "By the middle of the nineteenth century, Methodist and Baptist churches had splintered into a score of separate denominations, white and black" (Hatch 1989, 3). As the United States extended westward, the Awakening followed and its diverse adherents multiplied. By 1845, there was one minister for every 500 Americans, a remarkable number "given the spiraling population and the restless movement of peoples to occupy the land beyond the reach of any church organization" (Hatch 1989, 4).

The Second Great Awakening was fueled by "camp meetings," outdoor events where as many as 4,000 evangelicals gathered for four days to watch the performances by as many as 100 preachers. Participants spoke of the heat of "heavenly fire" or wrote that "sinners were struck as with hammer and fire, or like as if thunder flashes had smitten them" (Hatch 1989, 49, 2). Skeptics criticized the events for encouraging intemperate behavior. One New Englander wondered, "Must a man draw his mouth out of all shape, and bellow like a bull, in order to become a Christian?" (Hatch 1989, 55).

Many who attended the camp meetings came in search of salvation, but the gatherings also served as entertainment in an era when few amusements existed. The performers included a "whole range of rootless and visionary preachers, spurning conventional religious establishments and genteel routines" (Hatch 1989, 55–56). Many were earnest in their fervor to save souls but some were entrepreneurs who identified a market to be exploited.

The evangelical movement became inseparable from America's "manifest destiny" to dominate North America. In an 1847 speech to missionaries, the Congregationalist minister Horace Bushnell (1802–1876) promised, "The wilderness shall bud and blossom as the rose before us; and we will not cease, till a Christian nation throws up its temples of worship on every hill and plain . . . and the bands of a complete Christian commonwealth are seen to span the continent." He also expressed concern over the keepers of those temples and their potential for "moral and social disorganization" and "ignorance, wildness and social confusion" (Hatch 1989, 62). Although evangelicals shared an anti-establishment, anti-elite bias and a certain style of fervor, they often found little else in common. If everyone interpreted scripture according to his own lights, then each Christian was potentially his own denomination.

The rancorous disagreement over the meaning of Christianity forms the backdrop to the rise of a particular offshoot of evangelical Protestantism, the Church of Jesus Christ of Latter-day Saints or Mormons. Mormonism's founder, Joseph Smith (1805–1844), came of age in upstate New York's "Burned-over district," so called because the area seemed to be on fire with camp meetings and incendiary preachers. But for many, the fire left the ground barren. The Smith family had exhausted a number of unfulfilling religious choices, "their hopes for experiencing the divine confused by a cacophony of voices" (Hatch 1989, 59).

By 1827, Smith had claimed to have received divine revelations, including the discovery of a new scripture. *The Book of Mormon* supplemented the New Testament with a narrative involving the appearance of the resurrected Christ in the New World. Smith's message found converts but also opposition from all previous Christian sects as well as state authorities, in part because he preached polygamy in defiance of law and custom. Smith led his beleaguered followers to Kirtland, Ohio in 1831 but violent opposition from their new neighbors forced them further west to a Missouri town called Far West in 1838. Surviving the attack of an angry mob, the Mormons withdrew to Illinois where they established the town of Nauvoo, the largest city in the state. With their growing numbers threatening to gain influence over the new state, Smith announced his candidacy for president of the United States. In 1849, he was arrested for treason but never stood trial. A mob attacked the jail where he was held and killed him. Afterward, Smith's successor, Brigham Young (1801–1877), led the faithful on an exodus to Utah, where Mormonism established its enduring center, Salt Lake City. Several smaller groups, including the Shakers and the Oneida Community, also seceded from evangelical Protestantism and formed separate communities in remote regions of the United States, but only the Mormons succeeded in perpetuating their beliefs.

Evangelical Protestantism was also shaped by the debate over slavery. Many Northern evangelicals embraced the moral imperative of Abolitionism while Southerners found justification for slavery in the Bible. The argument led to denominational splits between Northern and Southern Baptists, Methodists, and Presbyterians in the 1830s and 1840s. As tensions rose over slavery, white Southerners came to view the Black churches with suspicion, especially after the 1831 slave revolt led by Nat Turner, a charismatic Black preacher (Gates 2021, 58).

New tensions broke out within American Protestantism in the decades following the Civil War. Holding on to literal interpretations of the Bible, conservatives tried to hold the line against liberals who harmonized new scientific findings on the age of the Earth and the evolution of species with Christianity. Especially in rural areas, in the Southern and Border States, conservative evangelical voices grew more strident and dominant in the face of modernism, secularism, and any effort to place the scriptures in their historical context. Typical of post-Civil War evangelical preachers, Samuel P. Jones (1847–1906) was a Georgia Methodist who traveled the South with an entertaining tent show. He denounced Christian "backsliders" as "flop-eared hounds, beer kegs, and whisky soaks" and called for the prohibition of alcohol (Kazin 2006, xvii).

The conservative movement became more conscious of itself and adopted a new name, fundamentalism, after a series of theological tracts, *The Fundamentals: A Testimony to the Truth* (1910–1915). The struggle over biblical interpretation took on greater urgency after World War I upset existing balances in American society and posed new challenges to old values. "In a postwar atmosphere of alarm, 'fundamentalism' emerged as a distinct phenomenon" with revivalism "at the center of the traditions carried on by fundamentalism" (Marsden 1980, 6).

Impassioned evangelical preachers, performing to audiences outdoors more than from pulpits, had been a fixture of American life since before the Revolution. The rise of fundamentalism was championed by such preachers, none more famous than Billy Sunday (1862–1935). He had been a

> **AIMEE SEMPLE MCPHERSON (1890–1944)**
>
> Most fundamentalist preachers have been men. Aimee Semple McPherson set a precedent for women in the pulpit. The flamboyant Canadian-born performer toured the Southern states by car in the 1910s preaching to crowds through a megaphone. She arrived in Los Angeles in 1918, where the message of her sermons resonated with the largely conservative, white Protestant population.
>
> McPherson came from the Pentecostal tradition of religious ecstasy and speaking in tongues and brought that faith from the backwaters into the mainstream. Through the 1920s and 1930s, she preached biblical literalism spiked with American exceptionalism to audiences comprising thousands. The idea of the United States as a divinely inspired commonwealth was crucial to her theology. She also claimed to be a faith healer and performed "miracles" for her audiences.
>
> Although she condemned theater and movies as the devil's work, her theatricality resembled Broadway shows and Hollywood musicals. McPherson was also a pioneer in Christian broadcasting and her Angelus Temple was America's original megachurch, claiming 10,000 parishioners. McPherson organized soup kitchens, food pantries, and other relief work for the poor in the 1920s and through the Great Depression. She endorsed Herbert Hoover in 1928 and Franklin D. Roosevelt in 1932, supported organized labor, condemned communism, and threw her support behind the war effort after Pearl Harbor.
>
> Her personal life gave rise to much-publicized rumors concerning extramarital affairs. In 1944, McPherson was found dead in her hotel room from an overdose of barbiturates.

professional baseball player and used his reputation in the sport to draw crowds. Sunday built his reputation as a preacher by working the "kerosene circuit," so called because the villages where he pitched his canvas circus tent had no electricity (Dorsett 1991, 58–63). Such was the fervor of Sunday's performances that he "pummeled sin with language and gestures that resembled a boxing match with the devil" (Kazin 2006, 131).

Not all evangelicals had a message as simple as Sunday's theme of sin and salvation. William Jennings Bryan (1860–1925) was considerably harder to categorize. He was a Democratic congressman from Nebraska and a three-time candidate for the presidency who resigned in 1915 as secretary of state, fearing that the United States under President Woodrow Wilson (1856–1924) was drifting toward entrance into World War I. During most of his public life, Bryan maintained a large, nationwide following as "a godly hero who preached that the duty of a true Christian was to transform a nation and world plagued by the arrogance of wealth and the pain of inequality" (Kazin 2006, xiii). However, a century after his death, he is remembered mostly for his role in the infamous "Scopes Monkey Trial" (1925) that prosecuted a public-school teacher in Dayton, Tennessee, for teaching Darwin's theory of evolution.

Bryan was far from the only voice in late-19th-century America who promoted populism and political reform in evangelical terms. It was an epoch when "evangelical rhetoric saturated every mass movement in America," including the Knights of Labor, the Women's Christian Temperance Union, and the Farmers Alliance (Kazin 2006, xv–xvi). Unlike most politicians of his era, Bryan intended to rock the ship of state if he was elected president. "Speaking to and for a legion of [lower and middle] class admirers, he voiced a romantic class-aware protest against an order increasingly being governed by the intellectual assumptions and material might of big corporations" (Kazin 2006, 45). By favoring a strong federal government and encouraging its intervention in policies once reserved for states and private interests, Bryan opened an ideological path for the Democratic Party that led to Franklin D. Roosevelt's New Deal measures to end the Great Depression.

Bryan was a star speaker on the Chautauqua circuit, the traveling shows that roamed the United States from 1903 to 1930 with programs of lectures and concerts. "The perennial message he delivered to Chautauqua crowds was a call to articulate and act upon convictions that married a faith in secular reform with the coming of the Kingdom of God" (Kazin 2006, 137). Left behind by the changing face of postwar politics, he turned his focus to religion. During the early 1920s, Bryan held Bible classes with audiences numbering into the thousands, delivered sermons from coast to coast, and was one of the first preachers to be heard on radio. "He debated, in person and in print, leading exponents of the modernist creed" (Kazin 2006, 263). He crusaded against Darwinism, not only because it appeared to violate the biblical account of creation but also because he feared that it opened the door to eugenics and a struggle for ascendance among different human races, even as he spoke in support of segregation (Kazin 2006, 275, 278).

Bryan lobbied for laws restricting the teaching of Darwin's theories in public schools. They were enacted only in the Southern and border states of Tennessee, Mississippi, Arkansas, and Florida, and in Oklahoma, home to large numbers of white Southern migrants. The issue was thrust into the national spotlight when Tennessee pressed charges against Dayton public-school teacher John Scopes (1900–1970). The high-school football coach's crime occurred when, substituting for an absent science teacher, he assigned the class to read a passage from their biology textbook on Darwinism. "Scopes volunteered to be tried in a test case meant to challenge the validity" of the newly enacted law. "He was hailed by some as a martyr, compared to the likes of Socrates and Galileo" (Shapiro 2013, 3–4). Unlike them, he wasn't in danger of life or vocation. In the end, Scopes was fined $100.

Journalists from across the nation flocked to Dayton, which had a population of 1,800. With a declining economy, civic leaders encouraged the case to move forward and tried to foster the image of Dayton as "every American town" with "an eye toward Dayton's economic revival" (Shapiro

2013, 8). Instead, the media caricatured Dayton as a backwater inhabited by fools. In his coverage of the trial for the prestigious *American Mercury* magazine, one of the nation's most famous commentators, H. L. Mencken (1880–1956), mocked "the resident yahoos" and caricatured Dayton as a town that progress had left behind (Mencken 2014, 544).

As a lawyer and America's most prominent anti-Darwinian, Bryan accepted the offer to join the prosecution team. He was opposed by a bevy of lawyers led by the country's most renowned defense attorney, Clarence Darrow (1857–1938). Scopes' defense was paid for by the American Civil Liberties Union as a free-speech case. The courtroom drama was depicted in newspaper accounts as a contest between religion and science with Bryan arguing the fundamentalist case. It was one of the early salvos in a culture war that continues a century later, and Bryan, in faltering health, lost the battle in the newspapers even as he won a conviction from the jury. He died in Dayton five days after the trial ended and is remembered today from the highly fictionalized film account of the Scopes trial, *Inherit the Wind* (1960).

While defeated in the minds of urban newspaper readers and the intelligentsia, Bryan remained a hero to his rural and small-town following. The funeral train that bore his casket from Dayton to Chattanooga and up through the Alleghenies into Virginia toward its final stop in Washington, D.C., was greeted at every station by "men in shirt-sleeves and overalls, women in gingham and barefoot children" (Kazin 2006, 296).

Evangelical Protestantism left an indelible mark on the literature of the American South, including *The Night of the Hunter*, and on the cultural life and music that emerged from the region. According to a historian of country music, "Although rural music bore some similarities all over the USA, that of the South was distinctly different from rural expressions in certain crucial ways" and "was strongly flavored by evangelical Protestant Christianity" (Kingsbury and Nash 2006, 17). Country wasn't the only music from that milieu that gained popularity across the world. Spiritual songs born in slavery gave rise to gospel music as rural Blacks moved to urban areas. Gospel was the fulcrum that led to rhythm and blues and soul music. Fusing the influences of country and blues together with gospel, Elvis Presley became the popularizer in the 1950s of the emerging music called rock and roll (Jeansonne, Luhrssen, and Sokolovic 2011, 29).

DEPICTION AND CULTURAL CONTEXT

The Night of the Hunter is unusual for weaving together a realistic picture of its time and place with a Christian parable and a dark fairy tale. The terrain in the early scenes of dirt roads and wooden houses clinging to hillsides replicates the small towns of southeast Ohio and West Virginia along the banks of the Ohio River. The Harpers' fictional hometown, Crespa's

Landing, has few modern conveniences aside from several Model T Fords and a small wooden structure marked Bijou. A paddle-wheeler steamboat sails past the fishing piers, a reminder of the Ohio River's linkage to the Mississippi.

The bank robbery that sets the story in motion rises from the dire economics of the Great Depression. When asked why he robbed the bank, Ben explains, "I got tired of seeing children in the woodlands without food, children roaming the highways in this here Depression, children sleeping in old, abandoned car bodies." Ben resorted to crime to provide for his family.

The prevalence of rural poverty in the Allegheny hill country and elsewhere during the early Depression years is apparent in *The Night of the Hunter*. The haggard farm woman who shares her meager ration of raw potatoes with the hungry children who come to her doorstep was modelled after the emaciated sharecroppers photographed by Walker Evans for Agee's book, *Let Us Now Praise Famous Men*. The children in Miz Cooper's care come from realistically diverse situations. Some are orphans. One girl was temporarily given to Miz Cooper by a mother unable to support herself and her child on a shop clerk's wages.

The limited economic choices of the lower class form a subtext to the story. After the hangman at the prison complains of his job to his wife after executing Ben, he adds, "Sometimes I wish I were back in the mine." She reminds him of the mine explosion in the 1920s that killed many of their friends and tells him to stick it out. The dangerous, unhealthy work of coal mining was the region's primary employer.

Although the American South and West had a long tradition of citizens bypassing the courts by meting out their own ideas of rough justice, lynching peaked at the end of the 19th century and declined afterward. Beginning with the Reconstruction, lynching was applied as a tool of oppression against Southern Blacks, but other minorities including Mexicans, Chinese, and Italians were singled out for execution by mob violence. According to one tabulation, 1,297 whites and 3,446 Blacks were lynched between 1882 and 1968 (Lynchings: By State and Race). However, during the 20th century, most lynchings were confined to the Deep South and the scene near the end of the film, showing a furious mob seeking to hang Powell before he could be legally executed, was unlikely in 1930s Ohio or West Virginia.

The film's dialogue echoes a culture whose language and imagination were shaped by the King James Version of the Bible, and this is true not only of Powell and Miz Cooper but of Uncle Birdie and other characters as well. Protestant religion was the guiding norm. Powell's black suit, parson's hat, and string tie formed the expected costume of the region's Protestant ministers, some of whom were, like Powell, itinerants with no fixed abode and of uncertain denominational affiliation. When Ben asks Powell which church he belongs to, the preacher replies, "The religion the Almighty worked out betwixt us." Like his real-life counterparts, Powell was a performer who drew from a familiar repertoire of Protestant hymns, such as "Leaning on the Everlasting Arms" and "Bringing in the Sheaves," and conducted fervent outdoor "revival meetings" by torchlight. Powell reflects the professed distaste of the era's fundamentalist Protestants for strong drink and sex without procreation.

The Christian parable of *The Night of the Hunter* is rooted in the warning by Jesus in the gospels, read by Miz Cooper as the film begins: "Beware of false prophets, which come to you in sheep's clothing, but inwardly they are ravenous wolves. Ye shall know them by their fruits" (Matthew 7: 15–16). Reverend Powell quotes large passages of scripture from memory and maintains a pious façade in the eyes of his rural audience, yet his actions are entirely opposed to the moral imperatives of Christianity. Miz Cooper's gift of discernment allows her to read his thoughts and see into his heart. The screenplay is true to Grubb's "allegory of the struggle between good and evil: a Christian mural, as he says, in which the Preacher has the part of the devil" (Callow 2000, 9).

Grubb and Laughton were both aware that they were transposing archetypal elements of age-old fairy tales into a 20th-century Southern milieu. Reverend Powell is the ogre stepfather, more monster than human, a Bluebeard who kills his wives. Although there is nothing explicitly supernatural in the story, a sense of the uncanny clings to Powell's pursuit of John and Pearl, whose river journey, a hero's quest for freedom, leads them to Miz Cooper in the protecting role of the Good Fairy.

"Fairy tales evoke every kind of violence, injustice, and mischance, but in order to declare it need not continue," writes folklorist Marina Warner (Warner 2014, xxiii). And like their models in the Brothers Grimm and elsewhere, a happy ending awaits the children of *The Night of the Hunter* after surviving many trials.

FURTHER READING

Callow, Simon. 2000. *The Night of the Hunter*. London: British Film Institute.
Crowther, Bosley. 1955. "Bogeyman Plus." *New York Times*, September 30, 1955. https://www.nytimes.com/reviews/movies?res=9407E2DE173DE53ABC4850DFBF66838E649EDE
Dorsett, Lyle W. 1991. *Billy Sunday and the Redemption of Urban America*. Grand Rapids, MI: W. B. Eerdmans.
Faulkner, William. 1936. *Absalom, Absalom*. New York: Random House.
Gates, Henry Louis, Jr. 2021. *The Black Church: This Is Our Story, This Is Our Song*. New York: Penguin Press.
Hatch, Nathan O. 1989. *The Democratization of American Christianity*. New Haven: Yale University Press.
Heimert, Alan. 1966. *Religion and the American Mind: From the Great Awakening to the Revolution*. Cambridge, MA: Harvard University Press.

Jeansonne, Glen, with David Luhrssen and Dan Sokolovic. 2011. *Elvis Presley, Reluctant Rebel: His Life and Our Times*. Santa Barbara, CA: Praeger.

Kazin, Michael. 2006. *A Godly Hero: The Life of William Jennings Bryan*. New York: Alfred A. Knopf.

Kerr, Elizabeth M. 1979. *William Faulkner's Gothic Domain*. Port Washington, NY: Kennikat Press.

Kingsbury, Paul, and Alanna Nash, eds. 2006. *Will the Circle Be Unbroken: Country Music in America*. London: DK.

Luhrssen, David. 2015. *Secret Societies and Clubs in American History*. Santa Barbara, CA: ABC-CLIO.

Lynchings: By State and Race, 1882–1968. *University of Missouri-Kansas City School of Law. Archived from the original on June 29, 2010. Retrieved July 26, 2010. Statistics provided by the Archives at Tuskegee Institute.*

Marsden, George M. 1980. *Fundamentalism and American Culture: The Shaping of a Twentieth Century Evangelicalism 1870–1925*. New York: Oxford University Press.

Mencken, H. L. 2014. "Inquisition." In *The Days Trilogy Expanded Edition*. New York: Library of America.

Plumley, William. 2014. "Davis Grubb." The West Virginia Encyclopedia. http://www.wvencyclopedia.org/articles/84

Rafferty, Terrence. 2010. "Holy Terror." In the booklet for *The Night of the Hunter*. Criterion Collection DVD release.

Shapiro, Adam R. 2013. *Trying Biology: The Scopes Trial, Textbooks, and the Antievolution Movement in American Schools*. Chicago: University of Chicago Press.

Smith, Margarita G., ed. 1972. *The Mortgaged Heart*. New York: Bantam Books.

Stragow, Michael. 2010. "Downriver and Heavenward with James Agee." In the booklet for *The Night of the Hunter*. Criterion Collection DVD release.

Thomson, David. 2010. *The New Biographical Dictionary of Film*. New York: Alfred A. Knopf.

Warner, Marina. 2014. *Once upon a Time: A Short History of Fairy Tale*. New York: Oxford University Press.

Chapter 6

They Shoot Horses, Don't They? (1969)

They Shoot Horses, Don't They? was released on December 10, 1969 by ABC Pictures. The film was produced by Robert Chartoff (1933–2015) and Irwin Winkler (1931–), partners who went on to produce the highly lucrative *Rocky* films of the 1970s. *They Shoot Horses, Don't They?* was based on a 1935 novel by crime fiction author Horace McCoy (1897–1955), who drew from his experience as a bouncer at Depression-era dance marathons in California (Martin 1994, xv).

The transition from page to screen took many years. In the early 1950s, producer Norman Lloyd (1914–2021) purchased rights to the book intending to cast Sydney Chaplin (1926–2009), son of film star Charlie Chaplin (1889–1977), as the protagonist and narrator Robert Syverton. But when the elder Chaplin went into exile after accusations of being pro-Communist, the project fell dormant (Persall 2008). Over a decade later, Chartoff and Winkler obtained rights and commissioned a script by James Poe (1921–1980), who hoped to direct. The screenplay, completed by Robert E. Thompson (1924–2004), retained much of the novel's terse dialogue but added new characters and gave histories to characters who had been granted little more than names and short speaking parts by McCoy. After firing Poe, Chartoff and Winkler hired director Sydney Pollack (1934–2008), a relatively young filmmaker who would earn his reputation from the movie's success. The film was likewise a turning point in the career of its star, Jane Fonda (1937–). Previously known for light comedies, Fonda's role as Gloria Beatty startled audiences at the time of the film's release. Her "performance heralded a new kind of acting: for the first time, she was willing to alienate viewers, rather than try to win them over" (Als 2011). She costarred with Michael Sarrazin (1940–2011), a Canadian actor whose career was also advanced by his role as the doomed protagonist Robert.

Unlike the novel, which begins with Robert on trial for murdering Gloria, his dance partner, the film focuses almost entirely on the marathon that led to the killing. In the novel, the couple are already friends, but in the film, they are strangers as the story begins. With nothing on his mind, Robert wanders from the beach into the Pacific Ballroom where a dance marathon is about to begin. Gloria is already in the contestants' line, desperate for the free food offered to dancers as well as the prize money. When the dance partner she arrived with is disqualified after a brief medical exam, the event's promoter and master of ceremonies, Rocky Gravo (Gig Young, 1913–1978), calls Robert over and asks him to partner with Gloria. She reluctantly accepts him.

They Shoot Horses, Don't They? follows Gloria and Robert through the dangerous repetition of the dance marathon, which will drag on until only one couple remains standing. She is sharp-tongued and bitter, a woman on the run from a bad past in Texas. He is compassionate and emotionally out of place in the doggedly competitive world of marathon dancing but is physically up for the challenge. Subplots are advanced through secondary characters played by a distinguished supporting cast, including Alice LeBlanc (Susannah York, 1939–2011), an emotionally unstable woman dreaming of Hollywood stardom; Harry Kline (Red Buttons, 1919–2006), a tough but amiable sailor; Ruby Bates (Bonnie Bedelia, 1948–), pregnant but dancing out of desperate poverty; her angry husband James (Bruce Dern, 1936–); and an elderly dance fan in the audience, Mrs. Laydon (Madge Kennedy, 1891–1987).

Robert and Gloria endure the marathon through many days and nights and have a chance to win, but Gloria, already suffering from depression, becomes despondent when Rocky informs her that "expenses" will be deducted from the prize money. Interspersed in the film are flash-forwards of Robert in a jail cell and on trial, the significance of which is understood only as the story reaches its climax. When Gloria produces a revolver from her purse and asks Robert to kill her, the meaning of those flash-forwards becomes clear. She wants to die to escape from a life that seems to have no future. When the police arrest him and ask why he killed her, he replies, "They shoot horses, don't they?" The film ends inside the ballroom with the final contestants as Rocky repeats one of his favorite phrases, "the marathon goes on and on and on," before fading to black.

The film cost $4.86 million to make, earning $12.6 million at box offices as well as general—if not universal—praise from critics. In his 1969 review, Vincent Canby of the *New York Times* called it an "epic of exhaustion and futility," a film "so disturbing in such important ways that I won't forget it very easily" (Canby 2006, 402, 404). The *New Yorker*'s Pauline Kael cited it, along with *Bonnie and Clyde* (1967) and *The Last Picture Show* (1971), as one of many Vietnam-era films that, while never mentioning Vietnam, shouted "the system is corrupt, that the whole thing stinks" (Kael 1994, 498). Although some critics found the story dire, they lavished praise on the cast. The entertainment trade paper *Variety* praised Fonda for "a dramatic performance that gives the film a personal focus and an emotionally gripping power" (*Variety* 1969). *TV Guide* responded similarly. "Although it is at times heavy-handed, *They Shoot Horses, Don't They?* is a tour de force of acting. Fonda here got her first chance to prove herself as a serious, dramatic actress" (*TV Guide* 1969). Fonda agreed. Looking back on her career, she wrote, "This was the first time in my life as an actor that I was working on a film about larger societal issues, and instead of my professional work feeling peripheral to life, it felt relevant" (Fonda 2006, 216).

They Shoot Horses, Don't They? was nominated for nine Academy Awards, including Best Director (Pollack), Best Actress (Fonda), Best Supporting Actress (York), and Best Adapted Screenplay (Thompson and Poe). It won for Best Supporting Actor (Young). York also won Best Supporting Actress from the British Academy of Film Awards. *They Shoot Horses, Don't They?* also received numerous other awards and nominations.

According to film historian David Thomson, today's audiences "will be amazed that so bleak and desperate a picture was attempted, let alone released" by a Hollywood studio. He adds that as a metaphor of the American Dream, *They Shoot Horses, Don't They?* demonstrates "how far show business itself was a corrupting energy that had driven the dream mad" (Thomson 2008, 876). Citing a 1993 reference by the *New York Times* to President Bill Clinton's politically difficult push for health-care reform as "the policy equivalent of the dance-marathon movie *They Shoot Horses, Don't They?*" Carol Martin, author of the pioneering 1994 academic study of dance marathons, commented on how the film single-handedly shaped public memory regarding those Depression-era marathons, writing, "Most people know of them only through a popular 1969 movie starring Jane Fonda" (Martin 1994, xv).

HISTORICAL BACKGROUND

According to Morris Dickstein, cultural historian of the Great Depression, the "glum marathon dancing in Horace McCoy's novel *They Shoot Horses, Don't They?*" was "a good metaphor for the whole era" (Dickstein 2009, 385). However, while marathon dancing is mainly remembered as a 1930s phenomenon, it was first popularized a decade earlier in a giddier time of relative prosperity, the Roaring Twenties.

The "endurance dances," as they were sometimes called, first surfaced in the early years of the 20th century but gained notoriety across the United

States only in 1923 (Calabria 1993, 5). At first, they were seen as just one of the many "crazes" of that era, which included flagpole sitting, swallowing goldfish and, in one unrepeated spectacle, the Texas man who spent 30 days pushing a peanut up Pike's Peak with his nose (Sann 1967, 76). Marathon dancing caught on more widely and persisted longer than other fads from the 1920s. One reason for the interest among audiences and participants was the intense public attention paid to the Olympic Games, whose modern revival began only in 1896 and whose contests stressed competition between teams and record-setting. Especially in their earliest phase, the marathons, whose name evoked the athletic endurance of the ancient Greeks, were "part of the craze to break world records" (Martin 1994, xvii).

Other explanations for dance marathons have been offered. With the closing of the American frontier, aside from the wilderness of Alaska, "feats of endurance were yet another kind of frontier where Americans could display their ability to prevail" (Martin 1994, 6). The marathons could also be understood as part of the effort to shake off the staid social values of the pre–World War I era in "the first strong nationwide rebellion against most important aspects of Victorianism" (Coben 1991, 35). Frenzied dancing might have signaled relief from wartime tension and the shaking off of old social norms. "For the young, the advanced spirit of the time was found in the foxtrot—dance music with a lively, accelerated tempo" (Miller 1991, 109).

In June 1923, the sole survivor of a contest that began with 22 couples set a record for dancing after 217 hours, including rest periods of 15 minutes every four hours. He was rewarded for his effort with a prize of $5,000. From the start, the marathons drew controversy as well as publicity. Religious groups condemned them for promoting lewd public behavior. Psychiatrists wondered whether the desire to compete in such tournaments was indicative of mental illness and physicians warned that marathons could cause permanent damage to muscles and the nervous system. Dance instructors opposed the marathons as "dangerous to health, useless as entertainment and a disgrace to the art and profession of dancing" (Martin 1994, 15).

The outstanding personality on the dance marathon circuit, Milton D. Crandall, wasn't a performer but a promoter. Resembling a stock character from a 1930s Hollywood comedy, Crandall was a pudgy, balding, glad-handing man whose affability cast a sinister shadow. He had a flair for gimmicks and knew how to hold the attention of the "boys" from the press. He was not the sole dance marathon promoter but was the most notorious one and became the model for other hustlers (Martin 1994, 25).

Crandall began in show business with a touring "panorama" reenacting the Great Dayton Flood of 1913 before moving on to Hollywood where he hired already passe stars for one-night shows in small towns (Sann 1967, 57). In 1927, he began promoting marathons in his Pittsburgh ballroom and expanded from there to Detroit, Minneapolis, Atlantic City, and Harlem. One year later, Crandall mounted the "Dance Derby of the Century" at New

York's Madison Square Garden, the event that became the model for dance marathons in the 1930s. Crandall's challenge was to make the marathons last as long as possible and generate more revenue by keeping audiences in the seats day after day. To extend the dancers' stamina, he established breaktime rules that granted them hour-long rest periods.

Participants in the Dance Derby passed a minimal medical examination involving a doctor listening to their hearts and a nurse taking their temperatures. Only one man was rejected. Each dancer signed a waiver releasing Crandall from responsibility for any injuries. Physical harm was anticipated. Red-and-white booths at the dance floor's perimeter sheltered medical stations and rest areas. Some dancers paid for their own masseurs who worked their tired bodies during breaks. A tugboat whistle signaled that breaktime was over and the dance was resumed (Martin 1994, 27–28). The Derby opened with 91 couples on June 10 after the master of ceremonies commended Crandall and the contestants for their "American spirit" and fired three blank shots in the air to start the dance. In accord with the patriotic theme, Madison Square Garden was decked out with red, white, and blue bunting. Crandall wanted to be certain that his marathon wasn't interpreted as entertainment for immigrants. "It was for those who were already situated, however poorly, in American life" (Martin 1994, 28).

As in theaters and opera houses, there were cheap seats for the masses and box seats where affluent patrons in evening wear enjoyed the show. Crandall even arranged tall potted plants around Madison Square Garden to suggest one of the city's posh ballrooms.

Crandall believed that all publicity was good publicity and relished the hint of scandal, the stern warnings from the medical profession, that clung to the marathons. His Dance Derby received daily coverage in Gotham's tabloids, including the *New York Daily News*, the *New York Evening Graphic*, and the Hearst chain's *Daily Mirror*. Photography played a key role. One dancer was shown having her hair done while taking a break for sleep. Barber chairs and a beauty parlor groomed contestants in full view of spectators (Martin 1994, 26–27).

Not unlike the producers of "reality television" in the 21st century, Crandall understood that unfiltered reality had a small audience at best. Watching couples dance hour after hour, as the dance instructors complained, was "useless as entertainment." To keep the crowds amused and encourage returning customers, each of his marathons developed an ongoing narrative, a storyline casting contestants in games of power and revenge, scenarios of comedy and melodrama and tense encounters among and between the dancing couples. Crandall encouraged certain contestants to become colorful characters, turning them into actors as well as dancers. He directed their antics, borrowing characterizations of the cad, the fool, the innocent, and the bully from pulp fiction, low-rent theater, and a new genre emerging on radio, the soap opera (Martin 1994, 22–24).

It's likely that Crandall and his imitators might have abandoned the marathons within a few years if not for the arrival of the Great Depression. "Dance marathons during the Depression were part of a culture of poverty. They relied on an audience that was out of work and on contestants who were willing to work for very little" (Martin 1994, 41). During the 1930s, the marathons were known by many names, including "dance derbies," "dance-a-thons," and "jitter-a-thons." They were often advertised as "walkathons," an apt description for the hobbled state of the performers after many hours on the floor (Calabria 1993, 17). They no longer danced but drooped, couples hung onto each other for support and shuffled their feet to maintain a semblance of motion. Cash prizes fell below the big money of the Roaring Twenties. In the 1930s, some top dancers received as little as $50 in addition to free meals. It was hard work for those who lasted. Marathons often lasted anywhere from six to twelve weeks and ran 24 hours a day (Martin 1994, 9, 46).

Although stardom eluded most dancers, several noteworthy performers did regular stints in the marathons, including Broadway and Hollywood actor June Havoc (1912–2010) (Havoc 1959, 7) and singer Onita O'Day (1919–2006) (O'Day and Eells 1981, 33). The entertainment industry trade paper *Billboard* included an "Endurance Show" section where promoters advertised for dancers. Comedian Red Skelton (1913–1997) was only the most famous of many unemployed vaudevillians who brought song-and-dance showmanship and a touch of slapstick to the marathons during the early Depression years (Calabria 1993, 9–10).

Along with hiring professional entertainers to alleviate the inherent boredom of dance marathons as a spectator sport, called "pageants of fatigue" by one writer, many promoters anticipated the antics of professional wrestling by crafting some of their performers into larger-than-life characters, often cast as heroes or villains (Calabria 1993, 9). Notorious among the latter on the marathon circuit was Chad Alviso, an unsmiling figure who ignited indignation among onlookers, elbowing female contestants and engaging in other transgressions (Martin 1994, 51).

In many places, local radio stations broadcasted live from the marathons at set times each day. Staged melodrama was generally reserved for moments when the microphones were live and announcers were broadcasting a play-by-play. Sometimes the floor judges, acting as referees, made deliberately outrageous calls and unfair decisions on the fate of dancers to rile the crowd. At least one floor judge had to be escorted out of a marathon by police to protect him from the angry mob (Martin 1994, 54–55). Promoters reached for other ways to publicize their shows. Many published "dope sheets," a term borrowed from horse-race betting, printed like newspapers and hawked outside of marathon venues with feature articles, profiles of dancers, and updates on who had been eliminated and who remained in the contest. In Winslow, Illinois, where few people owned radios in the early

1930s, a promoter engaged the local telephone exchange to notify customers with updates each morning about the previous day. Some promoters gave groceries to random customers on certain nights to drum up business (Martin 1994, 56–57).

Despite strenuous efforts by their promoters, the marathons were unable to sustain their peak of popularity past the first years of the Depression, a time when President Herbert Hoover failed to deliver a message of hope. Attendance declined when Franklin D. Roosevelt lifted glum spirits and initiated job programs that put many Americans back to work. "The long hours of the contests reflected the amount of time spectators had on their hands. Unemployed, bored, and sometimes angry, spectators spent days and nights watching the 'kids' make their endless rounds on the dance floor" (Martin 1994, xix).

The marathons faced growing opposition. The American Social Hygiene Association, dedicated to fighting prostitution and venereal disease, as well as religious and other groups actively campaigned against the dances. Marathons were outlawed in many states including Georgia, Indiana, Iowa, Kansas, North Dakota, and South Dakota and in cities such as Atlantic City, Los Angeles, Minneapolis, and Milwaukee. Texas, New Hampshire, New York, and Maine enacted laws limiting the hours of marathon events, shattering their round-the-clock business model. Other jurisdictions placed various licensing obstacles in their way (Martin 1994, 130, 147–148, 150). Ballrooms that regularly booked dance bands and cinema operators joined the chorus against the marathons. "Not only did they appear to many to attract 'undesirables,' they also seemingly posed a threat to the stable and permanent businesses upon which the community relied" (Martin 1994, 132).

In 1935, faced with declining ticket sales, the promoters formed the National Endurance Amusement Association to foster cooperation and promote a better image for the marathons, but it was already too late. Audiences continued to dwindle. Unlike baseball, there was no enduring interest in the records being set, and unlike movies or swing bands, the marathons produced no stars even if they temporarily sustained the careers of a few performers who would make their names elsewhere. Marathons continued sporadically into the 1940s, usually in small towns, but the phenomenon ended along with the Depression.

DEPICTION AND CULTURAL CONTEXT

They Shoot Horses, Don't They? benefits from its close adherence to the spirit and text of the novel, which dramatized people and situations witnessed by the author. The accurate sense of time and place begins with the hall where most of the film is set. Rising from a boardwalk and overlooking the ocean, the Pacific Ballroom typifies the shabby venues associated with dance marathons. They were held in inelegant but functional rooms whose open spaces could accommodate a hundred or more couples. Bleacher-style seating afforded good views to all spectators. Rocky's on-stage reference to Herbert Hoover's promise that "prosperity is just around the corner" places *They Shoot Horses, Don't They?* in the early Depression years of 1930 through 1932.

The realism begins as applicants for the film's "World's Greatest Dance Contest" line up to receive a perfunctory medical exam calculated to weed out only the weakest or most dangerous cases. Gloria's intended partner is diagnosed with a contagious infection and disqualified before spreading it to other participants. Another dancer is sent packing for bringing bottles of opiate-based "medicine" in his bag. Rocky explains that he wants no "hop-heads" because he already has enough trouble. This reflects the concern of promoters over the marathons' reputation among community groups and police as magnets for low life (Martin 1994, xvii, 27). Harry Kline is clearly too old for the rigorous competition but Rocky winks and looks the other way. "Rules were established at the beginning of every marathon, but they were subject to revision by promoters" at any time (Martin 1994, 34).

The waiver Rocky presses on his contestants replicates the usual contracts signed by dancers in the 1930s. The only assurance they were given against injury was the round-the-clock, on-site presence of a physician, a team of nurses to treat broken or fractured bones, and a "trainer" who is glimpsed in one scene massaging a contestant's knotted legs (Martin 1994, 28).

Promoters like Rocky did not always act as their own master of ceremonies, but Rocky embodies the hustling characteristics of both endeavors. The film doesn't delve into the logistics he surmounted by arranging and promoting the "World's Greatest Dance Contest" but hints that, like most marathon promoters, he's an itinerant. The clue to his backstory comes when he privately shares memories of his father's traveling show as a fake faith healer. He's a man without roots making a living from gullible customers. Like the era's real-life emcees, Rocky is a performer, "a man who could elicit laughter and tears from the audience by playing on the situations he saw in front of him" (Martin 1994, xx). A marathon on the scale of his Dance Contest would have required several second-string emcees for off-hours, but to avoid complicating the screenplay with additional secondary characters, Rocky is the only one visible on screen.

Rocky is an improviser and a manipulator, making the most of accidents and calling out incidents on the dance floor for the audience's entertainment. He also encourages flamboyant displays of skill, which occur less frequently as exhaustion takes hold of even the fittest dancers. In one scene, a contestant is shown lathering his face and shaving while dancing, a stunt familiar to marathon audiences (Martin 1994, 9). Rocky is shown encouraging Alice, an aspiring actress, to work up "that specialty bit," but if anything, the marathon at the heart of the movie is less contrived than many similar events of the 1930s where situations were often wholly staged to amuse the audiences. However, Rocky isn't above spontaneously inventing stories about his contestants. Seizing on the merchant seaman's suit Harry wears to the marathon, Rocky describes him to the audience as a naval hero from World War I, dancing despite the 32 pieces of shrapnel in his body. "It's the kind of grit and never-say-die spirit that made this a great country" Rocky proclaims.

Although his Dance Contest is in Los Angeles, Rocky makes passing references to dancers from other states, including one couple from as far away as Alaska. McCoy noted as much in the novel when Robert observes that "about half of the people in this contest were professionals. They made a business of going in marathon dances all over the country, some of them even hitch-hiking from town to town" (McCoy 1997, 118). Many promoters deliberately planted "professionals" pretending to be ordinary contenders among the amateurs, but this is not emphasized in the film. The cast of marathons in Los Angeles often included young Hollywood hopefuls, bit players with big dreams like Robert and Gloria. Alice, whose blond hair and costumes deliberately emulate one of the era's stars, Gene Harlow, exemplifies the "novices ambitious to become celebrities," hoping to be noticed by a director or producer in the audience (Martin 1994, 47).

However, many dancers were simply out of work or out of luck. "Just keep on thinking about those seven meals a day they're feeding us," James reminds his wife. In addition to the cash prize, all contestants were fed with four main meals and three light lunches. In the film, as in reality, they continued to perform even as they ate, shuffling their feet according to contest rules and eating in full view of the audience from tall sawhorses in the middle of the dance floor (Martin 1994, 57–58). The prize money for the winning couple of Rocky's marathon, $1,500, was at the high end for tournaments during the Depression, higher even than the $1,000 mentioned in McCoy's novel, but was not unrealistic.

Dancers could also pick up pocket money through the "silver showers," coins tossed at them by eager fans, usually after performing a specialty number such as Harry's tap dance routine. Many dancers were sponsored by local businesses. In exchange for wearing a sweater with a business's name stitched on the back, a couple received pairs of shoes and other items. Those new shoes were helpful because heals and soles wore down fast as the competition continued.

They Shoot Horses, Don't They? doesn't hide the reality of empty seats. Attendance was often sparse through the off hours, but the dances attracted regulars. Mrs. Laydon, the elderly woman who takes special interest in Robert and Gloria, represents the phenomenon of the "ringside ladies," daily attendees who brought gifts as well as encouragement to their favorite contenders (Martin 1994, 49–50). The progress of any show depended on a core of ticket buyers who returned to see how their favorites were faring.

In the evening, the live music also provided diversion for the audience. *They Shoot Horses, Don't They?* shows that various ensembles, including a three-piece combo and a medium-size orchestra, were employed to maintain the tempo during peak hours. Larger orchestras or "name bands" were usually beyond the budget of most promoters, but occasionally a bigger marathon would book Guy Lombardo or other well-known band leaders (Calabria 1993, 10). To keep down the cost of hiring musicians, off-hours were filled with recorded music blaring from Victrolas or radio sets as the dancers shuffled in time. Emcees such as Rocky sometimes called on the band to pick up the pace for an impromptu "sprint," forcing the dancers to kick up their heels in a lively whirl to hold the crowd's interest. Absent from *They Shoot Horses, Don't They?* are the comedians, wrestlers, and other acts that took the stage during rest breaks at many marathons, turning them into variety shows.

The interior of the film's Pacific Ballroom accurately recreates the atmosphere surrounding the marathons. Food vendors hawked hot dogs, popcorn, candy apples, and soda pop, but in those penny-counting times, some customers, like Mrs. Laydon, brought their own picnic baskets. Large signage above the band stand indicated the number of hours since the contest began and the number of couples who remained on the floor. The crowded backroom where contestants rested on cots is realistic, as is the use of

---

BENNY GOODMAN (1909–1986)

For many young Americans of the 1930s, Benny Goodman led the big band that set the rhythm for a new kind of dancing—the jitterbug. The media proclaimed him the "King of Swing," even though the structured syncopation of swing music had been pioneered earlier by African American bandleaders. Goodman acknowledged his debt, insisting on integrating some of his band lineups over the objection of nightclub owners and promoters.

Goodman's music was "hotter" and faster than the sweetly swaying dance bands of earlier years and opened an avenue for wider appreciation of Black music in the United States. Goodman became a professional musician at age 11 and eagerly absorbed the new music from New Orleans called jazz. He was a clarinetist and his "Oriental" tones occasionally recalled his heritage. As a child, Goodman had studied music at a Chicago synagogue.

The wild percussiveness and loud volume of Goodman's big band unnerved older observers and impacted audiences in a manner similar to rock music later in the 20th century. Goodman broke racial as well as sonic barriers as one of the few white musicians performing at Carnegie Hall's tribute to African American music, a multi-act concert called "Spirituals to Swing" (1939). When the big bands fell out of fashion after World War II, Goodman remained active in smaller combos and often performed as a classical musician.

bottled ammonia and ice baths to revive severely fatigued dancers (Martin 1994, 57).

Although it might seem improbable given the lack of privacy, fast and furtive sexual encounters occurred at marathons. As in *They Shoot Horses, Don't They?*, the curtains and dark corners of the ballroom provided temporary refuge. Women in the audience sometimes paired off with dancers during their break time (Martin 1994, 42). Such activity was frowned upon by promoters for fear of drawing attention from the vice squad or community groups.

The worst hurdles faced by dancers happened when the emcees decided to rouse the sleepy crowd with shows of athletic endurance. Late in the film, Rocky forces the remaining dancers to don track suits and run in a "derby," described by him as "the supreme test of energy and endurance." In this elimination contest, dancers run in rings around the dance floor, with the last three couples eliminated, but it's not as grueling as some marathons of the 1930s. Reports exist of contestants running more than 100 laps in a figure-eight pattern around pylons set at opposite ends of the dance floor. Other marathons boasted "zombie treadmills," "heel and toe races" and other tortures (Martin 1994, 55). Harry collapses at the end of the derby and is taken away. Pain was part of the show. "Spectators came to see the contestants hurt. They felt a vicarious pleasure, bordering on sadism" (Martin 1994, xxi). As early as the 1920s, some contestants died from heart attacks after many days of exertion on the dance floor (Calabria 1993, 6). Rocky justifies the competitive struggle as "the American way." For historian Carol Martin, the marathons "seem to epitomize the 'American dream' in one of its crazier and more contradictory manifestations" (Martin 1994, xv).

Down to many small details, *They Shoot Horses, Don't They?* is a plausible recreation of an early-1930s dance marathon. As the *New York Times'* critic mentioned when the film was released, "There are some small anachronisms, including a new Johnny Green song that recalls the 1940's or 1950's instead of the 1930's. These are not really important, however" (Canby 2006, 404). As critic Roger Ebert recalled, the film is "a masterful re-creation of the marathon era for audiences that are mostly unfamiliar with it," adding that it "holds our attention because it tells us something we didn't know about human nature and American society" (Ebert 2011).

FURTHER READING

Als, Hilton. 2011. "Queen Jane, Approximately: How Jane Fonda Found Her Way Back to Acting." *The New Yorker*, May 2, 2011.

Calabria, Frank M. 1993. *Dance of the Sleepwalkers: The Dance Marathon Fad.* Bowling Green, KY: Bowling Green State University Popular Press.

Canby, Vincent. 2006. *American Movie Critics: An Anthology from the Silents until Now*. Edited by Phillip Lopate. New York: Library of America.

Coben, Stanley. 1991. *Rebellion against Victorianism: The Impetus for Cultural Change in 1920s America*. New York: Oxford University Press.

Dickstein, Morris. 2009. *Dancing in the Dark: A Cultural History of the Great Depression*. New York: W.W. Norton.

Ebert, Roger. 2011. "They Shot Horses, Didn't They." rogerebert.com, January 16, 2011. https://archive.vn/sz1CS

Fonda, Jane. 2006. *My Life so Far*. New York: Random House.

Havoc, June. 1959. *Early Havoc*. New York: Simon & Schuster.

Kael, Pauline. 1994. *For Keeps: 30 Years at the Movies*. New York: Penguin Books.

Martin, Carol. 1994. *Dance Marathons: Performing American Culture in the 1920s and 1930s*. Jackson: University Press of Mississippi.

McCoy, Horace. 1997. "They Shoot Horses, Don't They?" In *Crime Novels: American Noir of the 1930s & 40s*. New York: Library of America.

Miller, William D. 1991. *Pretty Bubbles in the Air: America in 1919*. Urbana: University of Illinois Press.

O'Day, Anita, with George Eells. 1981. *High Times, Hard Times*. New York: G.P. Putnam's Sons.

Persall, Steve. 2008. "Who Is Norman Lloyd: Documentary Shows You." *St. Petersburg Times*, April 9, 2008. https://web.archive.org/web/20080410195436/http://www.tampabay.com/features/movies/article450062.ece#

Sann, Paul. 1967. *Fads, Fallacies and Delusions*. New York: Bonanza Books.

Thomson, David. 2008. *"Have You Seen…?": A Personal Introduction to 1,000 Films*. New York: Alfred A. Knopf.

TV Guide. 1969. "They Shoot Horses, Don't They?" https://archive.vn/tVJz

Variety. 1969. "They Shoot Horses, Don't They?" December 31, 1969. https://variety.com/1968/film/reviews/they-shoot-horses-don-t-they-1200421765/

Chapter 7

Sounder (1972)

Sounder was released to theaters on September 24, 1972, by 20th Century Fox. The film was produced by Robert B. Radnitz (1924–2010), "a maker of high-quality movies for children and their parents" (Nelson 2010), based on a bestselling book for young adults by novelist William H. Armstrong (1911–1999). *Sounder* was directed by Martin Ritt (1914–1990), an accomplished and socially conscious filmmaker who had been blacklisted from the entertainment industry from 1951 through 1957 for suspected communist sympathies (McGilligan and Buhle 1997, 561–562). Concerned over his role as a white filmmaker telling a Black story, Ritt turned to African American playwright Lonne Elder III (1927–1996) for the screenplay. "There's no way anyone can understand what it is like to be black unless you're black," Ritt explained. "Some of us make a pretty good facsimile thereof, and I hope I am one of those" (McGilligan and Buhle 1997, 565).

Armstrong's 1969 novel was focused on a dog called Sounder, owned by a family of Black sharecroppers. The novelist was a white Southerner who drew his characters and situations through observations of the Black folk with whom he grew up. Although obviously set in a Southern state at an earlier period than 1969, the author left the time and place unclear. After he won the Newberry Medal in 1970, the top prize for American children's literature, Hollywood took interest in his story.

Sounder stars Cicely Tyson (1924–2021) as Rebecca Morgan, the family's mother. At that time, she was one of the most familiar Black actresses to American audiences after two decades of pioneering roles in television and film as well as the fashion industry. She was not Ritt's original choice. Given her background as a model, he worried that she was too glamorous for the role. "I need a working class, peasant woman," he told her. She replied, "there are no blacks in this country more than one generation removed from that experience" (McGilligan and Buhle 1997, 565). Television actor Paul Winfield (1939–2004) costars as her husband, Nathan, and Kevin Hooks (1958–) as her adolescent son, David Lee. Other characters include Mrs. Boatwright (Carmen Matthews, 1911–1995), who employs Rebecca for housework; blues singer Ike Philips (Taj Mahal, 1942–); Sheriff Charlie Young (James Best, 1926–2015); and the plantation owner, Mr. Perkins (Ted Airhart, 1924–1996).

As the film begins, Nathan, David Lee, and their dog Sounder are out at night hunting racoons. Nathan fires a shot in the woods and misses, returning home empty-handed. Worried about feeding his family, he steals sausages from a nearby smokehouse. The theft is observed and he is arrested the following day. When Sounder tries to follow as the sheriff takes Nathan to jail, one of the deputies shoots the dog with buckshot. The Morgan family is deprived of their father and their pet for much of the story. Rebecca is denied permission to visit her husband by the sheriff, who allows only David Lee into the jail. The injustices continue. After Nathan is sentenced to one year of hard labor, the authorities refuse to tell the family which prison camp he's been sent to.

David Lee is a bright lad given special permission to attend a whites-only school through the influence of Mr. Perkins. He is also encouraged to read literature by Mrs. Boatwright, a kindly well-to-do white woman who reveals, despite the sheriff's demand for silence, where Nathan has been imprisoned. Sounder eventually returns to the family after his wounds heal. Injured while working with dynamite on a chain gang, Nathan is given early release and sent home. Although David Lee wants to help his injured father with the farm work, Nathan convinces him to take advantage of an opportunity to go to boarding school and escape the dead-end of rural poverty.

Released during the era of *Shaft* (1971), *Superfly* (1972), and other "blaxploitation" films depicting violent Black anti-heroes in contemporary urban settings, industry insiders worried that *Sounder* would be overshadowed by flashier competitors for Black audiences. In response to those concerns, 20th Century Fox marketed *Sounder* to schools and church groups and provided a study guide written by Roscoe Brown Jr. (1922–2016), director of New York University's Institute of Afro-American Affairs. The film became popular with all audiences, becoming the 10th highest grossing film at box offices for 1972. Produced on a modest budget of less than $1 million, *Sounder* grossed nearly $17 million in revenue (*Variety* 1974).

The *New York Times* gave the film a condescending review, calling it "an intelligent enough movie" that "avoids all the major pitfalls of its type" but lacking "the excitement that may have come from plumbing greater depths and discovering a few tougher, less accessible insights" (Greenspun 1972). However, most reviews were enthusiastic.

Roger Ebert called *Sounder* "a story simply told and universally moving" and "one of the most compassionate and truthful of movies," adding, "there's not a level where it doesn't succeed completely" (Ebert 1972). *New York* magazine's usually scornful critic John Simon praised *Sounder* as "a rare honest Hollywood movie about blacks, making it virtually unique" (Simon 1982, 91).

Sounder received Academy Award nominations for Best Picture, Best Actor, Best Actress, and Best Adapted Screenplay as well as nominations from the British Film Academy, the Golden Globes, the Directors Guild of America, and the Grammys (for Best Original Score Written for a Motion Picture). Elder was the first Black screenwriter honored with an Oscar nomination. Although she was already a familiar face from movies and television, Tyson's role as Rebecca elevated her to stardom (Bogle 2019, 147). Widely regarded as an exemplary cinematic depiction of the dignity and perseverance of Black folk under Jim Crow, *Sounder* found new audiences on television and home video but its success could not be replicated by its disappointing and forgettable sequel, *Sounder, Part 2* (1976).

African American film historian Donald Bogle praised *Sounder* for its positive portrayal of Black manhood and understanding of family life along with Ritt's sensitive direction and the convincing naturalism of Elder's screenplay (Bogle 2016, 223). "The film is pure emotion, huge, unforced, coming directly out of the characters' experiences," according to a recent essayist (O'Malley 2020). However, *Sounder*, along with other earnest liberal message movies, fell out of fashion in some circles. It is seldom mentioned in comprehensive film histories and its director has been dismissed for making "dull, amiable films" (Thomson 2010, 824).

HISTORICAL BACKGROUND

Slavery is as old as civilization and was practiced in societies across the world. However, the slavery Europeans imposed on the New World assumed a distinct form based on the skin color and origins of the enslaved. In ancient Egypt, Greece, and Rome, slaves often looked much like their masters. This would not be the situation in the Americas where slaves were imported from Africa for the heavy labor of exploiting the rich lands of the new colonial empires. Following the rise of the New World's slave economies, European natural philosophers began to contemplate theories of racial inequality and hierarchy. Ethnic and cultural prejudices were common throughout history, but racism in its modern form was conceived during the rise of European empires.

During the century before Christopher Columbus (1451–1506) opened the New World to colonization, European nations had already established a flourishing trade in slaves and other goods with the kingdoms of West

Africa. The trading posts they established on the coastline became conduits for human trafficking, which increased in scale as demand grew in the American colonies. Although the Spanish and Portuguese initially used Native Americans as slave labor on sugar plantations in South America and around the Caribbean, the indigenous population declined drastically through lack of immunity to European diseases, spurring the market for African slaves, deemed to belong to a hardier race. Joining the rush to claim the New World, France, Great Britain, and the Netherlands established profitable tobacco, coffee, and cotton plantations that required labor in large numbers. From the 1500s through the 1800s, some ten million Africans were shipped to the Western Hemisphere in the holds of slave ships. The cruel and unhealthy conditions resulted in as many as two million deaths of African captives at sea during the "middle passage" across the Atlantic (Mancke and Shammas 2005, 30–31).

In the colonies that became the United States, the institution of slavery developed alongside the evolution of the economy. Slavery arrived in 1619 when a Dutch trader sold 20 Africans to the British colony at Jamestown, Virginia, and more followed. Toiling in the fields alongside English and Irish indentured servants, the plantation laborers "lived and worked together in ways that blurred racial lines." Some of the early African arrivals "escaped bondage and secured a modest prosperity" (Berlin 1998, 29). In the early years, Britain's mainland North American colonies were societies with slaves, not slave societies. The distinction is that in slave societies, "slavery stood at the center of economic production" (Berlin 1998, 8). Slave societies came into being to exploit a labor-intensive commodity such as cotton or tobacco that could command an international market. In slave societies, "the number of slaves increased sharply, generally by direct importation from Africa, and enslaved people of African descent became the majority of the [agricultural] laboring class" (Berlin 1998, 9). In 1800, there were 900,000 slaves who labored in the United States. By 1860, this number had grown to four million.

The word "slavery" never appears in the U.S. Constitution, yet the issue was of concern to its authors and the founding document's role in perpetuating the institution has been a subject of debate almost since its ratification. Of the 11 clauses in the Constitution that have a bearing on slavery, 10 "protect slave property and the powers of masters. Only one, the international slave-trade clause, points to a possible future power by which, after 20 years, slavery might be curtailed—and it didn't work out that way at all" (Waldstreicher 2015). The clause abolishing the importation of slaves after 1808 implied that many of the Constitution's signers envisioned slavery's eventual demise. One provision, the "three-fifths clause," mandated that "all other persons" (meaning slaves) should be counted as three-fifths of a person for the purpose of establishing the size of each state's delegation to the U.S. House of Representatives. The clause allowed the South to gain congressional seats by counting people who were given no civil rights.

Slavery was less profitable and slaves less numerous in the North, a region of small farms where industry took hold early. As a result, by 1830, slavery ended in the Northern states even as it continued to expand in the South. In another indication that the republic's founders favored its gradual extinction, slavery was prohibited by the Northwest Ordinance (1787), the statute governing the territories that became Ohio, Illinois, Minnesota, Michigan, Indiana, and Wisconsin. However, equality under the law for Black people was not forthcoming in most Northern states. Although slavery was never allowed in Ohio, Black people weren't allowed to vote and could only reside in the state if two white landowners vouched for them. (Masur 2021, 10).

With its long hot summers and fertile river bottoms, the Southern states were ideal for raising cash crops such as cotton. After the introduction of the cotton gin in 1794, the commodity became even more valuable, spurring the cultivation of new lands. The brainchild of New England inventor Eli Whitney (1765–1825), the gin was a machine whose efficient separation of fiber from seeds transformed the cotton industry. Before the gin was introduced, a single person using his fingers could clean and produce a pound of cotton per day. The gin enabled one person to generate up to 50 pounds daily. As a result, Southern entrepreneurs pushed westward into Alabama, Mississippi, and Texas, hoping to increase the number of slave states. Before the start of the Civil War, cotton accounted for 40 percent of America's exports, much of it feeding Britain's burgeoning cotton mills.

Slaveholders in the slave societies that developed in the cotton- and tobacco-rich states of the American South dominated the local political systems and enacted codes giving them near-absolute sovereignty over their slaves. Conditions on plantations varied on the whim or conscience of the slave owner. Resistance by slaves to their enslavement through tardiness or sabotage was almost inevitable.

"The slaveholding South was synonymous with violence" with "whites of all economic stripes engaged in violent acts" against each other and Blacks. Slave owners resorted to the whip to "exert dominion over their chattel and perpetuate the institution of bondage." Slaves "occasionally struck back in individual acts of violent confrontation, and on very rare occasions, they rose up in concerted, coordinated rebellions against white authority" (Forret 2015, 1–2).

Anxiety over slave rebellions began during the colonial era as word came of insurrections among the European colonies of the Caribbean. The Declaration of Independence hadn't been debated, much less signed, in November 1775 when Virginia governor Lord Dunmore (1730–1809) promised freedom to slaves who turned on their masters and supported Great Britain if the revolution came. The fear of a slave uprising cast a deeper shadow across the slave states after the successful revolution in Saint-Domingue

(1791–1804). Hundreds of thousands died during a brutal war ending in the defeat of French colonists and the proclamation a new nation of freed slaves, Haiti.

Several slave uprisings occurred in the United States during the early decades of the 19th century. On July 2, 1822, Denmark Vesey (1767–1822), a formerly enslaved man, was hanged in Charleston, South Carolina, for plotting what might have been the largest insurrection against slaveholders in U.S. history had it occurred. Vesey had been enslaved but purchased his freedom after winning a lottery. Although he worked as a carpenter, he never earned enough money to purchase freedom for his wife and children. Vesey pointed to the Bible to justify the rising. While sentencing him to death, the magistrate accused Vesey not only of treason but also of "attempting to pervert the sacred words of God into a sanction for crimes of the blackest hue."

More famous was the insurrection led by Nat Turner (1800–1831), a slave in Southampton County, Virginia. Despite claiming guidance from God, Turner was a marginal figure in his community and had only four followers when he launched his revolt on August 21, 1831. After he killed a family of plantation owners, several dozen slaves rallied to his cause and the ensuing violence soon became "the bloodiest slave revolt in American history" (Breen 2015, 1). Exact death tolls have long been disputed. According to recent analysis of court records and census figures, as many as 40 slaves and 50 whites perished before the state militia restored order (Breen 2015, 89, 100). Determined to protect the human property of slave owners, the militia acted quickly to suppress revenge murders of slaves by the county's poor white residents while rounding up suspected participants in the rebellion. Slaves accused of "conspiring to rebel and make insurrection" were tried in court and given defense counsel. Fifteen were acquitted, and eighteen were hung, including Turner, captured after a two-month manhunt.

In the aftermath of the Turner rebellion, the Virginia legislature contemplated the eventual abolition of slavery in their state. Leading the effort was Thomas Jefferson Randolph (1792–1875), nephew of the founding father, who told his colleagues that abolition "must come." The proposal was defeated, marking the last time antebellum Southern politicians seriously considered ending the slave system. While most Northern abolitionists distanced themselves from the mayhem of Turner's uprising, activists such as William Lloyd Garrison (1805–1879) used the revolt as an occasion for editorials on the dangers of slavery. After Turner, the South dug in and prepared for a long struggle to keep slavery while anti-slavery opinion hardened in the North. "Nat Turner's revolt contributed to the radicalization of American politics that helped set the United States on its course toward the Civil War" (Breen 2015, 2).

The roots of Abolitionism can be traced to a protest by Pennsylvania Quakers in 1688. Quakers continued to play prominent roles in the movement as societies lobbying to end slavery formed in Northern cities.

Religious-minded reformers of other denominations took up the cause, sometimes linking it with an appeal for women's suffrage. Garrison's Boston newspaper, *The Liberator*, took a radical position by calling for the immediate emancipation of all slaves. In response to his fiery editorials, the Georgia legislature offered a $5,000 reward for his arrest.

However, *The Liberator* had a circulation of only 3,000 in a nation of 31 million and its editorial perspective wasn't widely shared. "It's hard to accept just how unpopular abolitionism was before the Civil War," a historian recently observed. "Even among Northerners who wanted to stop the spread of slavery, the idea of banning it altogether seemed fantastical" (Grinspan 2016, 347).

Although the appeals of the Abolitionists fell on many deaf ears, the movement had some practical results before the Civil War. Abolitionists operated the Underground Railroad, a chain of illegal safehouses that assisted escaped slaves in their trek across the border to freedom in Canada. The railroad ran in defiance of the Fugitive Slave Act (1850), a federal law mandating the return to their owners of escaped slaves, even slaves who made it to states where slavery was illegal. The law was part of the Compromise of 1850, a Congressional agreement whose provisions included the right of voters in the newly organized Kansas Territory to determine whether slavery would be allowed in their state. As a result, Kansas became a battleground between settlers from North and South. Active in the Kansas violence was the militant abolitionist John Brown (1800–1859). In October 1859, Brown led a raid on the federal arsenal in Harpers Ferry, Virginia, in a bid to seize the arsenal's weapons and distribute them to slaves, triggering a rebellion across the United States. But Brown's revolution ended before it began, with his capture. He was convicted of treason and hung, an incident that further radicalized the South and heightened tensions on the road to the Civil War.

Preserving slavery was the overriding issue for the Southern politicians who led the secession and formed a new nation, the Confederate States of America. However, abolishing slavery was not the foremost concern for most Northerners, including national leaders, as the Civil War began. Even years after the conflict ended, the Civil War monuments erected in towns and cities across the North were inscribed with words about "preserving the Union" and "putting down the Rebellion," not ending slavery. The reaction to the coming of war by Frederick Douglass (1817–1895), a former slave who became one of America's most outspoken Abolitionists, was proven correct. "Thank God!" he exclaimed. "The slaveholders themselves have saved our cause from ruin!" (Grinspan 2016, 343). As the war continued and Blacks volunteered to fight in the U.S. Army's "Colored Infantry" regiments, the sentiment for Blacks and against slavery grew. Without the Civil War, the Thirteenth Amendment to the Constitution, which outlawed slavery upon ratification in 1865, might never have been enacted.

Although he may not have believed in full equality for Blacks, President Abraham Lincoln (1809–1865) was morally opposed to slavery throughout his political career and said so privately and in public (Striner 2006, 2–4). But with widespread public and political support for abolition remaining uncertain, he waited and acted pragmatically despite pressure from Abolitionists.

On August 19, 1862, abolitionist Horace Greeley published an open letter to Lincoln demanding that he outlaw slavery immediately, not only in the Confederacy but in the "loyal states" of Delaware, Maryland, Kentucky, and Missouri where slavery continued. Lincoln responded with his own letter, writing, "My paramount objective in this struggle is to save the Union, and is not either to save or destroy slavery."

Recent historians have declared Lincoln's reply as "mere rhetoric, designed to placate Northern conservatives, and residents of the loyal slave states" at a time when he was laying plans to free more than three million slaves in the Confederacy. Lincoln prepared to dismantle slavery "as best he could, given the constraint of the Constitution and the necessity of winning the war." The language of the Constitution left him no choice. "Neither Congress nor the president had any power to liberate slaves in the loyal border states," he believed. "But Lincoln could use his power as commander-in-chief to strike at slavery in those Southern states that claimed to be out of the Union and were making war on the United States" (Finkelman 2016, 295). The Emancipation Proclamation (January 1, 1863) freed slaves in Confederate territory occupied by federal troops but did not abolish slavery elsewhere.

Even before the final shots were fired in the Civil War, politicians and pundits debated what was to be done with the defeated South. President Andrew Johnson (1808–1875), hastily sworn in after Lincoln's assassination, favored speedy readmission to the Union of the states that had seceded. However, not content with the Thirteenth Amendment, the anti-slavery Republican majority in Congress passed a series of enactments including the first federal civil rights law, the Civil Rights Act (1866), and the Fourteenth Amendment (1868), guaranteeing due process for all citizens and citizenship to anyone born in the United States. The Republicans were determined to prevent the South from returning to its old ways, giving African Americans "a millennial sense of living at the dawn of a new era" (Foner 1988, 281).

The new era was called the Reconstruction. The former Confederacy was placed under military occupation with the U.S. Army supervising state constitutional conventions and elections. Most white Southerners were horrified that full voting rights were accorded to Black males. During the Reconstruction, some 2,000 Black men were elected to public office at every level, including 2 members to the U.S. senate and 20 members to the U.S. House of Representatives (Gates 2019, 8).

The Republicans intended to go beyond the lifting of legal restrictions and to lift the social and economic status of Blacks through federal programs on a scale previously unimagined. "The process of Reconstruction involved nothing less than the monumental effort to create a biracial democracy out of the wreckage of the rebellion" (Gates 2019, 7). Along with the military, the agency primarily tasked with implementing the Reconstruction was the Bureau of Refugees, Freedmen, and Abandoned Lands (or Freedmen's Bureau). Established in 1865, the agency (with the assistance of Northern religious groups) provided food and shelter to newly freed slaves but had wider objectives including assisting the former slaves with education, health, legal issues, and land ownership. The agency's work was impeded by budget cutbacks and confronted by massive opposition from Southern whites well before it was abolished in 1872.

The dream of elevating former slaves into landowning farmers was frustrated by the economic demands of restoring the cotton trade to serve the international textile industry. "It took a multiyear struggle on plantations, in local courthouses, in state capitols, and in Washington to determine the outlines of a new system of labor in the cotton-growing regions." The planters held on to their land and "sought to restore a plantation world as close to slavery as possible." Although "contracts had to be made and wages paid ... life was to go on as before" (Beckert 2014, 278, 282).

Slavery was replaced by sharecropping. Much of the South's agricultural land was now worked by tenant farmers who paid their rent with crops, usually giving the planter half of their harvest (Grubbs 1971, 8). Poor whites also found themselves ensnared in the sharecropping system but life was worse for Blacks because of "an all-encompassing, suffocating white supremacist discourse ... one whose peculiar mode of reasoning and argumentation, with its own symbols and signs, would carry on long after slavery" (Gates 2019, 17)

White Southern resistance to the Reconstruction operated at two levels. On the ground, terrorist groups such as the Ku Klux Klan waged a second Civil War with the South as the victor. "African Americans were murdered and cowed, state officials were assassinated, and state militias sapped by hit and run raids" (Luhrssen 2015). While Southern leaders distanced themselves from the Klan, "most white Southerners were pleased by the new status quo" of a reimposed racial hierarchy (Luhrssen 2015, 63). Even before Reconstruction ended in 1877, the federal government, tired of endless bloodshed, washed its hands off responsibility for instilling a new social order in the South.

At a higher level, business interests lobbied to reintegrate the Southern states into the Union and war-weariness moved many Northerners to forgive the rebellion's participants and reembrace them as fellow citizens. Even leading figures such as Confederate president Jefferson Davis (1808–1898) and general Robert E. Lee (1807–1870) benefitted from Andrew Johnson's Christmas 1868 pardon to "every person who directly or indirectly participated in the late insurrection or rebellion." The financial crisis called the

Panic of 1873 and the economic depression that followed "further sapped the civic will and led many voters to cast blame on the party in charge in Washington since the Civil War: the Republican Party" (Gates 2019, 10).

Following the Reconstruction came the Redemption, so called because of the white Southern crusade to "redeem" their states on their terms. The new all-white state governments curtailed or eliminated voting rights and other legal guarantees for Black residents through Jim Crow laws. The term Jim Crow came from a song, "Jump Jim Crow," introduced in 1832 by a white New Yorker, Thomas Dartmouth Rice. Rice was the original blackface minstrel performer, and his song, a caricature of Black culture, circulated widely through sheet music and became one of the country's most familiar tunes (Strausbaugh 2006, 57–61).

Jim Crow laws mandated residential segregation as well as segregation in public facilities ranging from drinking fountains to hospital rooms. Jim Crow was upheld by the U.S. Supreme Court in *Plessy v. Ferguson* (1896). A Louisiana man of mixed heritage, Homer Plessy, sued after his arrest for riding in a whites-only railroad car. The court ruled that "separate but equal" facilities for whites and Blacks were constitutional. Despite this, accommodations for Blacks, especially in schools, seldom equaled what was afforded to whites.

With the Plessy ruling, progress toward civil rights was reversed and discriminatory practices grew more widespread throughout the nation, not only the South. The Black response to the worsening situation came to be defined through the work of three leaders, W. E. B. DuBois (1868–1963), Booker T. Washington (1856–1915), and Marcus Garvey (1887–1940).

DuBois was the first Black person to earn a doctorate at Harvard. An activist as well as a scholar, DuBois was a founding member of the NAACP and editor of its magazine, *The Crisis*. As author of seminal works such as *The Souls of Black Folk* (1903) and *Black Reconstruction in America* (1935), he is acknowledged as "the premier architect of the civil rights movement in the United States" and was "among the first to grasp the international implications of the struggle for racial justice." DuBois believed that through their accomplishments, a Black elite, the "Talented Tenth," would lift the race to full equality and famously predicted that "the problem of the twentieth century would be the problem of the color line" (Lewis 1993, 4).

In contrast to DuBois' call for intellectual excellence and his articulation of a radical vision for the future, Washington urged Blacks to accept current restrictions on political and social rights in exchange for action by white Southern leaders "to allow gradual progress in agriculture and business and to rein in the rednecks" (Lewis 1993, 175). Washington was a pragmatist who measured progress in gradual increments. Presenting a third alternative, Garvey, a charismatic Jamaican-born orator, reawakened the dream of Blacks returning en masse to Africa.

America's entry into World War I (1917) coincided with the start of the Great Migration that brought millions of Southern Blacks into Northern cities. Until 1910, 90 percent of Black Americans lived in the South. By 1934, that number had dropped to 79 percent. Between 1917 and 1925, Detroit saw its Black population increase by 611 percent, Chicago by 114 percent, and New York by 66 percent. In 1910, Harlem was 90 percent white. During the following decade, it became the world's most prominent Black city, home to the flourishing musical, literary, and artistic culture of the Harlem Renaissance (Gates 2019, 203).

The migrants were greeted in many places by white riots. In 1917, more than 100 Black people died in East St. Louis, Illinois, when mobs attacked their neighborhood as the National Guard looked the other way. During the "Red Summer" of 1919, deadly white mob violence erupted in Chicago, Washington, D.C., and Elaine, Arkansas. "Across the country black veterans in particular were targeted for lynching, as white mobs feared that the end of the Great War would put them in competition" for jobs. In one of the worst incidents, the 1921 Tulsa Race Massacre, Oklahoma whites destroyed Greenwood, one of the most prosperous Black communities in the United States, leaving its 10,000 residents homeless.

Sharecropping remained a common way of life for Southern African Americans who didn't embark on the Great Migration and their numbers had grown during the prosperous years of the 1920s. "The whites came down from the hills and the Negroes crossed the river from Mississippi to make a better living on the huge Delta plantations or in the humming sawmills." But as the Great Depression took hold, "the sawmills shut down, the price of cotton plummeted" as displaced sharecroppers "crowded into vacant shacks or lived along the river bottoms with the rats and mosquitoes" (Grubbs 1971, 4, 5).

Like slave owners in the previous century, the planters painted themselves "as sponsors of an agrarian welfare state. Religion, recreation, health and education all were alleged products of planter paternalism" (Grubbs 1971, 10–11). According to one study, most planters paid less than a dollar per year on the education of their tenants' children; for recreation, most planters hosted all-day picnics on holidays for the sharecroppers; many donated to churches attended by their sharecroppers.

Most plantations continued through the Great Depression despite the economic downturn—compounded by competition from cheap cotton grown in Egypt and India—that saw cotton prices drop from 20 cents a pound in 1927 to 5 cents in 1932. "Planters, once living quite comfortably, were now 'getting by'; sharecroppers, once subsisting, were now starving" (Grubbs 1971, 15).

The sharecropper system, "in reality a slave-labor system perpetuated with minor changes after the Civil War," remained in place through the Depression years because it had "become an inextricable part of a whole complex of cultural attitudes," including stereotyping the tenant farmers as "a good-for-nothing class on whom any systematic help would be wasted . . . Outmoded machinery can be replaced rapidly, but outmoded cultural patterns persist" (Grubbs 1971, 15).

DEPICTION AND CULTURAL CONTEXT

Although the novel was set in no definite time or place, the film opens with a caption establishing the setting as Louisiana in 1933. Ritt shot the film in rural Louisiana in places where dusty gravel roads still wound between woods and fields. Ritt and his cinematographer, John A. Alonzo (1934–2001), took visual inspiration from Walker Evans (1903–1975) and Dorothea Lange (1895–1965), Depression-era photographers who captured the desperate conditions of the poor. Also influential was the photography of Gordon Parks (1912–2006), who documented African American life years before directing Black-oriented films such as *Shaft* (O'Malley 2020). Without ever feeling slow-going, *Sounder* catches the muggy pace of Southern life in the 1930s. In *Sounder*, as in backwoods Depression-era Louisiana, automobiles are scarce. The Morgan family's donkey cart would not have been an uncommon sight.

The film subtly shows racial disparity by contrasting the town's steepled church where whites worship with the unpainted wooden structure serving as the Black church. The only white home visited in the film belongs to the affluent Mrs. Boatwright. White poverty is not observed. The Morgans' home was based on photographs of Southern sharecroppers. Their wooden shack is all hard unpainted surfaces, dimly lit in the evening by kerosene lamps. There is no running water or indoor plumbing. Water is drawn by hand from a well outside. The setting is realistic, yet some sharecroppers lived in far worse conditions. An Arkansas attorney traveling through cotton country in the 1930s described a house about 10 by 20 feet "made of corrugated tin and scraps of lumber. It was flat upon the ground and had only one or two openings" (Grubbs 1971, 5).

Sharecropper families sustained themselves as the Morgans do by gardening and hunting as well as purchasing coffee, sugar, and other goods on credit from the plantation commissary. The credit system was called "furnishing," because the commissary "furnished" what the sharecroppers needed but at interest with rates as high as 30 or 40 percent on some plantations. Their debt is subtracted from their earnings at harvest time, leaving them in perpetual poverty. As Nathan tells David Lee at the film's climax, the only escape is to get away.

David Lee's situation as a Black student in a white rural school, and his apparent acceptance by the teacher and fellow pupils, would have been unusual in the segregated South of the time and warrants more attention than it receives in the screenplay. Louisiana's schools were first integrated in 1960 against a backdrop of white boycotts, violence, and racial slurs. U.S. marshals escorted the first Black students into previously all-white schools (Reckdahl 2010).

The character Ike Phillips is the kind of figure familiar through much of the South in the 1930s, when many wandering blues musicians entertained at roadhouses or house parties. Some of them were able to record for record labels catering to the Black audience. A few became legendary. The film hints at but doesn't explore the conflict between Ike and the Black community's pastor. "Churchgoing folk" in those years "despised blues players . . . for their refusal to abide by 'traditional' values, their racy lyrics, the sexual innuendo of their rhythms, the goings-on where they perform, their references to black magic and other vestigial descendants of African belief systems" (Santoro 1994, 13–14). The film's soundtrack by the recording artist who played Ike, Taj Mahal, replicates the wordless moans of work songs as well as the gritty humor of the blues and the uplift of gospel music, presenting an accurate aural panorama of the Black rural South during the Great Depression.

MEMPHIS MINNIE (1897–1973)

Blues emerged as a distinct form of music at the beginning of the 20th century but with roots that ran deep, including memories of African syncopation and the groaning harmonies of work songs sung by farm laborers. Guitar, once an exotic instrument in the United States, became widely available through the Sears & Roebuck catalog by 1900 and was readily adopted by blues musicians. Although professional blues singers such as Bessie Smith worked the vaudeville circuit, the music was rural in origin. Crucial to the blues' development was the Mississippi Delta, a fertile country of big plantations worked by sharecroppers. Most blues singers from the region were men, given the rough juke joints and street corners where they performed. Memphis Minnie was the exception.

Born Lizzie Douglas, probably in Tunica County, Mississippi, she learned guitar by age 10 and began entertaining at parties. At age 13, she ran away from home for Memphis, whose Beale Street neighborhood was a flourishing hub of Black music and culture. She was discovered in 1929 by a Columbia Records talent scout and given the name Memphis Minnie. She made several recordings and settled in Chicago's growing South Side Black community. In that setting, blues was transformed from a rural to an urban music with a louder, more aggressive sound. By 1941, Memphis Minnie was playing electric guitar.

However, like many blues performers of her generation, she was unable or unwilling to make the next transition to R&B and rock and roll. She made her final recordings in the 1950s, retired from performing, and died in a nursing home. Rock fans know her from Led Zeppelin's version of one of her most powerful songs, "When the Levee Breaks."

Nathan's year of hard labor for stealing sausages to feed his family is realistic. Poor Southerners of all backgrounds were handed hard time for relatively small offenses, especially if committed against people of higher social status. Elvis Presley's father Vernon and his uncle Travis Smith, both sharecroppers, were sentenced to three years at Mississippi's infamous Parchman Farm for adding a zero to a four-dollar check. They were released eight months later upon the intervention of the local planter (Jeansonne, Luhrssen, and Sokolovic 2011, 9). However, law enforcement in the South weighed more heavily on Blacks and was often abetted by mob violence, especially when Black men were accused of giving offense to white women.

The injustice of life in the Jim Crow South is emphasized in *Sounder* but not the terror. The choice was intentional in a screenplay whose "rich texture of life... feels more authentic than an uninterrupted parade of misery." Lonnie Elder III's subtlety and sensitivity ensured that "the joy is as real as the misery" (O'Malley 2020).

Missing from *Sounder* is the harshness of the sharecropper's daily labor. Also unseen is the "riding boss," the mounted overseer whose word was law in the Southern fields. Work on the plantation was easy in midsummer but harvest time brought "hard labor [that] lasted seven days a week from 'can to can't'—from the time one can first see the sunrise until visibility fades after sunset" (Grubbs 1971, 9, 10).

During the Great Depression, many planters put wage laborers to work in their fields alongside the sharecroppers. "Their use signified an oversupply of labor so great that the planter no longer needed to fix his laborers to the soil" (Grubbs 1971, 8). The Depression and other great events of the early 1930s aren't registered in *Sounder* but that may be because the film is largely from the perspective of David Lee, a boy whose awareness of the world beyond the plantation and the nearest town has only just begun.

FURTHER READING

Beckert, Sven. 2014. *Empire of Cotton: A Global History*. New York: Vintage Books.

Berlin, Ira. 1998. *Many Thousands Gone: The First Two Centuries of Slavery in North America*. Cambridge, MA: The Belknap Press of Harvard University Press.

Bogle, Donald. 2016. *Toms, Coons, Mulattoes, Mammies, and Blacks: An Interpretive History of Blacks in American Films*. New York: Bloomsbury Academic.

Bogle, Donald. 2019. *Hollywood Black: The Stars, The Films, The Filmmakers*. Philadelphia: Running Press.

Breen, Patrick H. 2015. *The Land Shall be Deluged in Blood: A New History of the Nat Turner Revolt*. New York: Oxford University Press.

Ebert, Roger. 1972. "Sounder." *Chicago Sun-Times*, September 25, 1972. https://www.rogerebert.com/reviews/sounder-1972

Finkelman, Paul. 2016. "Lincoln's Letter to the Editor." In *The New York Times' Disunion: A History of the Civil War*, edited by Ted Widmer. New York: Oxford University Press.

Foner, Eric. 1988. *Reconstruction: America's Unfinished Revolution, 1863–1877*. New York: Harper and Row.
Forret, Jeff. 2015. *Slave Against Slave: Plantation Violence in the Old South*. Baton Rouge: Louisiana State University Press.
Gates, Henry Louis, Jr. 2019. *Stony the Road: Reconstruction, White Supremacy, and the Rise of Jim Crow*. New York: Penguin Press.
Greenspun, Roger. 1972. "'Sounder' Opens: Story of a Negro Boy in Louisiana of 1930's." *New York Times*, September 25, 1972. https://www.nytimes.com/1972/09/25/archives/screen-sounder-opensstory-of-a-negro-boy-in-louisiana-of-1930s.html
Grinspan, Jon. 2016. "Was Abolition a Failure?" In *The New York Times' Disunion: A History of the Civil War*, edited by Ted Widmer. New York: Oxford University Press.
Grubbs, Donald H. 1971. *Cry from the Cotton: The Southern Tenant Farmers' Union and the New Deal*. Chapel Hill: University of North Carolina Press.
Jeansonne, Glen, David Luhrssen, and Dan Sokolovic. 2011. *Elvis Presley, Reluctant Rebel: His Life and Our Times*. Santa Barbara, CA: Praeger.
Lewis, David Levering. 1993. *W.E.B. DuBois: Biography of a Race, 1868–1919*. New York: Henry Holt and Company.
Luhrssen, David. 2015. *Secret Societies and Clubs in American History*. Santa Barbara, CA: ABC-CLIO.
Mancke, Elizabeth, and Carole Shammas. 2005. *The Creation of the British Atlantic World*. Baltimore: Johns Hopkins University Press.
Masur, Kate. 2021. *Until Justice Be Done: America's First Civil Rights Movement, From the Revolution to Reconstruction*. New York: W.W. Norton.
McGilligan, Patrick, and Paul Buhle. 1997. *Tender Comrades: A Backstory of the Hollywood Blacklist*. New York: St. Martin's Press.
Nelson, Valerie J. 2010. "Obituary: Robert B. Radnitz, Producer of Oscar-nominated Family Films, Including 'Sounder.'" *Pittsburgh Post-Gazette*, June 12, 2010. https://old.post-gazette.com/pg/10163/1065115-122.stm
O'Malley, Sheila. 2020. "Sounder." Film Comment, September 27, 2020. https://www.tcm.com/tcmdb/title/90934/sounder#articles-reviews?articleId=020759
Reckdahl, Katy. 2010. "Fifty years later, students recall integrating New Orleans public schools." *New Orleans Times-Picayune*, November 13, 2010.
Santoro, Gene. 1994. *Dancing in Your Head: Jazz, Blues, Rock and Beyond*. New York: Oxford University Press.
Simon, John. 1982. *Reverse Angle: A Decade of American Film*. New York: Crown Publishers.
Strausbaugh, John. 2006. *Black Like You: Blackface, Whiteface, Insult & Imitation in American Popular Culture*. New York: Jeremy P. Tarcher/Penguin.
Striner, Richard. 2006. *Father Abraham: Lincoln's Relentless Struggle to End Slavery*. New York: Oxford University Press.
Thomson, David. 2010. *The New Biographical Dictionary of Film*. New York: Alfred A. Knopf.
Variety. "Big Rental Films of 1973." January 9, 1974.
Waldstreicher, David. 2015. "How Indeed the Constitution was Pro-Slavery." *The Atlantic*, September 19, 2015.

Chapter 8

Paper Moon (1973) and *The Sting* (1973)

In 1973, two memorable films set during the Great Depression appeared in cinemas. *Paper Moon* debuted in Hollywood on April 9, 1973 and was released widely on May 9 by Paramount Pictures. *The Sting* was released on December 25, 1973 by Universal Pictures.

The success that year of those films was not a coincidence. By 1973, the 1960s were already receding into the past and many moviegoers were eager to embrace nostalgia in films about supposedly simpler, less chaotic times—before the upheaval of the Vietnam War, the protests, the riots, and the rise of psychedelic drugs and counterculture. Director George Lucas's *American Graffiti*, also released in 1973, showcased teenage life in pre-Beatles, preprotest America and reflected on coming-of-age experiences for the first wave of baby boomers. The audience for films set in the Great Depression included, but was not limited to, moviegoers for whom the 1930s was a living memory. Baby boomers saw heroic or antiheroic images of themselves in the lead actors, Ryan O'Neal (1941–) in *Paper Moon* and Paul Newman (1925–2008) and Robert Redford (1936–) in *The Sting*.

Paper Moon was produced by a team of young upstarts in Hollywood, Frank Marshall (1946–) and Peter Bogdanovich (1939–). The screenplay was adapted from the novel by Joe David Brown (1915–1976), *Addie Pray* (1971), by television writer Alvin Sargent (1929–2019), who changed the story to give it an open-ended conclusion. Bogdanovich directed the film with an eye toward replicating the best elements of Hollywood from the era of *Paper Moon*'s setting, starting with the decision to shoot it in black and white. Although he was considered part of the American New Wave of filmmakers that emerged by the end of the 1960s and was in the generational cohort that included Francis Ford Coppola and Steven Spielberg, he preferred the company of golden age Hollywood directors such as Howard Hawks and George Cukor and was eager to gain pointers from them. "What I had been doing in my work was using the grammar and vocabulary of movies that I'd learned from . . . They showed me the way. I put myself through the best film school anyone's ever been through" (Eichenbaum 2014, 7).

After working with rising star Ryan O'Neal (1941–) on his previous hit, the comedy *What's Up, Doc?* (1972), Bogdanovich chose him for *Paper Moon*'s lead role as the wandering confidence man Moses "Moze" Pray. In an inspired act of casting, the director chose the star's nine-year-old daughter, Tatum O'Neal (1963–), to play Addie Loggins, Moze's willing partner in crime and possible daughter (Bogdanovich 2017). Madeleine Kahn (1942–1999) plays a supporting role as Trixie Delight, an exotic dancer Moze encounters at a carnival.

Paper Moon opens with the poorly attended funeral of Addie's mother. Arriving late, Moze plucks a bundle of flowers from another tomb and presents it at the gravesite. His jaunty ease establishes his role as a con man and his profession of selling Bibles reinforces confidence in his piety. However, despite his dishonesty, he shows signs of having a good heart by traveling some distance to this barren cemetery in rural Kansas because he once knew the deceased. The better angels of his nature argue with his greed when Moze accepts responsibility for taking Addie to her nearest relative in St. Joseph, Missouri. Rather than drive out of his way as promised, he intends to buy her a train ticket and send a telegram to her aunt alerting her of the girl's arrival.

Plans change when Moze sees an opportunity to shake down the owner of the town's grain elevator. That man's brother was responsible for the car crash that killed Addie's mother and Moze confronts him with the threat of bringing a lawsuit with a high-powered attorney. The blackmail nets Moze $200, but Addie overhears their discussion and demands the money. They come to an agreement. Moze will pay her from the proceeds of his small-scale con jobs. She becomes his willing assistant in the scams they pull off along the road to St. Joseph.

Addie believes that Moze might be her father because he met her mother "in a bar room" and they resemble each other physically. Moze denies her assertion, but it remains an open question throughout the film.

Paper Moon maintains a light-hearted tone as Moze and Addie pull off small capers in the small towns they pass through. The mood darkens when they steal crates of bonded whiskey from a local bootlegger's shed and sell it back to him. The bootlegger becomes aware of the scam and sends his brother, the sheriff, after them. They are treated brutally in the police station and held for illegal possession and transportation of alcohol.

Kansas was a "dry state" that continued to ban alcohol after the repeal of Prohibition (1933).

Although they escape and manage to cross the Missouri border, the sheriff and his deputies track them down, and while they have no authority to arrest them, they beat up Moze and leave him on the street. Afterward, Moze takes Addie to her aunt's house, but the girl decides to stay with him. *Paper Moon* closes with a final shot reminiscent of the endings of many Hollywood films made during the Great Depression. Addie and Moze are shown driving in a rickety Model T up a winding road toward the distant horizon of a hopeful future.

Paper Moon became popular with movie audiences, earning $30.9 million in domestic ticket sales, ranking in ninth place at box offices for 1973 (The Numbers). Most critics liked it as well. *Variety* singled out Tatum O'Neal's performance as "outstanding" and a "sensational screen debut" (*Variety* 1973). The *Chicago Sun-Times's* Roger Ebert was especially perceptive, praising Bogdanovich's skill in setting an entertaining film amid "the real poverty and desperation of Kansas and Missouri, circa 1936," adding that "Addie Loggins, the little girl, hardly ever smiles: She can see perfectly well there's nothing to smile about" (Ebert 1973a). His rival at the *Chicago Tribune*, Gene Siskell, didn't like it as much, complaining about Addie's "melodramatic dialogue," but gave it three-and-a-half stars out of four (Siskell 1973).

Paper Moon performed well during awards season. Tatum O'Neal became the youngest Academy Award–winner ever as Best Supporting Actress, defeating costar Madeleine Kahn. Some thought Tatum O'Neal should have won for Best Actress because she was the film's "mind, its conscience, its humor and fears" (Thomson 2008, 642). Along with Kahn and O'Neal, *Paper Moon* was nominated for Best Adapted Screenplay and Best Sound. At the Golden Globes, Kahn won Best Supporting Actress and O'Neal was Most Promising Newcomer–Female. The National Board of Review named *Paper Moon* as one of the year's top 10 films. Sargent's screenplay won the Writers Guild Award for Best Comedy Adapted from Another Medium.

The film is considered an enduring example of the sort of movies produced during Hollywood's "Second Golden Age" of the 1970s. Film historian David Thomson argues that *Paper Moon* presents "among the toughest views of children in the unduly sentimental range of American film" and that Bogdanovich had earned his place in "the pantheon of American moviemakers" (Thomson 2008, 642).

The Sting was produced by actor Tony Bill (1940–), Wall Street analyst Michael Phillips (1943–), and his wife Julia Phillips (1944–2002). The threesome dreamed of breaking into Hollywood production and raised $5,000 to develop *The Sting*'s screenplay with first-time writer David S. Ward (1945–) (*New York Magazine* 1975). Although Ward claimed he used many nonfiction books in researching the screenplay, he was sued by University of

Louisville linguistics professor David Maurer (1906–1981) who maintained that it was plagiarized from his book, *The Big Con* (1940). Universal settled out of court several years later. *The Sting* was directed by George Roy Hill (1921–2002) whose previous film, *Butch Cassidy and the Sundance Kid* (1969), had brought together Robert Redford and Paul Newman in starring roles. Hill regrouped them for lead roles in *The Sting*. Redford plays Johnny Hooker, a small-time grifter, with Newman as Henry Gondorff, a semiretired master of the "big con." The cast also includes Robert Earl Jones (1910–2006) as their friend Luther Coleman, Robert Shaw (1927–1978) as Irish mobster Doyle Lonnegan, Charles Durning (1923–2012) as police lieutenant William Snyder, Dana Elcar (1927–2005) as FBI special agent Polk, and Dimitra Arliss (1932–2012) as waitress-assassin Loretta Salino.

The Sting opens in Joliet, Illinois, in September 1936 as a suave man in clean suit and shoes strides along dirty streets and passes into an inconspicuous hub of activity, an illegal numbers operation. The man, a mob "runner" (currier), is handed $11,000 to convey to another point in the Chicago area racket. Once the runner is back on the street, his money is stolen during a quick con-job by a pair of grifters, Hooker and Luther.

America's addiction to gambling is a theme throughout *The Sting* and the game is always rigged by someone. When Hooker goes to a neighborhood bar with a roulette wheel in the back, he places $3,000 of his take on the table but the bar's owner presses a hidden button, causing the wheel to stop on a losing number. And when the manager of the Joliet numbers phones his boss in New York to report the $11,000 theft, the call reaches the kingpin in an exclusive club whose members are bent over cigars and cards. The boss, Lonnegan, orders that the grifters be found and "taken out . . . to discourage this sort of thing."

Luther plans to retire from grifting and advises Hooker to try a "big con" with one of the country's top con artists, Gondorff. Hooker leaves but is caught on the street by Lieutenant Snyder, who slaps him around and tells him that Lonnegan's gang is looking for him. Hooker pays him in counterfeit bills to keep silent. When Hooker returns to Luther's apartment, he finds his friend has been murdered by Lonnegan's men. Hooker heads to Chicago and tracks down Gondorff, who is laying low. The FBI is looking for him after he pulled a big con on a U.S. senator. Hooker wants Gondorff to organize a big con on Lonnegan to avenge the death of their friend Luther. Although reluctant at first, Gondorff agrees.

The Sting's plot takes many twists and turns. Posing as a bookie, Gondorff deliberately encounters Lonnegan on a train from New York to Chicago where the Irish mobster is known to play high-stakes poker with marked cards. Gondorff wins the game with his own marked deck. Hooker introduces himself as a disgruntled employee of Gondorff and proposes a money-making scheme to the mobster. Peeved at his loss in the card game, Lonnegan is interested. Hooker tells Lonnegan that he can obtain the names of winning horses a few minutes in advance of their public announcement at Gondorff's betting parlor with the connivance of a corrupt Western Union telegraph official. The scheme Gondorff and Hooker pull on Lonnegan is elaborate and includes setting up a complete betting parlor with bartenders, cashiers, a hat check girl, an announcer broadcasting races in progress, and a roomful of customers.

Hooker is nearly killed by Salino, a waitress who turns out to be a paid killer. Snyder continues to pursue Hooker but is drawn into what he thinks is an FBI operation to catch Gondorff. In the end, the FBI team is part of the big con. Snyder and Lonnegan are fooled. Gondorff and Hooker make a large sum of money on their big con and get their revenge.

The tone of *The Sting* is comedic, despite episodes of violence and police brutality. As antiheroes who take down reprehensible figures in the police and the underworld, Gondorff and Hooker appealed to the era's youthful antiestablishment audience as well as to older moviegoers who saw them as comparable to loveable rogues from traditional Hollywood pictures. *The Sting* was the second top-grossing movie of 1973, earning nearly $160 million at box offices (The Numbers). Most critics also liked the film. Roger Ebert gave it four stars and praised it as "seductive and witty" with "a nice, light-fingered style" (Ebert 1973b). The *New York Times*'s Vincent Canby wrote that "the film is so good-natured, so obviously aware of everything it's up to, even its own picturesque frauds, that I opt to go along with it. One forgives its unrelenting efforts to charm, if only because 'The Sting' itself is a kind of con game" (Canby 1973). The *New Yorker*'s Pauline Kael gave the dissenting view, deriding the movie as "harmless, inoffensive" and calling its success "a celebration of celebrity and stardom" of its lead actors, Redford and Newman (Kael 1994, 563, 570).

The Sting was nominated for 10 Academy Awards and won for 7, including Best Picture, Best Director, Best Film Editing, Best Original Screenplay, Best Art Direction, Best Costumes, and Best Music. The Directors Guild of America gave Hill its top award for the film.

In 2005, *The Sting* was added to the Library of Congress's National Film Registry for being "culturally, historically, or aesthetically significant."

HISTORICAL BACKGROUND

The trickster is integral to the mythologies of many cultures, playing an ambiguous role in the stories of gods and men. Swindlers gaining advantage and fortune by deception have lived in most societies, yet some have seen something distinctly American in their evolution. After all, the term "confidence man" originated in a much-reported incident on Broadway in New York City in 1849. A man calling himself William Thompson approached a stranger, asking, "Have you confidence in me to trust me with your watch until tomorrow?" Eager to prove his faith in fellow men, the mark, as con men call their victims, handed over his watch and waited in vain the next day for its return (Bergmann 1969).

Thompson, also known as Samuel Williams or William Thomas, continued to prey on strangers along the streets of Manhattan for several weeks until one of his marks recognized him and alerted a police patrolman. The *New York Herald* covered the story and coined the term "confidence man." Even before Thompson was sentenced to two-and-a-half years in prison, copycat criminals began to roam New York. The publicity surrounding the incident inspired Herman Melville to pen his satirically complicated final novel, *The Confidence Man: His Masquerade* (1857). By 1860, the New York police estimated that one out of every ten professional criminals in the city was a confidence man (Reading 2012, 25–26).

Not unlike the ancient trickster deities Hermes and Loki, America's confidence men provoked an ambiguous response of revulsion and admiration. Some scholars have found the original image of the confidence man in a familiar figure from early-19th-century America, the "Yankee peddler," an itinerant hustler who infused the can-do enterprise of the new republic with a measure of dishonesty (Hoffman 1961, 307). Perhaps the most familiar and benign fictional example of a trickster gaining advantage by fooling people came from Mark Twain's *Tom Sawyer* (1876), whose protagonist conned his friends into paying him for the privilege of doing his chores.

The sort of con men (and women) from *Paper Moon* and *The Sting*, familiar types that continue to populate more recent films such as *Dirty Rotten Scoundrels* (1988) and *American Hustle* (2013), "so often come across as buoyant enterprisers, cut from the same cloth as the American ideal of the self-made man" (Harnett 2017). America's ethic of success has always been elastic enough, in some minds, to embrace scoundrels.

One of the country's most beloved scoundrels, P. T. Barnum (1810–1891), brought deceit together with entertainment through traveling shows and exhibits. His career culminated in "Barnum and Bailey's Greatest Show on Earth," known later after an additional merger as "Ringling Brothers Barnum and Bailey Circus." A largely shameless manipulator of human curiosity and credulity, Barnum disparaged the grim Puritanism of early America in his autobiography, *The Life of P. T. Barnum* (1854), and claimed that the "great defect in our American civilization is a severe and drudging practicalness (sic)" that "concentrates itself upon dry and technical ideas of duty" (Saxon 1989, 11).

The journalist-turned-impresario was the self-professed "King of Humbug" who allegedly said, "There's a sucker born every minute." Defining humbug differently than the dictionaries, he called it "putting on glittering appearances . . . by which to suddenly arrest public attention and attract the public's eye and ear" (Saxon 1989, 77). His humbug could also define the emerging advertising industry, enabled in the early 19th century by mass-circulation newspapers, and raise questions about the relationship between marketing and confidence games. His circuses employed bait and switch by promising one thing and delivering something else. To cite one example, customers paid admission to view the "Feejee Mermaid," pictured as a beautiful half-woman sea creature on a placard outside the tent. Once inside, they found instead a grotesque thing fashioned from the head and torso of a dead monkey joined to the body of a fish. Before the Civil War, Barnum displayed a blind, elderly Black woman called Joice Heth, claiming she was 161 years old and had "nursed" George Washington (Saxon 1989, 10, 74).

Little wonder then that many con men emerged from the ranks of traveling circuses. According to Maurer, "The American circus was a grifter's paradise on wheels. Until about 1950 most circuses carried grifters as a matter of course . . . circuses carried their own private menders (fixers) who cooled out any irate citizens who might cause trouble for the show" (Maurer 1974, 148). The grifters paid circus managers a fixed percentage of their take and shared meals and accommodations with management.

During the 19th century, America's often lawless frontier became fertile ground for new breeds of con men eager to relieve a restless migrant population of their money. The origin of the brand of confidence game played in *The Sting*, the "big store," has been traced to one man in one location. In 1867 Benjamin Marks, "a familiar sight on river steamboats, at land openings and on the streets of frontier towns," arrived in Cheyenne, Wyoming (Maurer 1974, 8). He was already known for playing a gambling game that originated in Mexico, three-card monte, in which players bet against the dealer. Skilled at entertaining crowds on the street with card tricks, Marks threw three cards face down on a board and asked onlookers to pick the queen. He worked with a shill, a covert collaborator who placed a dollar bet on the correct card and won. As a result of his apparent success, "more and larger bets were taken" until the participating onlookers lost most of their money (Maurer 1974, 8–9).

The competition on the bustling streets of Cheyenne encouraged Marks to innovate with an idea that became "the backbone of all big-time confidence games" by setting up a shop. He called it The Dollar Store because it displayed merchandise on sale for one dollar per item, a relatively expensive price in a nickel-and-dime world. However, Marks wasn't interested in selling dry goods but used the store as a gathering place where many monte games could go on simultaneously. Several shills milled around, encouraging customers through their wins.

David Maurer, who spent many years studying various underworlds close-up, identified Marks's Dollar Store as the prototype for increasingly elaborate con games after 1900. In the new century, the big store shed its frontier origins and often took the form of "the swanky gambling club or fake brokerage establishment" in schemes intended to swindle customers.

Some big stores assumed the appearance of legitimate wholesalers, especially in the cotton or garment industries. Farmers were lured into the establishment by lectures on suppressing the boll weevil and stayed afterward for crooked card games. Through the early years of the big store, Marks could be discerned in the background. His operations spread beyond Cheyenne and many successful grifters apprenticed under him. The chain of big stores became a colorful subculture led by ringleaders whose monikers included the Keystone Kid, the Narrow Gauge Kid, and Pretty Billy (Maurer 1974, 10–13, 16).

Also prominent in the new century was a Marks associate called Buck Boatwright who began with stores in Joplin and Webb City, Missouri and Galena, Kansas. "Buck introduced the idea of furnishing the mark with part of the money for the play," usually boxing or other sports betting, to encourage the mark's belief that luck was with him. Boatwright's victims always lost in the end (Maurer 1974, 15).

Technology enabled the next innovation in the confidence racket—called "playing the wire," it was a "racing swindle in which the con men convinced the victim that, with the connivance of a corrupt Western Union official, they could delay the race results long enough for him to place a bet after the race had been won, before the bookmakers received the results" (Maurer 1974, 17). Similarly, a stock market con was played whose victims thought the con man was connected to a prominent Wall Street firm. Here the con man sold sure-thing investments in make-believe offices furnished with ticker tapes and telephones and staffed by brokers, clerks, and customers (Maurer 1974, 18).

The first known wire store was established in New York in 1898 by Christy Tracy. Within two years a half dozen other stores were running in the city under men with names like Larry the Lug, 102nd Street George, and Limehouse Chappie. Most remained in business for many years. In 1902, the wire spread to Chicago in shops run by Jim the Rooter, Barney the Patch, and Yellow Kid Weil. Limehouse Chappie soon shifted his operation to the Windy City. Altogether, wire stores in New York and Chicago regularly employed many hundreds of people including "ropers," who were tasked with finding and bringing marks through the door. And there was no lack of marks. Because they were transit hubs and economic centers, New York and Chicago were logical places for the wire to flourish. "However, as the politicians demanded increasingly large payments, as the police grew ever more avaricious in their shakedown tactics ... many con men of the better class chose to find smaller cities which could be easily righted up" for easy profits (Maurer 1974, 21).

One of the most notorious con-jobs occurred in 1919 when Texas rancher J. Frank Norfleet (1865–1967) lost his fortune in a stock market swindle. While in Dallas to cut a land purchase deal, he was spotted by a team of confidence artists in a hotel lobby. The pitchman, Reno Hamlin, introduced himself as a fellow rural Texan in the big city. With abundant feelings of fellowship, Hamlin brought Norfleet to his friend W. B. Spencer, posing as an agent for a Minneapolis real estate company scouting land in Texas. Spencer in turn introduced him to his purported boss, Garret Thompson (Reading 2012, 6–8)

Friendly discussion began around purchasing Norfleet's land, but this was never the con-men's objective. Their plot advanced when they pulled off a "wallet drop," planting a pocketbook for Norfleet to discover. The wallet belonged to another guest in the hotel, Big Joe Furey, "the cleverest bunco artist in the country." The grateful Furey claimed to work for a Wall Street syndicate with clandestine arrangements to manipulate the market. Furey's job involved buying and selling according to encrypted telegrams sent from New York operatives (Reading 2012, 10).

Furey was the trigger setting the big con in motion. Addressing Norfleet, he said, "My brother, you refused to accept the $100.00 reward which I offered you for finding my pocketbook. Would you mind placing that money on the market and would you accept any money it might earn?" Norfleet agreed. Furey pretended he had an appointment with a Dallas broker to buy stock and returned later that day with $800 for Norfleet, claiming he earned it in stock trading (Reading 2012, 11).

Norfleet gladly took the money "and as soon as he accepted it, he also accepted the logic of the game." The tactic "works even on marks who are not fundamentally motivated by greed, because it exploits empiricism ... all the swindler must do is embed a rigged proof in his script" (Reading 2012, 11–12).

Script is not a word carelessly used because, in reality as in movies, a big con game is "a tightly scripted drama" with multiple acts that climax with fleecing the mark of his money. "Confidence men took inordinate pride in the structured nature of their profession. Instead of the violence and mayhem of other kinds of theft, they relied solely on a perfectly constructed piece of theater" (Reading 2012, 7–8).

The next day, Furey made a show of sending Spencer on an errand so that he could speak privately with Norfleet, a gesture directly addressing the victim's sense of importance. Furey confessed that he was in financial trouble but his firm's rules barred him from placing his own money on the syndicate's stock picks. He then asked Norfleet for a favor: could he take advantage of his insider knowledge of the market and buy some stock in Norfleet's name? He would share the proceeds. Norfleet heartily agreed to the proposal. The game had entered its final innings in an increasingly elaborate set of charades involving all five con artists. They took Norfleet for $45,000, much of it borrowed from his brother-in-law, a sum worth nearly $600,000 in today's money. The rancher didn't realize what had happened until after the con artists had left Dallas by train (Reading 2012, 16–23).

"Once a victim is fleeced he often proves to be a most reluctant and untruthful witness against the men who have taken his money" (Maurer 1974, 3). Shame and embarrassment are magnified. "A confidence man prospers only because of the fundamental dishonesty of his victim" (Maurer 1974, 2). Norfleet was aware that the game he was playing was off-the-books and possibly illegal but played it until he realized he had lost. However, unlike most marks, Norfleet was determined to even the score with his con men.

Norfleet considered himself as an American success story. Starting as a ranch hand, he saved and invested until he owned his own ranch. After being swindled, he said, "With us of the Plains country, a man's word was his bond . . . If I was gullible, I was simply following the reasoning habits I had acquired in my lifetime of experience" (Reading 2012, 54). Like a character from a Hollywood western or the dime novels of that era, Norfleet had lived by a code, and when that code was violated, he reached for his gun.

The law had already intervened in the case before Norfleet began his vengeance quest. Two minor players were arrested by chance, and their leads sent the rancher to California looking for the ringleaders. Claiming that he carried a revolver in his pocket and a suitcase of disguises, Norfleet crisscrossed the continental United States searching for them. His case drew newspaper headlines and eventually his own published memoir, *Norfleet: The Actual Experiences of a Texas Rancher's 30,000 Mile Transcontinental Chase After Five Confidence Men* (1924).

Norfleet's tireless efforts led to arrests and convictions. However, his biographer is skeptical about many details from his cross-continent adventure narrative. "Norfleet justifies his vigilante quest as an attempt to restore his cowboy values that had been so summarily violated by the urban tricksters," but with many of the deeds he recounts in his memoir, "he starts to resemble his enemies more than he realized." If Norfleet "is conning us, do we mind?" she asks, adding that Americans show a "particular pleasure of accepting an invitation into a story they know might be false, only to be immersed in it completely and then duped at the end by what they thought was true" (Reading 2012, 674–65).

By the end of the 1930s, the sort of big cons depicted in *The Sting* had become less common due to the growing power of the FBI to enforce more rigorous federal laws governing interstate crime. According to Maurer, some con artists moved outside the continental United States. "Many of the older big-con men with spectacular records . . . now settle for quiet little rackets which bring in a steady income but which do not carry so much risk of a jolt in federal stir" (Maurer 1974, 5). But while the elaborate confidence schemes of the early 20th century are unlikely to occur today, technology has enabled new forms of swindling that can be just as devastating to the victims. In the 21st century, con men seldom see their marks face-to-face but fleece their victims by phone or internet in scenarios that lack the potential for the drama and human interest of *Paper Moon* and *The Sting*.

DEPICTION AND CULTURAL CONTEXT

University of Louisville linguistics professor David Maurer may seem like an unlikely source of insider information on grifters, but as a "strong, broad shouldered man" as comfortable in a pool room or a betting shop as the lecture hall, the professor "earned the intimate confidence of many vulnerable and close-mouthed miscreants, people who would not have opened up to journalists" (Sante 1995, viii, ix). Following the example of cultural anthropologists such as Margaret Mead (1901–1978), Maurer's research involved immersion within the subculture he studied through the 1930s as he gathered material for his pathfinding book, *The Big Con* (1940). Maurer divided confidence games into two categories, the short con and the long con. Moze from *Paper Moon* is a short con man, while Hooker and Gondorff play the long con in *The Sting*.

Moze's cheerful, can-do optimism is emblematic of a short-con artist. "A confidence man must have plenty of ego. Once he loses his self-confidence, he is a failure" (Maurer 1974, 145). Working a Midwest circuit where Protestant fundamentalism holds sway, he establishes the necessary aura of confidence by posing as a pious entrepreneur, a Bible salesman. Moze realizes soon enough that Addie, a disarming nine-year-old, is an ideal partner in scams that leverage the confidence of his victims,

Paper Moon's setting is recreated with a meticulous eye for detail. Bogdanovich benefitted from finding that many Depression-era buildings and bridges continued to stand in the Kansas and Missouri locations where the movie was filmed. *Paper Moon* takes place in small towns strung along rail lines; the roads that Moze drives on are dusty, often unpaved, and pitch black at night. The grain elevators of Addie's hometown are authentic and recall the images of agriculture and industry beloved by the 1930s artists employed by the New Deal Works Progress Administration. Moze and Addie pass a cinema whose marquee advertises a picture by America's top comedian of the mid-1930s, Will Rogers (1879–1935), for 15 cents admission. The diner, hotel rooms, and five-and-dime stores are realistically worn out at a time when money for improvements was scarce.

Bogdanovich paid close attention to the accuracy of the music and all aspects of the era's popular culture. Discarding the name of the novel he adapted for the screen, Bogdanovich called the film *Paper Moon* after a hit song, "It's Only a Paper Moon," recorded by several artists in the 1930s and heard in the movie's soundtrack. The lyric by Yip Harburg (1896–1981) and Billy Rose (1899–1966) includes the key line, "It's a Barnum and Bailey world, just as phony as it could be." Bogdanovich recreated period advertisements painted on the sides of buildings; Addie drinks Nehi, a soda pop brand during the Depression; Addie and Moze listen to comedian Jack Benny (1894–1974) performing on the radio, which had already become the most popular form of home entertainment.

The automobiles Moze drives through the movie indicate his status and aspirations. He first appears in a Ford Model A, a car already several years old but a respectable choice for America's middle-class in the 1930s. He buys a sharper, newer vehicle, a Ford V8 De Luxe convertible, to impress Trixie Delight. But to avoid capture by the Kansas sheriff, he trades the De Luxe for a broken-down Model T.

While *The Sting*'s scenario may seem too fantastic for real life, the film took much of its inspiration from the research Maurer conducted during the Great Depression. Much of the screenplay's colorful language and antics derives from Maurer's discovery that the con men's slang and methods are more complex than elsewhere in the American underworld, covering an "enormous range of situations, nuances, and subtleties . . . confidence men are after all artists, laden with idiosyncrasies that distinguish their work" (Sante 1995, ix).

The big con Hooker and Gondorff play on Lonnegan mirrors Maurer's explanation of how wire scams operated as well as his description of how grifters recruited large teams of professional crooks to achieve their schemes. "The mobs are organized," Maurer wrote. "Even though their members are loosely held together and the functioning units are often flung far afield, there is a remarkable sense of professional unity." He added, "A highly developed group solidarity keeps intact a strong morale" (Maurer 1974, 142).

AL CAPONE (1899–1947)

The child of Italian immigrants, Alphonse Capone became the most notorious gangster of the Prohibition era. He came to Chicago in the 1920s as bodyguard to Johnny Torrio (1882–1957), the supplier of bootleg alcohol for much of the Windy City. After he was shot in 1925 during a failed assassination by rival gangsters, Torrio retired to Italy and left his underworld empire to Capone.

Capone expanded Torrio's operation and enjoyed friendly relations with Chicago's mayor and police chief. He was popular with many Chicagoans for his acts of charity as well as for circumventing the hated Prohibition laws. Public opinion began to shift after he ordered the killing of rivals in the St. Valentine's Day Massacre (1929).

In 1931, the federal government responded by trying Capone for tax evasion. He was indicted on 22 counts, convicted of 5, and sentenced to 11 years. He was released after 8 years due to his failing health, diagnosed as neurosyphilis. In 1942, he was one of the first Americans to be treated with an experimental drug, penicillin, which slowed his decline without curing him. Capone spent his last years surrounded by family at his Florida mansion. His pinstriped suits and Italian accent became Hollywood's model for depicting mobsters.

Gondorff makes first contact with Lonnegan aboard the 20th Century Limited, a fast train connecting New York with Chicago and notorious for high-stakes card games conducted in private compartments. Seemingly incredible antics, such as Gondorff's temporary use of a real Western Union telegraph office to fool Lonnegan, were tactics that grifters employed. *The Sting*'s largely benign characterizations of Hooker and Gondorff are accurate. A con man "never employs violence to separate the mark from his money." They aren't crooks in the ordinary sense but are "suave, slick and capable. Their depredations are very much on the genteel side" (Maurer 1974, 1).

While *The Sting*'s director George Roy Hill prepared for the filming by watching 1930s crime movies, he was less concerned than Bogdanovich with getting the scenery correct (Horton 1984, 100). Like Bogdanovich, Hill wanted to reflect certain aspects of Golden Age Hollywood but unlike him, he was less concerned with the correct depiction of the world that inspired Hollywood fantasies from the 1930s. The *New York Times* review noted that many of *The Sting*'s period details "aren't too firmly anchored in time" (Canby 1973). Hill brought an exaggerated flair to his filming, making everything a bit sharper in cut and color than reality. As film historian David Thomson put it, *The Sting* inhabits "a strange, abstract world" more suitable for a musical than a realistic drama (Thomson 2008, 831). Most of *The Sting* was not filmed on location but shot in the Universal Studios back lot.

The most noticeable misplacement in time was the music chosen for the film's soundtrack. Hill encouraged cinema music composer Marvin Hamlisch (1944–2012) to set the mood with ragtime, an African American genre that fell out of favor by the end of World War I. In its day, ragtime was condemned for promoting licentiousness and Black culture in a white Anglo-Saxon Protestant society, but by the 1930s, the music had disappeared, pushed aside by jazz and big dance orchestras (Doggett 2015, 43). Ragtime's prevalence in the film suggests that Hill was concerned only with evoking a generalized nostalgia for early-20th-century America, not with getting the details nailed down.

However, Hill's decision had an impact on musical culture. *The Sting*'s theme song, "The Entertainer," reached No. 3 on *Billboard* magazine's pop music chart and spent No. 1 on the trade magazine's easy listening chart (Whitburn 2002, 110). "The Entertainer" was a 1902 melody by ragtime's most accomplished composer, Scott Joplin (1868–1917), and an unlikely contender in the hit parade of the 1970s. Interest in Joplin's music had grown in academic circles in the years before *The Sting*, but Hamlisch's soundtrack recording stirred a full-tilt revival among the general public. The film had another enduring influence by popularizing the word "sting" to describe a carefully orchestrated covert operation. However, unlike in the movie, the term is usually applied to police undercover projects to lure and catch criminals.

FURTHER READING

Bergmann, Johannes Dietrich. 1969. "The Original Confidence Man." *American Quarterly* 21:3, Autumn 1969. https://www.jstor.org/stable/2711934?seq=1

Bogdanovich, Peter. 2017. Special Feature for *Paper Moon* Paramount DVD release.

Canby, Vincent. 1973. "1930's Confidence Men are Heroes of 'Sting.'" *New York Times*, December 26, 1973. https://www.nytimes.com/1973/12/26/archives/film1930s-confidence-men-are-heroes-of-sting.html

Doggett, Peter. 2015. *Electric Shock from the Gramophone to the iPhone: 125 Years of Pop Music*. London: The Bodley Head.

Ebert, Roger. 1973a. "Paper Moon." *Chicago Sun-Times*, June 15, 1973. https://www.rogerebert.com/reviews/paper-moon-1973

Ebert, Roger. 1973b. "The Sting." *Chicago-Sun Times*, December 27, 1973. https://www.rogerebert.com/reviews/the-sting-1973

Eichenbaum, Rose. 2014. *The Director Within: Storytellers of Stage and Screen*. Middletown, CT: Wesleyan University Press.

Harnett, Emily. 2017. "Sympathy for the Con Man." *The Atlantic*, March 20, 2017. https://www.theatlantic.com/entertainment/archive/2017/03/con-artists-the-catch-imposters-sneaky-pete/520125/

Hoffman, Daniel. 1961. *Form and Fable in American Fiction*. New York: Oxford University Press.

Horton, Andrew. 1984. *The Films of George Roy Hill*. Jefferson, NC: McFarland & Company.

Kael, Pauline. 1994. *For Keeps: 30 Years at the Movies*. New York: Dutton.

Maurer, David W. 1974. *The American Confidence Man*. Springfield, IL: Charles C. Thomas.

New York Magazine. "The Sting of Success." January 27, 1975. https://books.google.com/books?id=6OgCAAAAMBAJ&pg=PA30&lpg=PA30&dq=%22Michael+Phillips#v=onepage&q=%22Michael%20Phillips&f=false

"The Numbers: Where Data and the Movie Business Meet." the-numbers.com. https://www.the-numbers.com/market/1973/top-grossing-movies

Reading, Amy. 2012. *The Mark Inside: A Perfect Swindle, A Cunning Revenge, and a Small History of the Big Con*. New York: Alfred A. Knopf.

Sante, Luc. 1995. Introduction to David W. Maurer, *The Big Con: The Story of the Confidence Man*. New York: Anchor Books.

Saxon, A. H. 1989. *P.T. Barnum: The Legend and the Man*. New York: Columbia University Press.

Siskell, Gene. 1973. "He's Just Mad About Addie." *Chicago Tribune*, June 15, 1973. https://www.newspapers.com/clip/37501983/gene-siskel-movie-reviewpaper-moon/

Thomson, David. 2008. *"Have You Seen...?": A Personal Introduction to 1,000 Films*. New York: Alfred A. Knopf.

Variety. 1973. "Paper Moon." December 31, 1973.

Whitburn, Joel. 2002. *Top Adult Contemporary: 1961–2001*. Menomonee Falls, WI: Record Research.

Chapter 9

Chinatown (1974)

Chinatown was released on June 20, 1974 by Paramount Pictures. The idea for the film was conceived by screenwriter Robert Towne (1934–) and midwifed by producer Robert Evans (1930–2019), who chose director Roman Polanski (1933–) based on his experience working with the Polish émigré on a previous box office hit, *Rosemary's Baby* (1968). "I wanted a European vision" on an American story, Evans explained (*Chinatown Revisited*, 1999). After Towne wrote the screenplay for *The Last Detail* (1973), starring Jack Nicholson (1937–), the writer brought the actor into the *Chinatown* project. Evans pushed the film forward against the opposition of Paramount executives who doubted Nicholson's potential as a romantic leading man and disliked the script (Eaton 1998, 8–9). The studio wanted to cast Jane Fonda (1937–) as lead actress but Polanski insisted on Faye Dunaway (1941–), who had starred in a recent movie set in the same period, *Bonnie and Clyde* (1967) (*Chinatown Revisited*, 1999).

Towne's original screenplay for *Chinatown* was longer than the version finally screened and had a more upbeat ending. Although Polanski trimmed the story to a manageable running time of two hours and ten minutes, the plot followed the twists and turns of the Raymond Chandler detective novels that had inspired Towne and was considerably more complicated than was usual in a Hollywood crime drama. In *Chinatown*, a private detective in Los Angeles named Jake Gittes, played by Nicholson, takes what initially appears to be a case of marital infidelity. He is drawn instead into a murderous struggle for wealth and resources playing out behind the scenes. The struggle centers on control over water and real estate. Hollis Mulray, played by Darrell Zwerling (1928–2014), LA's chief engineer for power and water, turns up dead. Gittes eventually develops a professional and personal relationship with Mulray's widow, Evelyn (Dunaway), the daughter of the corrupt millionaire Noah Cross (John Huston, 1906–1987).

Hindering Gittes's investigation is Claude Mulvihill (Roy Jenson, 1927–2007), a thuggish power and water department security chief in league with Cross, and a short man in a white suit (played by Polanski) who slashes Gittes's nose with a knife in a memorable scene. The private investigator keeps his distance from the Los Angeles Police Department, represented by Lieutenant Lou Escobar (Perry Lopez, 1929–2008) and Detective Loach (Dick Bakalyan, 1931–2015). Gittes comes across evidence that water is being diverted from farmers outside the city for the purpose of forcing them to sell their land cheaply to anonymous investors led by Cross.

Chinatown's shocking revelation comes when Evelyn reveals that the girl Mulray was seen with was not his mistress but her daughter Katherine (Belinda Palmer), born after her father raped her at age 15.

Sympathetic after learning of her troubled past, Gittes urges Evelyn to take Katherine to the home of her butler, Kahn (James Hong, 1929–), in LA's Chinatown. From there, she could slip undetected from the city. Escobar arrives in response to Gittes's call after she leaves; unsatisfied with his explanations, he arrests Gittes for concealing evidence and other charges. Gittes convinces Escobar that Evelyn is hiding in the home of her maid in San Pedro and offers to take him there. The house where he brings the police actually belongs to his client Curly. With Curly's help, Gittes evades Escobar and meets with Cross, confronting him with the bifocals from the pond where Mulray was drowned. They are identical to the pair worn by the old man, who admits he is Katherine's father. Existing within a moral universe different than any Gittes has encountered, he concedes no wrongdoing. With Mulvihill holding a gun on Gittes, Cross learns the whereabouts of his two daughters.

The film's climax occurs in Chinatown and brings together the significant, surviving characters. Escobar and Loach wait outside Kahn's home with Gittes's operatives under arrest and in handcuffs. Cross and Mulvihill arrive with Gittes who is then arrested. Gittes tries to tell Escobar that Cross is "the bird you're after—he's rich. He thinks he can get away with anything." Cross looks on unperturbed. He is above the law. When Evelyn arrives with Katherine, Cross identifies himself to the young girl, hesitating as he chooses his words, "I'm your grandfather." Evelyn draws a gun, wounds her father and tries to make a getaway with the terrified Katherine. She hopes to flee to Mexico but never gets beyond the end of the block. Escobar and Loach shoot at the speeding car, killing Evelyn. Katherine falls into Cross's hands. Flustered by events, Escobar frees Gittes, saying "Go home Jake, I'm doing you a favor."

Chinatown is among the few successful Hollywood movies with scarcely a glimmer of a happy ending. However, its downbeat tone matched the mood of a nation grappling with the Watergate scandal and the post-Vietnam malaise. Made on a budget of $6 million, *Chinatown* grossed over $29 million at U.S. box offices through a long theatrical run. The film was generally well received by critics. Writing in the *Chicago Sun-Times*, Roger Ebert called *Chinatown* "a tour de force; it's a period movie with all the right cars and clothes and props, but we forget that after the first ten minutes." He added that the audience is drawn into its "web of mystery" because "we care about these people and want to see what happens to them" (Ebert 1974). However, the *New York Times* was less favorable, reserving most of its praise for Nicholson, "who wears an air of comic, lazy, very vulnerable sophistication that is this film's major contribution to the genre" (Canby 1974). Honored by the movie industry for helping revitalize the familiar genre of private detective films, *Chinatown* was nominated for 11 Academy Awards including Best Picture, Best Director, Best Actor, and Best Actress but won only for Best Original Screenplay.

Chinatown's reputation has grown over time. In 1991, the Library of Congress added it to the National Film Registry. Film historian David Thomson called it "a perfect thriller" and credited the cast, especially John Huston, whose "Cross is so attractive, so winning, so loathsome" and praised the set designers for recreating the appearance of *Chinatown* during the 1930s. "The craft work, the details are things to dream on. We are in 1937," he wrote (Thomson 2008, 165). In 2008, the American Film Institute ranked *Chinatown* as Hollywood's second-best mystery film, bested only by Alfred Hitchcock's *Vertigo* (1958). Two years later, Britain's *Guardian* newspaper named *Chinatown* "The Best Film of All Time" (Pulver 2010).

HISTORICAL BACKGROUND

Chinatown is built on popular memory of the underside of Los Angeles during the 1930s and 1940s as derived from Hollywood movies and the hardboiled crime fiction that inspired filmmakers. Crucial to defining the city's dark image was the author "often considered that city's epic poet," Raymond Chandler (Jameson 1996, 98). Like Polanski, the Anglo-American writer "brought to his work a European sensibility" by examining the city as an outsider (Speir 1981, vii). *Chinatown*'s depiction mirrored Chandler's "treacherous lights and crooked streets of Los Angeles" and "the unrelenting sun of California only intensifies the shadiness" of a depraved, soulless world (Iyer 1988).

From 1934 through 1938, the period in which *Chinatown* is set, Chandler published 15 short stories in *Black Mask* and other pulp fiction magazines. His stories reinvented the detective genre and led to his career as a novelist and Hollywood screenwriter. Emerging from his stories was the protagonist who shaped the characterization of Jack Gittes, private detective Philip Marlowe.

> **RAYMOND CHANDLER (1888–1959)**
>
> Dashiell Hammett (1894–1961) had already elevated the hardcore crime genre a decade before Raymond Chandler published his first novel, *The Big Sleep* (1939). Chandler would never have tried his hand at crime writing if he hadn't been fired from his job at a Los Angeles-based oil company in 1932, the worst year of the Great Depression. As a young man, Chandler had written poetry and literary criticism. Realizing there was little money in either, he studied pulp crime fiction magazines for their style and content and sold his first short story to *Black Mask* in 1933.
>
> Chandler came from an unusual Anglo-American background. Born in the United States, he grew up in England and served in the Canadian army during World War I. He brought an outsider's distance and an insider's experience to his tough stories of Los Angeles, whose society he depicted as hopelessly corrupt. Chandler's fictional private investigator, Philip Marlowe, was wisecracking and cynical yet in pursuit of justice. Alongside Hammett's Sam Spade, Marlowe defined the popular conception of private investigators.
>
> Chandler's success as an author led to work as a Hollywood screenwriter, notably for the film noir classic *Double Indemnity* (1944) and an adaptation of his own novel, *The Big Sleep* (1946). Dissipated by alcohol and depression, he wrote little during the final years of his life.

Chinatown's screenwriter Robert Towne changed certain details—Marlowe operated from a shabbier office than Gittes and refused to accept divorce cases. Otherwise, the similarities are striking. Like Marlowe, Gittes was an investigator for the District Attorney's office before striking out on his own. Both characters brought a wisecracking wit and detached irony to their cases and carried themselves in a suave manner. Marlowe's chivalry was armored in cynicism as he pursued justice in an underworld where scheming politicians, crooked cops, and powerful rackets overlapped. Much like Gittes at *Chinatown*'s conclusion, Marlowe "illuminates the way in which characters are alternately responsible for the world in which they live and trapped by that world" (Speir 1981, viii).

Chinatown's political and social backdrop is summarized by the screenplay's final line, "Forget it Jake, it's Chinatown." Producer Robert Evans recalled Towne describing his Chinatown as not a neighborhood but "a state of mind," a moral twilight zone (Evans 1994, 257). Towne said that he got the idea from a Los Angeles vice squad detective assigned to Chinatown who told him, "You don't know who's a crook and who's not a crook" and the best police response is to do nothing (Biskind 1994).

During the time Chandler lived in Los Angeles, the city's population exploded, rising from 300,000 in 1912 to 2.2 million in 1932 with no end in sight to the migration (Marling 1986, 28). Much of the growth was spurred by the Los Angeles Chamber of Commerce, which organized exhibits throughout the United States touting Southern California as the "Land of Plenty, the Cornucopia of the World" for its sunshine, oranges, and vineyards. "During the period, no other city in the United States was given so much publicity and the migrants kept flocking in" (Marchand 1986, 64).

Land speculation was LA's major enterprise until oil fields were exploited and the nascent movie industry established itself in the rustic suburb of Hollywood. Real estate development was abetted by local politicians. Confined to segregated districts and schools, Asians, Hispanics, and Blacks were deemed second-class at best by a majority population drawn from white Anglo-Saxon Protestant migrants from the Midwest and Western states. Those arrivals considered themselves "true Americans," whose conservative views were coupled with "an anxious need for law and order" (Marchand 1986, 65). Militant political conservatism kept unions at bay; the city fathers prescribed widespread home ownership as a vaccination against the spread of organized labor.

Unlike major cities in the East and Midwest that saw an influx of Jews, Roman Catholics, and other immigrants from Southern and Eastern Europe, "Los Angeles was divided between an overwhelming native white majority and a sizeable colored minority" (Fogelson 1967, 83). Outside of Hollywood, Jewish influence over the city's financial and commercial life retreated in the early 20th century in the face of rising anti-Semitism from white Anglo-Saxon Protestant migrants. Wealthy Jews withdrew into their own segregated country clubs and many hotels were "restricted" against Jewish occupancy. Hollywood studios played down the ethnic background of their founders and addressed Jewish issues cryptically if at all. Roman Catholic influence also declined against "the political supremacy of militant Protestantism" (Davis 1990, 116).

Oil increased the city's prosperity and drew additional migrants. In 1920, Standard Oil opened a well at Huntington Beach and soon afterward Unocal struck oil near Whittier and Shell at Long Beach. Derricks sprouted in Santa Monica, Beverly Hills, and Venice. By 1930, the Los Angeles region accounted for 5 percent of world oil production with the industry employing some 5,000 workers (Marchand 1986, 66). Chandler was employed by the South Basin Oil Company until he was fired in 1932 for alcoholism and absenteeism. Industries relevant to the oil boom sprang up in the city, including auto plants, steel mills, and rubber factories processing raw materials shipped from Asia through the port of Los Angeles.

Although Los Angeles became emblematic of America's car culture, the physical growth of the city in the early decades of the 20th century was spurred by the Pacific Electric Railway, whose trolleys, the "Red Cars," enabled residents to travel easily between far flung neighborhoods. The city expanded into the surrounding foothills and the farmland, ranches, and desert beyond, carving out neighborhoods that were "homogenous, clean and orderly" and lined with single-family homes on inexpensive, modestly sized lots (Marchand 1986, 68). The city center was relatively small.

The movie business was crucial to LA's image and rapidly became its largest industry as well as a dominant shaper of mores and dreams in the United States and across the world. Filming in Hollywood began in a barn on the corner of Sunset Boulevard and Comer Avenue in 1910; by 1930, the studios employed some 15,000 people. The major studios were founded by first- and second-generation immigrants, mostly Jews from Central and Eastern Europe. They were entrepreneurs with an outlaw streak. The original generation of Hollywood moguls came to California not so much for the sunlight but to escape the clutches of Thomas Edison's Motion Picture Patents Trust, which sought to retain control of the new industry and collect fees on all aspects of moviemaking and projecting.

The major Hollywood movie studios, including Metro-Goldwyn-Mayer (MGM), RKO Pictures, 20th Century Fox, Columbia, Paramount, Warner Brothers, and Universal, were sprawling and virtually self-governing districts. Typical of those facilities was Universal City as that studio's lot was called. Constructed on the site of a 230-acre ranch, the complex included its own restaurants, shops, and police force along with production facilities enabling the studio to manufacture a steady stream of films from idea through finished product. Universal even had its own zoo to house exotic animals needed in stories set in Africa and Asia (Schatz 1988, 16–18).

Even before Hitler took power in 1933, Hollywood attracted talented European filmmakers, actors, and writers with the lure of money and large audiences. After 1933, emigres, many of them Central European Jews with reason to fear persecution, poured into Hollywood, forming what one refugee later recalled as a "ghetto under Pacific palms" (Reinhardt 1979, 303). While grateful for work and sanctuary, many of the emigres compared Los Angeles unfavorably to their homelands. German author Erich Maria Remarque (1898–1970), whose antiwar novel *All Quiet on the Western Front* was adapted into an Oscar-winning movie (and banned in Nazi Germany), complained that "real and false were fused here so perfectly that they became a new substance, just as copper and zinc become brass that looks like gold." Conceding that the city was home to great artists, he countered that it "was also filled with spiritualists, religious nuts and swindlers. It devoured everyone, and whoever was unable to save himself in time, would lose his identity" (Davis 1990, 50). *Chinatown* advances Remarque's critique. Beneath the love story and detective work, the film's subtext is of how greed shaped Los Angeles (Eaton 1998, 8).

The dreamworld of Hollywood movies magnified the fantasy, marketed by the Chamber of Commerce, that transformed Los Angeles into a mecca for Americans seeking escape from the sooty cities and hard winters of the East and Midwest. The advertising campaign for the city and its real estate conjured a "promised land of a millenarian Anglo-Saxon racial odyssey," a paradise for whites on the far edge of the New World, America's final frontier. "Their imagery, motifs, values and legends were in turn endlessly reproduced by Hollywood" (Davis 1990, 20). The underlying ideology was plainly stated by University of Southern California president Joseph Widley (1841–1938). In his book *Race Life of the Aryan Peoples* (1907), Widley argued that it was the "manifest destiny" of the "Aryan Americans" to establish a world empire with Los Angeles as one of its principal cities.

During the 1930s, the Los Angeles area became the nucleus for the post–World War II aerospace industry with scientists and engineers gathered at the newly founded California Institute of Technology (Cal Tech). The campus's Pasadena location was chosen in part for the promise by the Southern California Edison power company to provide a high-voltage laboratory for atomic experiments. Some 60 millionaires from the region formed a support group, the California Institute Associates. Cal Tech's first president, the Nobel Prize–winning physicist Robert A. Millikan (1868–1953), reflected the prevalent ideology of his prominent backers from Los Angeles. According to Millikan, Southern California "is today, as was England two hundred years ago, the westernmost outpost of Nordic civilization" with "a population which is twice as Anglo-Saxon as that existing in New York, Chicago or any of the great cities of this country" (Davis 1990, 56). During the 1930s, Cal Tech's faculty and students tested the prototype of Donald Douglas's DC-3 in their wind tunnel and consulted with LA's oil industry. Their experiments in rocketry coalesced into the Jet Propulsion Laboratory.

The contrariness of LA's intelligentsia toward the city's utopian image found expression in the stories of Chandler, the novels of Nathaniel West (1903–1940), and the works of other writers. In his book *Los Angeles* (1933), satirist Morrow Mayo (1896–1983) called the metropolis "an artificial city which has been pumped up under forced draught" and complained that it "never imparted an urban character to its incoming population for the simple reason that it never had any urban character to impart," having "retained the manners, culture, and general outlook of a huge country village" (Mayo 1933, 327).

Although still equipped with functioning mass transit, by the 1930s Los Angeles was already a city of automobiles, a widely spread metropolis whose residents drove from their tract homes to shopping and work. Pedestrians are seldom glimpsed in *Chinatown* outside the densely packed Chinese neighborhood where the film concludes.

DEPICTION AND CULTURAL CONTEXT

Aside from portraits of Franklin D. Roosevelt in several scenes and Gittes's slur against farmers in the valley outside Los Angeles as "dumb Oakies," a reference to the rural refugees of the Dust Bowl who poured into California during this era, the Great Depression is virtually invisible in the circles Gittes travels in in *Chinatown*. This coheres with the attitude of the city's leading citizens through the 1930s. Their mouthpiece, the *Los Angeles Times*, declared that "much of the Depression is psychological." Mayor John C. Potter regarded bad news as heresy to the city's cult of boosterism. "We do not find it necessary to feed our unemployed men," he said, "In San Francisco I saw free soup kitchens. There are none here" (Weaver 1980, 110).

Chinatown's story of water rights and urban sprawl is inspired by actual events and characters. A native "Angelino" intent on exposing the city's corrupt foundations, Towne was fascinated by the subject but realized he had no chance of making a film about how water reached Los Angeles. He "transformed an unsellable history which clearly outraged him into a pitchable genre yarn" in the form of a Raymond Chandler–like detective story (Eaton 1998, 27). To accommodate that genre, Towne shifted the timeline, moving the 1906–1926 struggle over water and real estate forward to the heart of the Great Depression.

The central historical figure in the LA water wars, William Mulholland (1855–1935), was a remarkable man whose principal accomplishments correspond to the career of *Chinatown*'s Hollis Mulray. Mulholland emerged as the head of a privately owned water company before running the operation in the public interest as chief engineer of the Los Angeles Bureau of Water Works and Supply. Mulholland was responsible for constructing a dam that collapsed with great loss of life. As in the movie, political corruption and private chicanery brought water to Los Angeles over the objection of farmers and against the backdrop of drought and violence.

Mulholland's story was one of the "impossible rags-to-riches tales" that emerged from the lives of immigrants who poured across the United States during the second half of the 19th century (Standiford 2015, 26). Born in Belfast, Mulholland was a merchant seaman who jumped ship in New York and made his way across America earning his keep by sharpening knives and mending clocks. When he arrived in Los Angeles in 1877, it was still a frontier town of only 9,000 inhabitants. He found work as a ditch tender for the Los Angeles City Water Company, a private firm contracted by the city board to provide residents with water (Standiford 2015, 29–32).

The unreliable Los Angeles River and a Spanish colonial canal, the Zanja Madre, barely sufficed to supply Los Angeles with water when the city was still an insignificant outpost. The problem became acute as the population soared, reaching 102,000 by 1900. Insufficient water was an obstacle to the city fathers' ambitious plans for growth and Mulholland became their reliable ally as his ambition and talent moved him up the ladder of influence. Cleaning the Zanja Madre with a shovel was not a job he had for long. Mulholland soon became foreman of the ditch tenders and then was put in charge of laying pipes to supply running water to the city's commercial and residential buildings. Although he never completed high school, Mulholland had a keen mind for problem-solving and anything mechanical. "All of Mulholland's engineering training came either on the job or through his own reading" (Standiford 2015, 39). Soon enough the Water Company promoted him to supervisor, answerable only to its shareholders. As the company's highest-ranking employee, he continued to expand the water infrastructure.

The chief source of political intrigue in Los Angeles through the 1890s was the conflict between the Water Company's owners and municipal leaders seeking public control over the city's water supply. After a while the sticking point came down to the sale price, which rose to $2 million. Like the Los Angeles of *Chinatown*, the machinations occurred during a drought and as in the movie, a special election was held to approve a bond issue critical to funding the future of the city's water. When the City of Los Angeles finally acquired the Water Company in February 1902, it retained the company's supervisor, retitling him as chief engineer and encouraging an even more ambitious agenda for expansion. "When the city bought the works, they bought me along with it," Mulholland said (Standiford 2015, 58).

Mulholland worked in partnership with several key players, starting with Fred Eaton (1856–1934), who preceded him as the Water Company's supervisor but resigned to become LA's chief engineer and was later elected mayor. The two men remained close. Despite his background in private enterprise, Eaton "knew the city could not be held hostage to private interests when it came to water" (Standiford 2015, 54).

Other models than Eaton for *Chinatown*'s Noah Cross can be sought among the oligarchs who largely controlled the city from the Korean War through World War II. The dynasty established by General Harrison Otis (1837–1917) and his son-in-law Harry Chandler (1864–1944) involved intertwined families that presided over "one of the most centralized— indeed, militarized—municipal power-structures in the United States." With the aid of police and private security and cooperative associations of local businesses, they enforced "open shop" laws that made union organizing difficult, expelled Jews from the social register, and "looted the region through one great real-estate syndication after another" (Davis 1990, 101).

The lurking sense of repression and violence is captured in *Chinatown*. "Manipulating water politics and captive city officials, Otis, Chandler" and their associates "joined in syndicates to monopolize the subdivision of Hollywood, the San Fernando Valley and much of north eastern Los Angeles" (Davis 1990, 113–114). Reform-minded activists received death threats by mail; their businesses were disrupted by stink bombs; they were beaten by police and arrested for vagrancy; their phones and offices were wire tapped; homes were bombed and one activist was killed by a car bomb. By 1939, a less-corrupt regime was in place under a newly elected mayor, Judge Fletcher Bowron, who fired the police chief and sent racketeers packing to Las Vegas (Nadeau 1960, 260–263).

Water remained a public issue in 1930s Los Angeles as city leaders moved to secure water rights from the Colorado River over the objections of Arizona to supply the growing needs of the metropolis. However, Noah Cross's scheme, involving expanding the city limits as well as bringing water to Los Angeles, is based on actions that occurred early in the 20th century. Los Angeles hungrily annexed adjacent property in transactions that enriched a handful of insiders and by 1926 became the largest city in the United States by land area. The key to that development was the aqueduct Mulholland completed in 1913 to bring water from California's mountains down to Los Angeles. As a feat of engineering, the project compared to the Panama Canal.

The expansion, which came in several stages and was more complicated than shown in *Chinatown*, began as early as 1906 when Eaton began buying up much of Owens Valley. Acquiring much of it at 20 percent of its value while acting as an agent of the city, he raised cattle and chickens on the land but "had known of the value of the property as a potential reservoir site" from the beginning (Standiford 2015, 220). When it came time to negotiate for water rights in the 1920s, Mulholland expressed disapproval regarding Eaton's high asking price. "I'll buy Long Valley three years after Fred Eaton is dead," Mulholland reportedly said, referring to Eaton's enormous Long Valley Ranch in the Owens Valley (Standiford 2015, 219). Mulholland was also faced with a consortium led by Owens Valley bankers Wilfred and Mark Watterson, who controlled all credit in the valley and were determined to drive up land prices.

On May 21, 1924, the dispute between contending interest groups turned violent when a portion of the aqueduct north of Lone Pine in Owens Valley was knocked out by dynamite. Despite a $10,000 reward, the saboteurs, presumed to be disgruntled residents of the valley, were never identified. Mulholland acknowledged that farmers were being displaced by water diversions from the Owens River to Los Angeles but argued for the greater good of the greatest number of people. He complained, "There is a movement afoot to force us into accepting rights in the Owens River Valley at prices which we have not been willing to consider" (Standiford 2015, 225).

The attack on Jake Gittes by valley farmers had several real-life counterparts. On August 27, 1924, a local attorney responsible for organizing land sales to the city was kidnapped and nearly lynched. He avoided the noose only because he was a fellow lodge member with several Masons in the hanging party. He fled Owens Valley and never returned (Standiford 2015, 225–226). Mulholland received many death threats as negotiations with local landowners continued. In November, several hundred Owens Valley residents including entire families briefly occupied a portion of the aqueduct and sent water through the sluices into the valley.

Violence continued into 1926 with dynamite attacks on the aqueduct and city employees held at gunpoint when they entered the valley. Mulvihill and his band of thugs in *Chinatown* represent the armed war veterans sent into Owens Valley by Los Angeles to protect its investment in water (Eaton 1998, 25). Resistance in the valley ceased after Wilfred and Mark Watterson were convicted of embezzlement and sentenced to San Quentin. "With the disgrace and fall of the Wattersons, organized resistance to the City of Los Angeles was at an end" (Standiford 2015, 234).

While rebuking the mayor in *Chinatown*'s City Hall scene, Mulray refers to a dam he had constructed that collapsed several years earlier with great loss of life. This is based on the March 1926 collapse of the St. Francis Dam, which claimed 450 lives in the resulting flood. Only days earlier, Mulholland had overruled his engineers and maintained that the dam was sound. Like Mulray, Mulholland felt deep guilt and acknowledged his responsibility. "If there was an error in human judgement, I was the human, and I won't try to fasten it [the blame] on anyone else" (Standiford 2015, 8).

Despite a shelf of nonfiction books on the subject, including a biography of Mulholland by his granddaughter, public memory of how water came to Los Angeles continues to be shaped by the historical fiction conceived by Robert Towne and filmed by Roman Polanski (Standiford 2015, xvi). However, despite its visually and even psychologically accurate depiction of Los Angeles during the Great Depression, the history behind the film's fiction took place in an earlier era.

FURTHER READING

Biskind, Peter. 1994. "The Low Road to Chinatown.' *Premiere*, June 1994.
Canby, Vincent. 1974. "Chinatown." *New York Times*, June 21, 1974.
Chinatown Revisited. 1999. Special feature included on the Paramount DVD release of *Chinatown*.
Davis, Mike. 1990. *City of Quartz: Excavating the Future in Los Angeles*. London: Verso.
Eaton, Michael. 1998. *Chinatown*. London: British Film Institute.
Ebert, Roger. 1974. "Chinatown." *Chicago Sun-Times*, June 1, 1974.
Evans, Robert. 1994. *The Kid Stays in the Picture: A Notorious Life*. London: Autumn Press.
Fogelson, Robert. 1967. *The Fragmented Metropolis: Los Angeles 1850-1930*. Cambridge, MA: Harvard University Press.
Iyer, Pico. 1988. "Private Eye, Public Conscience." *Time*, December 12, 1988.
Jameson, Fredric. 1996. "The Synoptic Chandler." In *Shades of Noir: A Reader*, edited by Joan Copjec. New York: Verso.
Marchand, B. 1986. *The Emergence of Los Angeles: Population and Housing in the City of Dreams 1940–1970*. London: Pion.
Marling, William. 1986. *Raymond Chandler*. Boston: Twayne.
Mayo, Morrow. 1933. *Los Angeles*. New York: Alfred A. Knopf.
Nadeau, Remi. 1960. *Los Angeles from Mission to Modern City*. New York: Longmans, Green.

Pulver, Andrew. 2010. "Chinatown: The Best Film of All Time." *The Guardian*, October 22, 2010.
Reinhardt, Gottfried. 1979. *The Genius: A Memoir of Max Reinhardt by His Son*. New York: Alfred A. Knopf.
Schatz, Thomas. 1988. *The Genius of the System: Hollywood Filmmaking in the Studio Era*. New York: Pantheon.
Speir, Jerry. 1981. *Raymond Chandler*. New York: Frederick Ungar.
Standiford, Les. 2015. *Water to the Angels: William Mulholland, His Monumental Aqueduct, and the Rise of Los Angeles*. New York: Ecco.
Thomson, David. 2008. *"Have You Seen . . .?" A Personal Introduction to 1,000 Films*. New York: Alfred A. Knopf.
Weaver, John D. 1980. *Los Angeles: The Enormous Village 1781–1981*. Santa Barbara, CA: Capra Press.

Chapter 10

Bound for Glory (1976)

Bound for Glory was released on December 5, 1976, by United Artists. It was directed by Hal Ashby (1929–1988)—considered part of Hollywood's "New Wave" of European-influenced and socially daring directors for previous films such as *Harold and Maude* (1971) and *The Last Detail* (1973)—and produced by Hollywood veteran Robert F. Blumofe (1909–2003) and Harold Leventhal (1919–2005), onetime manager of the film's subject, folksinger Woody Guthrie (1919–1967).

The screenplay, written by Robert Gretchell (1936–2017), was a loose adaptation of Guthrie's memoir of the Great Depression years, *Bound for Glory* (1943). Respected cinematographer Haskell Wexler (1922–2015) strove to give the production an authentic period look. *Bound for Glory* stars David Carradine (1936–2009) as Guthrie, Ronny Cox (1938–) as folksinger Ozark Bule, and Melinda Dillon (1939–) in a double role as Guthrie's wife Mary and his singing partner Memphis Sue.

The film opens with Woody Guthrie living in a small town, Pampa, Texas, that is crumbling from the blows of the Great Depression and the Dust Bowl. He is married with children and hard-pressed to make a living as a sign painter and playing fiddle for a country music band. As the dust storms increase in intensity, Guthrie joins the increasingly large throng of migrants seeking a better life in California.

Much of the film depicts Guthrie on the road in a long odyssey from Texas through desolate countryside and over the California border to Los Angeles. He has no discernable political or social ideas at the start of his journey, but by the time he reaches LA, he has witnessed the cruelty of institutions and their agents, including churches, corporations and the police, and decides to become a force for change in American life. He becomes an activist in the left-wing movement to organize California's farm workers and conveys his messages through songs.

With the help of singer–labor activist Ozark Bule, Guthrie lands a regular show on a Los Angeles radio station and sends for his wife Mary and their children. He irritates the station's owner by his refusal to avoid political controversy in his material. He refuses offers by an agent to place him on national radio and in good paying hotel nightclubs. He also angers his wife by his irresponsible attitude toward earning a living. He abandons his family and California, riding the rails like a hobo on the way to New York, where fame awaits him.

Bound for Glory was not a hit at box offices but received respectable reviews from critics and within the movie industry, winning Academy Awards for Best Cinematography (for Wexler) and Best Music/Adaptation Score for Hollywood composer Leonard Rosenman (1924–2008). It was nominated for four other Oscars, including Best Picture, Best Screenplay Based on Material from Another Medium, Best Costume Design, and Best Film Editing. Film critic Roger Ebert praised *Bound for Glory* for its beautiful imagery, adding that it "has a grave dignity, which is good, but it often seems to lack life, which would be better" (Ebert 1977). The entertainment industry trade publication *Variety* called *Bound for Glory* "outstanding biographical cinema, not only of the late Woody Guthrie but also of the 1930s Depression era which served to disillusion, inspire and radicalize him and millions of other Americans" (*Variety* 1976).

HISTORICAL BACKGROUND

According to Pete Seeger (1919–2014), Woody Guthrie's biggest musical influences were the Carter Family and Jimmie Rodgers (1897–1933), two of country music's biggest stars in the 1920s and 1930s (Seeger and Santelli 1983, 25). Guthrie cowrote "Oklahoma Hills," number one on the country music charts in 1945 as recorded by his cousin, Jack Guthrie (1915–1948). Guthrie got his start playing fiddle in a country band and became well-known singing on the radio in a country duo, yet he is always remembered as a folk singer. He even claimed he never heard the term "folk" or "folk song" until he fell in with a sophisticated New York crowd in the 1940s, although this might have been another example of his tendency of pretending to be naiver than he was in reality (Szwed 2010, 158).

"Country music did not exist prior to the 1920s" but had roots that reach as far as medieval Britain and West Africa. "Country music is a commercial art form that coalesced only after rural American music met the technologies of radio and records" (Malone 2006, 14). Country music was initially constructed out of the folk music of the American South. Its performers were white but despite Jim Crow, poor Southern whites and Blacks lived separately yet close together. The banjo is an instrument of African origin while the guitar came to America from Europe. Whites and Blacks heard each other's music and "shared a folk culture with a common body of songs, dances, and instruments" (Malone 2006, 17).

In the 19th century, folk culture and music became a field of academic study in America and throughout Europe, driven by scholars searching for the "essence" of their national culture in pockets of cultural isolation relatively unaffected by modernization, especially the ancient tales and songs of rural communities. In the United States, Harvard's James Russell Lowell (1819–1891) and Francis James Child (1825–1896) began collecting the texts of traditional ballads. Their interest was literary and historical; they valued the lyrics as poetry but believed that folk balladry had already ended and was an extinct tradition. However, from 1916 through 1918, British folklorist Cecil Sharp (1859–1924) travelled through Appalachia and "found an extensive body of songs from the Child canon still being sung by the people who lived there" (Malone 2006, 15). His *English Folk Songs from the Southern Appalachians* (1917, revised and expanded in 1932) became a foundational text in what became the mid-20th-century folk music revival.

The folk songs of the American South had no individual composers. They traveled with immigrants across the ocean and were passed down from generation to generation, evolving to echo local conditions. Ballads often recalled specific events, whether a hanging or a train wreck, and were set to tunes pulled from a legacy of inherited melodies. The music was like the air, owned by no one but sustaining everyone. Whereas British settlers arrived with intact families and sometimes entire communities, planting their folk culture in New World soil, slaves from various African cultures speaking different languages were thrown together and unable to transplant their societies in America. They brought few songs with them but contributed distinct traditions of rhythm and singing.

The evolution of the folk ballad tradition was stimulated and accompanied by the continuous arrival of new songs into the South. Even "Dixie" was introduced on the New York stage before the Civil War. Before radio, most middle-class homes had a piano and families entertained themselves and guests playing songs from sheet music. Demand for new songs was supplied by the sheet music industry, centered along New York's Tin Pan Alley, and its wares were widely available in the South and performed by the traveling minstrel shows that entertained the lower classes. Idealized images of the South figured in many Tin Pan Alley songs during the late 19th and early 20th centuries. "No other regions of the United States inspired songwriters or their publishers to produce anywhere near the number of songs as those about Dixie" (Jones 2015, 2). Many of them found their way into the repertoires of early country singers.

The record companies responsible for the birth of country music worked much like the folklorists who collected folk songs, but with a different agenda. Like the scholarly song collectors, the record labels sent scouts into the Southern back country looking for talent, but their motivation was not to document an endangered tradition—it was to exploit the potential for "a healthy market for country music," usually called "hillbilly" or "old-time music" in the early years. "The motherlode of these prospecting trips was mined" by Victor Records' Ralph Peer (1892–1960) (Wolfe 2006, 52).

In 1927, Peer set up a temporary recording studio in an empty building by the railroad tracks in Bristol, Tennessee. Unlike the wandering folklorists, he advertised for talent in the local newspaper and auditioned all comers. His two great discoveries left an indelible impression on country music. First was the Carter Family, a trio consisting of A. P. Carter (1891–1960), his wife Sara (1898–1979), and her cousin Maybelle (1909–1978), who sang in traditional harmonies of a nostalgic rural world fast fading due to industrialization and urbanization. The second discovery, Jimmie Rodgers, brought country music up to date, performing in "a genre he virtually invented— white blues" (Wolfe 2006, 58).

The terminology remained confusing for many years. In 1944, *Billboard* magazine debuted its "Folk Records" chart, which it described as a weekly ranking of the most played "hillbilly" records. As a result, Hank Williams and Eddy Arnold were filed under folk music by the music industry's leading mouthpiece. *Billboard* replaced the term "folk" with "country and western" in the 1950s. While country has usually tended toward social and political conservatism, it continually evolved musically in step with the interests of record buyers. For many years, folk music was politically progressive but musically conservative, clinging to a vision of the past until shaken into the 1960s by Bob Dylan (1941–).

While Guthrie certainly heard many hit records by the Carter Family and Jimmie Rodgers, he may have been unaware of how American music traditions were understood by students of Child and Sharp, whose views differed sharply from listeners of "The Grand Ole Opry." He may have thought of himself as a hillbilly singer but by the time he arrived in New York, he discovered that he was a folk artist.

The emergence of the movement that came to be called the "folk revival" or, more inclusively, the "folk blues revival," came against the backdrop of New Deal cultural policies as expressed through the Works Progress Administration, whose federally funded theater, murals, and regional guidebooks served the idealistic goal of ennobling the experience of everyday Americans and the agenda of the Communist-inspired Popular Front, which sought to mobilize proletarian culture in the United States.

Alongside larger social forces responding to the Great Depression, the folk revival was guided by a small circle of enthusiasts. At their center was a quarreling father-and-son team of folklorists, the politically conservative John Lomax (1867–1948) and his left-leaning son, Alan (1915–2002).

Alan's political persuasion was more representative of the audience that embraced their work as "collectors" of American songs.

John Lomax was among the pioneers in the study of American folk songs. His *Cowboy Songs and Other Frontier Ballads* (1910) was written while lecturing at the University of Texas at Austin. Contrary to Cecil Sharp's contention that cowboy ballads were the "despoiled ... inheritance of traditional song," Lomax accepted that folk songs could develop and reflect the lives of contemporary Americans.

The Lomaxes, "like every other family, were hit hard" by the Great Depression. The need for income as much as genuine interest inspired John to seek financial support for an expedition with Allan to the American South in search of songs. In 1933, John received a modest grant from the Library of Congress, including money for gas and food and use of a car and recording equipment. Despite chronic arguments with his socialist son, John looked forward to "bumming across the country, but doing so with noble goals and legitimacy of the highest order" (Szwed 2010, 31, 35).

The Lomaxes traveled in a Model A Ford and often camped out to save money. They sometimes stopped along the roadside to record a singer on cylinders, transferred to discs later at the Library of Congress. For their second trip in 1934, they obtained a machine that recorded directly onto discs. Sometimes their song collecting was done with a nod from the local planter. Near Huntington, Texas, "they stopped at the Smithers Plantation and approached the manager with their plans for collecting songs, stressing that they wanted to hear locally 'made-up' songs, not spirituals or pop tunes" (Szwed 2010, 36).

The planter summoned entire families of Black tenants who waited patiently that night in a schoolhouse lit only by a single oil lamp. With no other whites in the room but the Lomaxes, one singer, a man called Blue, gathered his courage and sang about the impoverishment of sharecroppers. When the song concluded, he added, apparently believing that the Lomaxes had the ear of Franklin D. Roosevelt, "Now, Mr. President, you don't know how bad they're treating us folks down here. I'm singing to you so I hope you will come down here and [do] something for us poor folks in Texas." Alan later said that the experience "totally changed my life. I saw what I had to do." Folk music would become a tool for social activism (Szwed 2010, 36–37).

John, however, saw a financial opportunity when they visited Angola Prison, a Louisiana work camp where convicts in striped garb labored in the heat. They discovered a Black prisoner, Huddie Ledbetter (1888–1949), known as Lead Belly. Convicted on a dubious murder charge, Lead Belly led Angola's work gangs in song as they bent to pick cotton and was a repository of old songs from many sources. In 1934, after convincing Governor O. K. Allen (1882–1936) to pardon Lead Belly, or so went the legend, John hired the singer as his driver and became his manager, an arrangement that led to disagreement over money. He presented Lead Belly to a conference of the Modern Language Association in Philadelphia and a concert at Bryn Mawr College before bringing him to New York. Lead Belly was seen as exotic and dangerous, as reflected in a *New York Herald Tribune* headline: "Sweet Singer of the Swamplands Here to Do a Few Tunes Between Homicides" (Place 2015, 28).

On December 31, 1934, John and Alan Lomax brought Lead Belly to a New Year's Eve party in Greenwich Village, where he performed "for a mix of New York tastemakers, Village intellectuals and artists, reporters, and faculty from Columbia and New York University" (Szwed 2010, 65).

The New York intelligentsia established a Lead Belly legend that both contrasted and complemented the tabloid life of the singer *Time* magazine called the "Murderous Minstrel." For them he was a noble exemplar of the folk tradition and the oppression endured by Southern Blacks; they wanted to present him as a leftist. The reality was more complicated. Lead Belly's repertoire included jazz, pop tunes, and anything he felt like playing and in 1940, he wrote a campaign song for Republican presidential candidate Wendell Willkie because Willkie, a centrist, supported civil rights.

Guthrie was among Lead Belly's fans from the New York left. Pete Seeger recalls Guthrie saying, "The best and loudest singer that I ever run into his name was Huddie Ledbetter and we all called him Lead Belly his arms was like big stove pipes, and his face was powerful and he picked the twelve-string guitar" (Seeger 1972, 27).

The potential of folk songs rewritten with a political slant or as rallying cries in the struggle against oppression had its own tradition stemming from the "broadside ballads." From the 16th century through the 19th century, broadsides were the cheaply printed street literature of Great Britain and America and often included song lyrics commenting on the news of the day. They were "the dim forerunners of modern commercial popular music," whose anonymous authors fed the folk culture of their time (Wilentz and Marcus 2005, 1). To the audience of those broadsides, "recognition counted for more than innovation." The words were meant to be sung to familiar tunes (Halker 1991, 81).

The songbooks of political groups as distinct as the Abolitionists and the Ku Klux Klan followed the same principle of setting messages to melodies that everyone could sing. The labor movement provided an especially fertile source of inspiration for the folk revival. As early as 1799, a Philadelphia strike was celebrated in a broadside ballad that proclaimed: "Arouse! The time has come! When our rights shall be fully protected!" The Knights of Labor, a 19th-century workingmen's society that was the forerunner of organized labor, distributed broadside ballads in great numbers. During that era, "labor broadsides surfaced during the struggles of coal miners, among whom song-poetry enjoyed a long history and song-poets commanded great respect" (Halker 1991, 81).

In the early years of the 20th century, labor broadsides were especially associated with the Industrial Workers of the World (IWW), an anarchist syndicate promoting the goal of "one big union" for all workers. Especially celebrated were the songs of Joe Hill (1879–1915), who like his anonymous predecessors appropriated melodies from Protestant hymns and other familiar music for his scathingly satirical numbers, including "The Preacher and the Slave," "The Rebel Girl," and "There Is Power in a Union." Hill was executed by firing squad in Utah, elevating him in left-wing circles to the status of a martyr (Adler 2011, 12–13, 206).

The Communist Party was initially skeptical about the potential of folk music transplanted from Appalachia to urban America. One party official scolded Pete Seeger, "If you are going to work with the workers of New York City, you should be in the jazz field" (Luhrssen and Larson 2017, 134). But big band jazz was associated with the capitalist music industry in the minds of the radical intelligentsia and in any event required too much musicianship. Folk music appeared easy to learn and democratic in its accessibility.

This was the political environment Guthrie gravitated to by the time of his first arrival in New York. On February 25, 1940, he was one of several performers at a Mecca Temple benefit concert for loyalist refugees from the Spanish Civil War. Alan Lomax discovered him that night, "drawn to the rustic cool of his performance and the ease with which his speech and song flowed together" (Szwed 2010, 157).

Lomax had encountered real back-porch performers of old song traditions while traveling the South and understood that Guthrie wasn't a remnant from the past to be cataloged but "a new idiom" representing a world of "new highways and power lines and Dust Bowl migrants and all that." According to Lomax, "His guitar has the sound of a big truck going down the highway with the riders bouncing around in the front seat" (Szwed 2010, 158).

Lomax played a significant role in elevating Guthrie from obscurity to national recognition. Before the singer could drift back onto the road, Lomax gave him a regular guest spot on his *American School of the Air* radio program and archived many of his songs during a three-day recording session at the U.S. Interior Department in Washington. At Lomax's suggestion, Guthrie was commissioned to write songs celebrating the Bonneville Power Administration, one of several New Deal projects that extended the electric grid into rural areas. From this project came several of his most memorable songs, including "Roll on Columbia," "Hard Travelin'," and "Grand Coulee Dam."

Guthrie's arrival in New York coincided with the release of *The Grapes of Wrath*. He carried himself like a character from the film and endorsed the movie, saying it "had more thinkin' in it than 99% of the celluloid that we're tangled up in the moving pictures today" (Denning 1996, 270). Victor Records, one of America's major record labels, released an album of Guthrie songs "to capitalize on the popularity of the film." Victor gave *Dust Bowl Ballads* the deluxe treatment normally accorded in those years to classical recordings under a prestigious conductor, complete with a booklet explaining the lyrics. The label asked Guthrie to write a song explicitly about *The Grapes of Wrath* and he obliged with "Tom Joad," its melody borrowed from the outlaw ballad "John Hardy," a 1928 hit for the Carter Family.

The other songs "were products of Guthrie's performances for the migrants" before he left California (Denning 1996, 271). They include "I Ain't Got No Home in This World Anymore," his adaptation of a Baptist hymn that had also been recorded by the Carter Family, and perhaps his most poetic lyric, a paean to agricultural works called "Pastures of Plenty."

While in New York, Guthrie fell in with the man who became his most eager acolyte, Pete Seeger, performing with him for the first time at a March 3, 1940 benefit for migrant workers. He sometimes played with Seeger's group, The Almanac Singers. In July 1941, they drove across the country to Los Angeles in a car they purchased with a $250 advance from a record label and "sang their way back to the East Coast the following year" (Aldin 1999, 9). Guthrie served in the merchant marine and married a dancer, Marjorie Greenblatt (1917–1983). They had three children, including Arlo Guthrie (1947–), who became a popular folksinger in the 1960s. In 1947, their four-year-old daughter, Cathy Ann, died in a fire in another of the bizarre accidents that dogged Guthrie's life.

PETE SEEGER (1919–2014)

The son of a politically progressive musicologist, Pete Seeger seemed to be born for his life's work in music and social activism. Seeger's mission to champion the music of America's working class and ethnic minorities in tandem with promoting left-wing causes remained his mainstay throughout his life.

In 1938, he brought his guitar and banjo to New York City where he became prominent in the emerging folk music scene. He assisted musicologist Alan Lomax in his documentary work for the Library of Congress's Archive of American Folk Music but never lost sight of his role as a performer. In 1940, he formed The Almanac Singers with Woody Guthrie. Regrouping in 1949 without Guthrie as The Weavers, Seeger and team took the folk music repertoire to nightclubs and concert halls and enjoyed several hit records, including "Goodnight Irene."

The Weavers' success was cut short in the McCarthy era over allegations of Communist sympathies. Seeger was blacklisted and could perform only at private or political functions. He sold albums released on small record labels and toured incessantly, unfazed by American Legion picket lines and an indictment for contempt of Congress.

With the shifting cultural and political climate of the 1960s, Seeger became an esteemed figure in American music while remaining committed to liberal causes.

Although he continued to record and perform, "the onset of Huntington's disease was already at work in his system; constant movement was becoming more urgent even as it became more difficult, and Marjorie saw less and less of him as his travels took him away for longer periods of time" (Aldin 1999, 11).

Seeger's new group, The Weavers, had a hit in 1950 with Guthrie's "So Long, It's Been Good to Know You," just before being blacklisted for their Communist ties. Unable to record for several years for major record labels or perform in concert halls or nightclubs, they traveled a circuit of rented rooms organized by sympathizers. Guthrie eluded the blacklist due to his failing health; even Joe McCarthy might have hesitated before outlawing the author of "This Land Is Your Land." The singer was admitted in 1952 to the hospital where he spent the rest of his life, "trapped in a body he could no longer control" (Aldin 1999, 11) but visited like a saint by many admirers. One of them was a young Bob Dylan, who arrived in New York in 1961 with a vocal style and persona copied from Guthrie. When Dylan became one of the most significant songwriters of the 1960s, inspiring artists as far afield as The Beatles and The Byrds, Guthrie's musical DNA filtered into rock music and remains influential today even among musicians who never listened to him.

DEPICTION AND CULTURAL CONTEXT

Bound for Glory was loosely drawn from Woody Guthrie's memoir of the same name, a folksy chronicle from an unreliable narrator who used his life and times as material for storytelling. He made up stories in performance, in between songs, and *Bound for Glory* was written in that fashion. Whether on paper or on stage, he was his own protagonist, a wisely naïve minstrel befriending the good common people forced to share America with their antagonists, the affluent manipulators growing fat from an unfair economy. Their henchmen were the cops and bullies who kept the working class down with the blunt end of their clubs.

Guthrie "could play the hillbilly to perfection when it suited him," wrote the biographer of Alan Lomax, the Library of Congress folklorist who helped raise the singer to national prominence. "Woody could drive those around him crazy with his offstage posturing, sleeping on the floor, refusing to eat at a table, declining to bathe." On one occasion, Lomax told Guthrie: "Grow up!" (Szwed 2010, 159). Moses Asch (1905–1986), who produced some of Guthrie's enduring recordings, described him as "a very serious and articulate person" who, when "he's not putting on or making fun," spoke in "common English" instead of rustic dialect. In public, Asch said, Guthrie was an "actor acting out the role of the folk singer from Oklahoma" (Carlin 2008, 45).

Bound for Glory was originally published in 1943 and spans more of Guthrie's life than was included in the screenplay. The film omits his early years and upbringing in Oklahoma and ends as he begins his journey to New York City. In the memoir, he arrives in New York and then heads back west, preparing to do his part for the war effort. The book suggests that Guthrie was thinking about finding work in a shipyard but instead, he served through the end of World War II in the merchant marine.

The film begins in 1936 in Pampa, Texas. The depiction of the place is true to Guthrie's description of "a little old low-built little town . . . jumped up big when the oil boom hit. Now eleven years later it had up and died" (Guthrie 1983, 191). The nearby derricks were pumping oil with diminished outcomes during the Great Depression, and the Dust Bowl had reduced Pampa's population and appearance. The film recreates the thin gray transparency that covered the sky on the sunniest of days and dramatically recreates the black wall of dust that rushed toward the town, blotting out the sun and leaving the townsfolk choking under masks, stopping the cracks in doors and windows as best they could with cloth. It was an experience endured by many residents of the southern plains during the Dust Bowl (Duncan and Burns 2012, 42).

Guthrie grew up in Okemah, Oklahoma. His father, Charles Edward Guthrie (1879–1956), was a cowboy before becoming a district court clerk and a local politician. His mother, Nora Belle Sherman Guthrie (1888–1929), sang to her children a repertoire of the folk songs, murder ballads, and popular tunes that became the foundation of country music. "Woody's childhood was full of strange, inexplicable occurrences," including his sister's death from a coal stove explosion and his mother's apparent dementia (she died in a mental hospital) (Aldin 1999, 3–4). At age 16, Guthrie dropped out of high school and followed his father to Pampa. The film includes a glimpse of the extended Guthrie family that migrated to the boom town.

David Carradine plays the role of Guthrie as the singer depicted himself, walking with a casual slouch as if to the rhythm of a song. Carradine's Guthrie is laconic but well-spoken in the folk dialect of the southern plains. He is also keenly observant of the people and society around him, a gift that allowed him to be mistaken for a "fortune teller" or mind reader, much as shown in the film (Guthrie 1983, 179–182). Guthrie had three children with his first wife, Mary Jennings (1917–2014), but the film shows only two. The necessity of transforming Guthrie's manuscript, of around 300 pages, into a two-hour feature film resulted in trimming details, condensing events and distilling the rambling, digressing account into a simpler narrative.

One of the most significant modifications was the implication that Guthrie, at loose ends in Pampa and finding insufficient work as a sign painter, finally hit the road in 1936. In reality, he had already been roaming for several years, sending money home "when he remembered." He took "short trips at first, then longer ones, and soon he was gone for months at a time"

(Aldin 1999, 5). He was already writing verses for songs and scribbling cartoons on scraps of paper. Guthrie wasn't fleeing the Dust Bowl but chasing a dream and along the way caught sight of the unfolding environmental catastrophe and got to know its victims. His first song, written in 1935, "Dusty Old Dust," was set to the melody of a hit by country singer Carson Robinson (1890–1957), "Ballad of Billy the Kid." "This set a pattern of reworking existing melodies with his own original words that would continue throughout his life" (Aldin 1999, 5–6).

Bound for Glory moves to the slow rhythm of small-town life in an unprosperous time. The faces of the film's Dust Bowl refugees reflect the influence of Depression-era photo documentarians such as Dorothea Lange (1895–1965), and many of *Bound for Glory*'s other visuals are accurate. While in Pampa, Guthrie played fiddle in the Junior Chamber of Commerce Band. A photograph shows him dressed in a big white Stetson hat and gaudy cowpoke garb, similar to what he wears in a scene from the film in which that band entertained square-dancing couples at the local dance hall (Aldin 1999, 6).

Along with his work as a musician, Guthrie earned money painting signs for local businesses, as in the movie, but the screenplay ignored Guthrie's wider talent for drawing in pencil, ink, watercolor, and gouache. "Clearly, expressing himself in pictures was an independent creative activity" for the singer, whose sketches later accompanied his "Woody Sez" column for the Los Angeles Communist Party paper, *People's World* (Landau 1999, 83). However, Guthrie valued his music more than his visual art, saying, "A picture you buy once, but you can sing a song and then sing it again" (Yurchenko 1970, 61–62).

Several specific incidents recounted in Guthrie's memoir recur unchanged or abbreviated in the film, including the mentally ill man he befriended. After talking to the stranger who had escaped from an asylum, Guthrie pronounced him as saner than the people who confined him. When the man said, "I always did think that maybe I'd like to paint some of this stuff I see inside my head," Guthrie gave him some of his paint brushes (Guthrie 1983, 186–187).

Unlike the screenplay, in Guthrie's memoir he talked politics in Pampa with the crowds that gathered around his house from his reputation as a mind reader. "I told them, 'Hitler an' Mussolini is out ta make a chaingang slage outta you, outta me, outta ever'body else! An kill ever'body that gits in their road!' " he wrote. Guthrie went on at the gathering to condemn the racism of the great dictators. "Bible says ta love yer neighbor! Don't say any certain color!" When asked if the end of the world was at hand, he replied, "Mebbe th' old one is . . . but a new one's in th' mail!" (Guthrie 1983, 188).

In this respect, the film was more accurate than the book; Guthrie's political and social activism came gradually and resulted from the influence of people he met in California. He grew up in a segregated environment, his father "participated in several lynchings," and as late as 1937, he wrote and performed aggressively racist songs on his Los Angeles radio show. But after receiving a letter from a Black listener, he apologized on the air and deleted those songs from his repertoire. Guthrie's manager Harold Leventhal said the singer was "educated" on the subject of race by actor Will Greer (1902–1978) (Marsh 1999, 172).

As in the movie, Guthrie recalled making his way from Pampa to California by hitchhiking, on foot when no cars pulled over, and sometimes by jumping onto passing freight trains. Among the hobo stories picked up in the screenplay is the incident where railroad police forced the hobos they flushed from the freight cars to spend what little money they had to purchase tickets on the next passenger train (Guthrie 1983, 216–217). In the book, the encounter was not as violent as in the film, but the railroad police were notorious for using clubs and guns against hobos (Watkins 1993, 60).

Guthrie recalled arriving in California in another freight car of hobos (Guthrie 1983, 222). But the film recapitulates a scene from *The Grapes of Wrath*, placing Guthrie in a truck with a family of Dust Bowl refugees at the state line where police had set up checkpoints to discourage the influx of migrants. By the time he reaches Los Angeles, the film version of *Bound for Glory* appears to be influenced more by *The Grapes of Wrath* than by Guthrie's memoir. The book devotes few words to the fruit pickers of California but the film spends long stretches in their camps, with Guthrie transformed into a union organizer, risking his neck at the hands of orchard owners' thugs to preach working-class solidarity in the struggle for better wages and a better world. In reality, by 1939 Guthrie did play at migrant camps and strikes in the San Joaquin Valley, often as part of performances organized by Greer (Denning 1996, 269).

The film picks up on biographical points less explored in the book. Guthrie did become the cohost of a popular show on a Los Angeles radio station, KFVD, where he performed live with a female partner, Lefty Lou (she's called Memphis Sue in the movie). With the regular earnings from radio giving him a comfortable income, he sent for Mary and the children. The movie doesn't show that "Woody, who had evidently forgotten they were coming, showed up to collect them at the train station several hours late" (Aldin 1999, 7).

The film's character Ozark Bule, the labor activist and singer who gets Guthrie his radio job, is fictional but loosely inspired by Cisco Houston (1918–1961), a singer, leftist songwriter, and frequent Guthrie collaborator. His real companions in Los Angeles—also unmentioned in the film—included his cousin, Leon "Jack" Guthrie (1915–1948), with whom he cowrote songs, and Will Greer, who allowed the singer to sleep in his one-room cabin in Topanga Canyon. The cabin became "a place of pilgrimage for folk music fans" decades later (Aldin 1999, 6).

In the film, Guthrie is determined to do things his own way almost to the point of madness. While in Pampa he is fired for refusing to change the color of a shop sign; in Los Angeles, the radio station fires him for refusing to drop political songs from his show. He also rebuffs offers to perform on a CBS coast-to-coast radio show and at a fancy hotel because he doesn't want to be an entertainer. In reality, Guthrie was happy to perform anywhere, whether in a train car with hobos or a posh nightclub for wealthy clientele. As for CBS, he bragged that the network was "giving me money so fast I'm using it to sleep under" (Klein 1980, 167). His cantankerous nature was part of the legend maintained by his associates. Decades after his death, Pete Seeger claimed that Guthrie quit a New York radio show in the 1940s after a couple of weeks when the sponsor, Model Tobacco, told him what to sing.

Bound for Glory presents a mythologized version of Guthrie's life that departs in many scenes even from the singer's own legend-making. It presents his early career as many of his fans, and fans of the musicians he inspired, wanted to remember him. *Bound for Glory* doesn't ignore his personal irresponsibility but minimizes it; it emphasizes his social conscience, making him a heroic fighter on behalf of the common man and woman.

David Carradine's characterization vividly brings to life the impression Guthrie made on his acolytes. The actor's role-playing corresponds exactly to folksinger Pete Seeger's recollection of Guthrie as a "wiry guy with a mop of curly hair under a cowboy hat . . . with his guitar slung on his back, spinning out stories like Will Rogers, with a faint, wry grin" (Seeger 1983, vii).

FURTHER READING

Adler, William M. 2011. *The Man Who Never Died: The Life and Times of Joe Hill, American Labor Icon*. New York: Bloomsbury.
Aldin, Mary Katherine. "Way Down Yonder in the Indian Nation: Woody Guthrie, an American Troubadour," 1999. In *Hard Travelin': The Life and Legacy of Woody Guthrie*, edited by Robert Santelli and Emily Davidson. Middletown, CT: Wesleyan University Press.
Carlin, Richard. 2008. *Worlds of Sound: The Story of Smithsonian Folkways*. New York: Collins.
Denning, Michael. 1996. *The Cultural Front: The Laboring of American Culture in the Twentieth Century*. London: Verso.
Duncan, Dayton, and Ken Burns. 2012. *The Dust Bowl: An Illustrated History*. San Francisco: Chronicle Books.
Ebert, Roger. 1997. "Bound for Glory." *Chicago Sun-Times*, March 9, 1977. https://www.rogerebert.com/reviews/bound-for-glory-1977
Guthrie, Woody. 1983. *Bound for Glory: The Hard-Driving, Truth-Telling Autobiography of America's Great Poet-Folk Singer*. New York: Plume.
Halker, Clark D. 1991. *For Democracy, Workers, and God: Labor Song-Poems and Labor Protest, 1865–1895*. Urbana: University of Illinois Press.
Jones, John Bush. 2015. *Reinventing Dixie: Tin Pan Alley's Songs and the Creation of the Mythic South*. Baton Rouge: Louisiana State University Press.

Klein, Joe. 1980. *Woody Guthrie: A Life*. New York: Alfred A. Knopf.
Landau, Ellen G. 1999. "Classic in Its Own Way: The Art of Woody Guthrie." In *Hard Travelin': The Life and Legacy of Woody Guthrie*, edited by Robert Santelli and Emily Davidson. Middletown, CT: Wesleyan University Press.
Luhrssen, David, with Michael Larson. 2017. *Encyclopedia of Classic Rock*. Santa Barbara, CA: Greenwood.
Malone, Bill C. 2006. "Turkey in the Straw: The Roots of Commercial Country Music." In *Will the Circle Be Unbroken: Country Music in America*, edited by Paul Kingsbury and Alanna Nash. London: DK.
Marsh, Dave. 1999. "Deportees: Woody Guthrie's Unfinished Business." In *Hard Travelin': The Life and Legacy of Woody Guthrie*, edited by Robert Santelli and Emily Davidson. Middletown, CT: Wesleyan University Press.
Place, Jeff. 2015. "The Life and Legacy of Lead Belly." In booklet for the Smithsonian Folkways CD, *Lead Belly*.
Seeger, Pete. 1972. *The Incomplete Folk Singer*. New York: Simon & Schuster.
Seeger, Pete. 1983. "So Long, Woody, It's Been Good to Know Ya." In *Bound for Glory: The Hard-Driving, Truth-Telling Autobiography of America's Great Poet-Folk Singer*, edited by Woody Guthrie. New York: Plume.
Seeger, Pete, with Robert Santelli. 1983. "Hobo's Lullaby." In *Hard Travelin': The Life and Legacy of Woody Guthrie*, edited by Robert Santelli and Emily Davidson. Middletown, CT: Wesleyan University Press.
Szwed, John. 2010. *Alan Lomax, The Man Who Recorded the World: A Biography*. New York: Viking.
Variety. 1976. "Bound for Glory." December 31, 1976. https://variety.com/1975/film/reviews/bound-for-glory-3-1200423759/
Watkins, T. H. 1993. *The Great Depression: America in the 1930s*. Boston: Little, Brown.
Wilentz, Sean, and Greil Marcus, eds. 2005. *The Rose & The Briar: Death, Love and Liberty in the American Ballad*. New York: W.W. Norton.
Wolfe, Charles K. 2006. "Red Hot and Rarin' to Go: The Commercial Beginnings, 1922–1930." In *Will the Circle Be Unbroken: Country Music in America*, edited by Paul Kingsbury and Alanna Nash. London: DK.
Yurchenko, Henrietta. 1970. *A Mighty Hard Road: The Woody Guthrie Story*. New York: McGraw-Hill.

Chapter 11

The Lindbergh Kidnapping Case (1976)

The Lindbergh Kidnapping Case is a made-for-television movie that first aired on February 26, 1976 on NBC. The Columbia Pictures production was directed by Buzz Kulik (1922–1999), a prolific figure in the television industry whose résumé included episodes of *The Twilight Zone* and *Perry Mason* as well as numerous television miniseries and movies. The screenplay was penned by veteran television writer JP Miller (1919–2001).

The Lindbergh Kidnapping Case opens with archival footage of the historic 1927 flight across the Atlantic Ocean by Charles Lindbergh (1902–1974) before shifting to its subject—the dramatization of the 1932 kidnapping of Lindbergh's infant son. In this production, the child's mother, Anne Morrow Lindbergh (Sian Barbara Allen, 1946–), is alerted by her nurse, Betty Gow (Kate Woodville, 1938–2013), that the baby is missing. A ransom note is found in the nursery. Charles Lindbergh (Cliff DeYoung, 1945–) tells the butler to call the police.

The New Jersey State Police under Colonel Norman Schwarzkopf (Peter Donat, 1928–2018) discover a ladder that might have been used by the kidnapper to climb into the second-floor nursery along with some footprints near the ladder. They establish a command center at the Lindbergh estate. Because of Lindbergh's celebrity status, the press descends upon his home and conducts a campaign of lurid rumormongering. The police suspect the Lindberghs' maid, Violet Sharp (Denise Alexander, 1939–), who commits suicide. The New York Police Department investigates the kidnapping's possible ties to organized crime and contends with a concerned citizen from the Bronx, Dr. John Condon (Joseph Cotton, 1905–1994), who becomes an intermediary between the Lindberghs and the kidnapper. Condon delivers the ransom money at a New York cemetery but the instructions left by the kidnapper, a man speaking with a German accent, lead nowhere. The Lindbergh baby's body is soon found two miles from the family's estate.

New York police detective James J. Finn (Tony Roberts, 1939–) identifies a suspect by tracing the serial numbers on the ransom money. After passing one of the bills from the ransom payment at a gas station, Bruno Hauptmann (Anthony Hopkins, 1937–), a German immigrant working as a carpenter, becomes the prime suspect. The police arrest Hauptmann and find part of the ransom money in his garage. Hauptmann's wife, Anna (Christa Lang, 1943–), appears shocked and unaware of her husband's kidnapping scheme. The case is prosecuted by New Jersey Attorney General David Wilentz (David Spielberg, 1939–) in the court of Judge Trenchard (Walter Pidgeon, 1897–1984). Although pleading innocence through the end, Hauptmann is convicted and despite a brief reprieve from Governor Hal Hoffman (Laurence Luckinbill, 1934–), he is executed in the electric chair.

The attention and accolades surrounding Lindbergh's death two years before the film was broadcast ensured a large audience for *The Lindbergh Kidnapping Case*. The *New York Times* panned the production as "buried under long stretches of dramatic tedium," adding, "the producers are trapped into wandering over several different aspects of the case, and the result is less complexity than diffusion" (O'Connor 1976). However, Hopkins, a British actor still relatively unknown in America, won an Emmy Award for Outstanding Lead Actor in a Miniseries or Movie for his performance. *The Lindbergh Kidnapping Case* also received a Golden Globe nomination for Best Motion Picture Made for TV. It remained the best-known dramatization of the Lindberg kidnapping until the broadcast, 20 years later, of another made-for-television movie, *Crime of the Century* (1996).

HISTORICAL BACKGROUND

Few American reputations have flown so high and fallen so low, rebounding only to fall again, as that of Charles Lindbergh. He became an international hero in 1927 as the first person to fly across the Atlantic Ocean and was admired in many circles, including Nazi Germany. As Europe lurched into World War II, Lindbergh leveraged his celebrity to advocate for U.S. neutrality in the conflict as spokesman for the America First Committee. When the United States entered the war, his ties to Germany put him under suspicion. In the postwar decades, Lindbergh was celebrated once again as an aviation pioneer but in the 21st century, his avowed racism and sympathy for Nazi Germany in the prewar years drew renewed scrutiny.

Lindbergh spent much of his youth roaming his family's sprawling homestead on the Mississippi River near Little Falls, Minnesota. His father was a Swedish immigrant whose law practice and investments made him one of the area's wealthiest men. After 1906 when his father was elected to the U.S. House of Representatives, Lindbergh spent many months each year in Washington, D.C. as well as with his mother's family in Detroit and in the family acreage in Little Falls. Because he attended 11 schools and never completed a full year in any one of them, he was seldom a good student. His mind wandered from the classroom to the outdoors and all things mechanical, inspired by his eccentric grandfather, an inventor (Denenberg 1996, 8–10).

Lindbergh's interest in the mechanics of modern life was stimulated by the social transformation he lived through—the rapid changes powered by steam turbines and electric motors that led to transportation and communication revolutions through automobiles and telephones. He drove his father's Model T Ford at age 11 in a time before drivers' licenses were required in Minnesota. He loved changing tires and adjusting carburetors. Lindbergh also received his political direction from his isolationist father, who blamed banks and big business for pushing America into World War I (Hixon 1996, 7–8).

Once war was declared, Lindbergh earned his high-school degree under a government program that allowed seniors who worked fulltime on food-producing farms to graduate without attending classes (Denenberg 1996, 14). Afterward came two academically unimpressive years studying engineering at the University of Wisconsin. He excelled only in the Reserve Officers Training Corps, where he won a national competition for shooting, and spent most of his college time riding his motorcycle "recklessly through the surrounding countryside" (Denenberg 1996, 16).

The daredevil aspect of his character led him from motorcycles to airplanes. "A career in aviation would allow him the opportunity to do the things he valued most in life—use his skills, avail himself of modern technology, and seek adventure" (Hixon 1996, 14). In 1922, he went to Lincoln, Nebraska, for lessons at Ray Page's Flying School and was thrilled by the sensation of being airborne. Only two months after first sitting in a cockpit, Lindbergh went to work for Erold Bahl (1894–1930), a pilot who entertained Midwest audiences with dangerous aerial acrobatics known as "barnstorming." As Bahl flew low over a new town, Lindbergh helped attract paying customers by standing on a wing of the plane, waving at the folks below. He also learned to parachute, still a novelty and a crowd-pleasing stunt in the early 1920s (Denenberg 1996, 24–28).

By July 1922, Lindbergh had signed on with another barnstormer, Harold J. "Shorty" Lynch, for a tour of county fairs in Kansas, Colorado, Montana, and Wyoming. He was Lynch's mechanic as well as wing-walker and parachute jumper. In April 1923, Lindbergh purchased a World War I surplus Curtis Jenny, a light-weight plane that tested his ability to handle headwinds and downdrafts. He crashed several times early on but was undaunted, suffering no serious injuries or irreparable damage to the Jenny. That summer,

"Daredevil Lindbergh" became the star of his own aerial show (Denenberg 1996, 29–30).

Unsatisfied with the obsolescent aircraft at his disposal, Lindbergh was determined to learn to fly the latest models. For that reason, he joined the U.S. Army, enrolling in the Air Service Cadet Program in San Antonio, Texas in March 1924. Structured learning had never been Lindbergh's strong suit but for once, he found the challenges sufficiently compelling and accepted classroom discipline. He graduated at the top of his class as a second lieutenant. However, with few active roles to play in America's shrunken postwar military, Lindbergh was relegated to the reserves (Hixon 1996, 19–20).

"The accumulated air hours, drills, and classroom knowledge gained in the Army air school made Lindbergh one of the most capable young pilots in the country" (Hixon 1996, 21). He easily found work in a new and dangerous endeavor. By 1920, transcontinental airmail delivery was established between New York and San Francisco with feeder lines to other cities, but the distances and fragility of the aircraft at high altitude over mountains and in unpredictable weather took a heavy toll. Thirty-one of the first 40 airmail pilots died in crashes (Denenberg 1996, 35). Undaunted, Lindbergh was hired by Robertson Aircraft Company, a St. Louis–based postal contractor. He flew five round trips each week between St. Louis and Chicago in an open, twin-cockpit plane. The work remained hazardous but Lindbergh continued to look for greater challenges. He wanted to bring the world closer together by crossing the Atlantic in an airplane.

Although gas-inflated dirigibles were already capable of traveling long distances, airplanes were limited by their short range and fragile construction. Aviation enthusiasts worked to change that unsatisfying situation. As early as 1919, Raymond Orteig (1870–1939), a French-born New York hotel owner, offered a $25,000 prize to the first aviator to fly nonstop from New York to Paris or Paris to New York. Although in the first years after he made the offer no airplane could survive the journey, steady improvements in aeronautical design and increasingly powerful engines brought the adventure closer to feasibility.

Several much-publicized attempts were made but all ended in failure. Colonel René Fonck (1894–1953), a French World War I fighter ace, designed an elaborate tri-motor plane with a three-man crew that tumbled off the runway and exploded. Fonck and his navigator survived but his radio operator died. Lieutenant Commander Richard Byrd (1888–1957), the American who was first to fly over the North Pole, also hoped to cross the Atlantic in a large tri-motor plane but crashed during a test flight. Lieutenant Commander Noel Davis (1891–1927), a U.S. Navy airman, was killed when his large plane lost altitude and crashed shortly after takeoff. French wartime fighter ace Charles Nungesser (1892–1927) had a better idea than his predecessors. Accompanied by only a copilot, he flew a small single-engine plane stripped down to just the essentials to minimize fuel consumption and wind resistance. He even removed the landing gear in hopes of touching down in New York harbor. Nungesser was last sighted over Ireland and disappeared on his way to the New World. Two weeks later, Lindbergh made the journey in a plane he called *The Spirit of St. Louis.*

Once he was captivated by the idea, Lindbergh worked methodically to prepare for the flight. He enlisted the support of St. Louis businessmen and the local chamber of commerce, convincing them that his success could be a tool for raising the city's image. He obtained money to purchase and customize a plane named in the city's honor. Unlike some of his failed predecessors, Lindbergh reasoned that a one-engine aircraft would be safer because of fewer opportunities for mechanical breakdown while in flight. He was determined to fly solo to keep the plane light, despite the possibility of falling prey to 30 sleepless hours of disorientation while crossing the Atlantic. Most aircraft manufacturers were wary of his project, fearing harm to their brand name if Lindbergh crashed or disappeared over the ocean. Finally, in February 1927, the Ryan Airlines Corporation of San Diego agreed to build him the plane that became *The Spirit of St. Louis.*

Everyone involved was aware that they were racing against time. Many other aviators dreamed of being first across the Atlantic and were laying their own plans for the journey. Lindbergh worked closely with Ryan's engineers on the design and the company's workers, "sensing they were participating in something special, worked morning, noon and night, seven days a week" to build *The Spirit of St. Louis* (Denenberg 1996, 47). Although based on an existing Ryan model, the new plane was given extra fuel tanks and an increased wingspan for the 4,000-mile trip.

Every item on the plane was carefully considered because every pound of weight was a burden to overcome. Lindbergh eliminated the radio, placing him out of contact with the world as he flew. He threw out the parachute, giving him no way of bailing out if trouble occurred. Navigation lights and gas gauges were never installed and he refused to bring a sextant. He would fly by dead reckoning. Lindbergh even designed a pair of lightweight boots to wear in the cockpit.

One advantage he enjoyed was the opportunity to test the plane's endurance through a long preliminary flight. On May 10, 1927, Lindbergh took off from San Diego in *The Spirit of St. Louis* and headed to St. Louis. From there, he flew to Curtis Field on Long Island, setting a record for fastest transcontinental flight. He was met by the popping flashbulbs of cameras, a mob of news reporters shouting out questions, and newsreel cameras recording the event. "He appeared on the scene the all-American hero; the underdog, going up against famous aviators supported by powerful financial groups, piloting huge, well-equipped multiengine planes" (Denenberg 1996, 57). Lindbergh discovered that he was photogenic with a charming smile that signaled to the public all that was best in the American character. The press dubbed him "The Lone Eagle" and "Lucky Lindy," a name he disliked because he believed that preparation, not luck, would see him through. Crowds gathered in New York City wherever he went.

Although long-range weather forecasting was far from an exact science, Lindbergh was glued to weather reports, waiting for fog and storms to clear. Despite the persistence of bad weather, he took off against a strong headwind on the morning of May 20. The world held its breath as newspapers on both sides of the Atlantic prepared headlines for success or failure.

The excitement surrounding Lindbergh's arrival in Paris on May 21, 1927 after 33 hours in the air can only be compared to the anticipation and thrill four decades later of the first moon landing. His solo flight was an act of heroism and resourcefulness and a source of national pride that resonated on a deeper level. "Lindbergh symbolized the triumph of technology over geography and the human spirit over the barrier of space" (Jeansonne and Luhrssen 2008). The enthusiastic crowd that surged onto the tarmac of Le Bourget Aerodrome outside of Paris carried Lindbergh out of his cockpit. "For nearly half an hour I was unable to touch the ground during which time I was ardently carried around in what seemed to be a very small area, and in every position it is possible to be in" (Lindbergh 1927, 225–226).

After a whirlwind tour of Paris, London, and Brussels, Lindbergh was called home by President Calvin Coolidge (1872–1933) who sent a cruiser to bring him back across the Atlantic. Some 30 million Americans listened on the radio as Coolidge awarded him the Distinguished Flying Cross in a ceremony at the Washington Monument. He was promoted to colonel. The U.S. Post Office issued an airmail stamp with his likeness, the first time a living American had been so honored. When he arrived in New York City for a tickertape parade, the stock exchange closed and more than 3 million people jammed the streets for a glimpse of the aviator (Hixon 1996, 39). The prize money and fees he earned by telling his story made Lindbergh a wealthy man.

Lindbergh was never entirely comfortable in the public eye but capitalized on his celebrity to build support and confidence in commercial aviation. He flew *The Spirit of St. Louis* across the country and spoke in many cities, drawing large crowds wherever he went. "By the end of his 48 state tour, Lindbergh had achieved one of his major goals" by raising millions of dollars to be used for constructing a nationwide network of airports (Hixon 1996, 47).

Lindbergh gathered prominent supporters for the aviation industry, including Harry Guggenheim (1890–1971), the philanthropist who underwrote Lindbergh's tour, and David Morrow (1873–1931), a partner at the J. P. Morgan banking house who arranged favorable investment deals for the aviator. After Morrow became U.S. ambassador to Mexico, he invited Lindbergh on a goodwill tour of that country with *The Spirit of St. Louis*. The flight was a diplomatic success but had a more important long-term significance for Lindbergh. In Mexico City he met the woman who became his wife for the remainder of his life, Morrow's daughter Anne (1906–2001). Returning to the United States after flying *The Spirit of St. Louis* across the Caribbean, he received the Congressional Medal of Honor, the first non-wartime hero to be so awarded (Hixon 1996, 45–52).

At age 26, he was America's most eligible bachelor, a brighter star than any luminary in Hollywood. He approached the problem of finding a wife methodically, with a checklist, "much as he might plan one of his adventures" (Hixon 1996, 54). His thoughts turned to Anne Morrow, attractive, athletic, and intellectual. They married privately in 1929, announcing their union to the press only afterward. "After the honeymoon, Lindbergh hoped to avoid public scrutiny so that he might focus his attention on the two things that now mattered most to him, family life and commercial aviation" (Hixon 1996, 57).

"The Lindberghs were a model modern couple, at the cutting edge of technological developments" (Jeansonne and Luhrssen 2008). As a consultant to America's leading airlines, Trans-World Airlines (TWA) and Pan American Airways, Lindbergh helped shape the development of commercial aviation in the United States. With Anne as his copilot, Lindbergh flew the first leg of TWA's inaugural transcontinental passenger route in July 1929. Their many accomplishments around the world were celebrated in the news media. Working together, they pioneered the use of aerial photography to identify archeological sites in Central America. Anne was copilot, radio operator, and navigator as her husband flew to East Asia in 1931, scouting for U.S.-China air routes.

Reclusive by nature despite their penchant for highly publicized events, Charles and Anne resented the almost incessant attention of reporters hungry for a story or willing to make one up. Newspapers offered bribes to servants for gossip, tapped the Lindbergh's phone, and tried to infiltrate their staff. To avoid cameras, Anne gave birth to their first child in their New York apartment (Hixon 1996, 58). Charles Jr. was born on June 22, 1930.

That same year, the Lindberghs purchased 400 acres in the relatively remote setting of Sourland Mountain near Hopewell, New Jersey. They constructed a house on the property along with a runway for a 20-minute flight to New York. In the winter of 1932, they moved into their new home but were given little time to enjoy it. On March 1, 1932, Charles Jr., 20 months old, was kidnapped.

The Lindbergh kidnapping was only the most notorious incident in a wider trend. During the early years of the Great Depression, criminal gangs revisited the ancient pursuit of a "king's ransom" by kidnapping the rich or their children. Not that kidnapping was unknown among professional criminals before the stock market crash of October 1929. Earlier that year in Detroit, Joseph "Legs" Laman set an example for other gangs by orchestrating the kidnapping of David Cass, son of Detroit real estate developer Gerson Cass. The kidnappers demanded $4,000 (about $60,000 in 2021) and insisted that he did not involve the police. However, the police were tipped off by an informer and arrived as Cass delivered the money, shooting and capturing Laman. His gang was eventually rounded up but not before they panicked and killed their hostage, dumping the body in the Flint River (Cox 2021, 1–2).

Laman perfected a kidnapping method the underworld called "the System," which identified specific tasks and assigned them to specific gang members. The "finger man" identified a potential victim with money and learned about his daily routine. Two to four masked "pickup men" abducted the victim, usually when he was out walking or driving alone. In the hideout, "the castle," a small group of "keepers" stood guard and gave the hostage food and drink. Great care was taken that the victim never saw his kidnappers' faces (Cox 2021, 3–4).

Because telephones were easy to monitor, the kidnappers often negotiated after making initial contact through go-betweens. Those intermediaries could be attorneys with underworld clients or known individuals in the community. "When the System functioned properly, the victim's representatives never saw the kidnappers, and the police never knew who to watch or wiretap to lead them to the kidnappers" (Cox 2021, 4).

The crushing of Laman's gang was touted by police but clearly, other kidnapping gangs had begun to apply the System in Detroit, St. Louis, Kansas City, Chicago, and even smaller cities like Peoria. The virus became a nationwide epidemic as it spread to the east and west coasts. Kidnapping was a profitable business, especially for criminals locked out of such larger rackets as bootlegging, rum running, prostitution, and gambling (Cox 2021, 5).

Some kidnappings were planned not by professional criminals but by criminally minded amateurs. In August 1931, Dr. Dee Keelley, a prominent St. Louis physician, was lured out of his house at night by a request for medical assistance and taken at gunpoint by two men. In an odd twist, the seizure took place outside the home of one of Lindbergh's business associates, Preston Sultan, who witnessed the event but was unable to provide useful information to the police. The kidnappers blindfolded Keelley and changed cars to confuse him regarding his whereabouts. After an evening in an attic, they brought him to the "castle." By the sound of the toll gate, Keelley recognized that they had crossed the Mississippi River bridge into East St. Louis, Illinois (Cox 2021, 9–13).

The scheme was orchestrated by a woman, the owner of an exclusive St. Louis dress shop, Nellie Tipton Muench. She was also an accomplished pianist familiar with the city's high society, yet she resented her wealthy clients who excluded her from their inner circles because she was "in trade" and not from old money. After the bankruptcy of her shop, Muench frequented St. Louis' speakeasies and gambling joints. True to her Baptist upbringing, she neither drank nor smoked but overlooked the commandment against stealing. Befriending gangsters, Muench put the System to work against Keelley, a member of St. Louis' high society. He was forced to write ransom notes to his wife, asking for $250,000 (more than $4.2 million in 2021) (Cox 2021, 13–17).

Keelley's wife Kathleen contacted her brother-in-law who convened what he called an "executive committee" of lawyers and friends to negotiate her husband's release. The committee told the local press that the family would pay but only if the kidnappers proved Keelley was alive. One of the family's lawyers received a phone call saying that a package waited for them in a certain mailbox in rural St. Louis County. They found Keelley's pearl tie pin and a written note asking the family to contact St. Louis criminal attorney Sigmund Bass to be the intermediary.

For their part, the family hired Charles A. Karch (1875–1932), East St. Louis' representative in the U.S. Congress and an attorney who had defended gangsters in court. A third party became involved at the family's request—John Rogers, who covered the crime beat for the *St. Louis Post-Dispatch* and had many sources in the local underworld. Rogers was eventually entrusted with the task of bringing Keelley home. The family denied that they had paid the ransom but were not believed and were criticized for their secrecy and willingness to work behind the back of the police (Cox 2021, 17–22).

As the kidnapping wave continued, a United Press article headlined "Kidnappers Have Taken a Heavy Toll in Middlewest in Recent Months" pointed to more than 20 incidents that had "so alarmed midwestern citizens that [vigilante] movements are under way in many cities for an organized offensive against what police say has become one of the most lucrative of all 'rackets'" (Cox 2021, 25–26).

In some places, the rich armed their chauffeurs and made their movements less conspicuous. The St. Louis Chamber of Commerce established a Crime Investigations Bureau to assist the police with private detectives and paid informers. While President Herbert Hoover (1874–1964) and other conservatives continued to argue that the U.S. Constitution gave little allowance to the federal government for prosecuting crimes under state jurisdiction, a movement was building for expanding federal jurisdiction, especially of crimes committed across state lines. The automobile made it easy for criminals to dart across borders. Given the endemic corruption of the Prohibition era, confidence in local law enforcement was at a low ebb. "In some instances, information given to peace officers in other states is tantamount to communicating the same facts to the criminals," complained St. Louis police commissioner Arthur Freund (Cox 2021, 30). The extension of federal police powers had to wait until the Lindbergh kidnapping case seized headlines and public attention from coast to coast.

While the press was filled with accounts of kidnapping, the victims had previously been little known outside their hometowns. Lindbergh was an international hero, idolized as a symbol of American distinction, and the kidnapping of his child, Charles Jr., came at "a time when the nation seemed to have lost its grip on the future" (Gardner 2004). The investigation and prosecution of the case coincided with "a steady increase of state power at all levels, while Americans watched with shocked fascination as the underworld rose to the surface to challenge civic authority in cities and countryside" (Gardner 2004, 1–2).

The kidnapping finally moved conservative politicians to act. On the day that would have been Charles Jr.'s second birthday, June 22, 1932, President Hoover signed the Federal Kidnapping Act. Under the "Lindbergh Law," as it was popularly known, transporting a kidnap victim across state lines became a federal crime. The Extortion Act, signed on July 8, made sending a ransom note by U.S. Mail a federal crime.

During the first year after the Lindbergh Law was enacted, the FBI was involved in only two kidnapping cases because most were committed within state boundaries. Soon enough, FBI director J. Edgar Hoover (1895–1972) decided to seize the initiative by investigating cases that *might* eventually violate federal law. In 1933, Hoover invited the public to report every kidnapping directly to his office and published a phone number that was answered round the clock. Calls were sometimes forwarded to his home, giving the impression that Hoover personally directed each case (Cox 2021, 115).

Hoover also began working with state and local authorities by offering the agency's assistance through its modern crime laboratory and enormous collection of fingerprints. He was willing to dispatch agents to anywhere in

J. EDGAR HOOVER (1895–1972)

J. Edgar Hoover was an ambitious civil servant who became the most powerful—and feared—administrator in the federal government. He went to work in 1917 for the U.S. Justice Department and by 1919 became head of the department's campaign against radical political organizations. He carried out a series of raids in 1919 and 1920 which led to the arrest of 3,000 suspected anarchists, communists, and socialists. More than 500 were deported.

In 1924, Hoover became chief of the department's Bureau of Investigation and began the expansion that led to its reorganization in 1935 as the Federal Bureau of Investigation (FBI). As FBI director, Hoover capitalized on public fear resulting from Depression-era crime waves of kidnapping and bank robbing, wartime anxiety over Axis subversion, and postwar fears of Communist agents of the Soviet Union.

His ambitions also benefitted from the need for broader federal powers over law enforcement, spurred in part by faster transportation and Prohibition. The automobile allowed criminals to cross state lines easily and Prohibition financed the growth of powerful crime syndicates that bribed local authorities to look the other way. Hoover's extensive network of informants kept tabs not only on suspected criminals but on anyone suspected of radical political views. His agents even compiled reports on the political content of Hollywood movies. Several presidents considered firing Hoover but he was deemed too powerful to be removed.

During the 1960s, the FBI monitored the civil rights movement and conducted secret campaigns to disrupt and discredit leftist organizations. Hoover remained FBI director until he died in his home of a heart attack.

the United States. Local police tended to resent the FBI's intrusion, yet the agency's resources were "a gift they usually couldn't refuse—and another masterstroke" of public relations by Hoover who increased his agency's power through his Depression-era battles with kidnappers and bank robbers (Cox 2021, 115–116).

Hauptmann's widow continued to maintain her husband's innocence and charged the authorities with bribing and coercing witnesses. She mounted numerous failed lawsuits charging New Jersey with wrongful conviction.

Although eager to leave the past behind, Lindbergh continued to make history after the kidnapping trial ended. In 1936, he went to Germany at the request of the U.S. military attaché in Berlin, Major Truman Smith (1893–1970), who asked him to report on German airpower. The Nazis treated him as an honored guest. Following that visit, he returned to Germany on several occasions and warned that the Luftwaffe was the most powerful air force in Europe.

Returning to the United States in April 1939, he became the leading spokesperson for America First, an organization that opposed America's involvement in World War II until Pearl Harbor. Because of his ties to Nazi Germany, he was suspected of disloyalty during the war years. His reputation rebounded afterward with advisory roles in the newly created U.S. Air Force and a promotion to brigadier general.

During the last years of his life, Lindbergh emerged as an advocate for environmentalism. Among other things, the onetime champion of aviation tried to ban U.S. landing rights for the supersonic Concorde airliner for the environmental damage it could cause. "His name gained him the ear of government and corporate officers who might have ignored the pleas of lesser-known ecological activists" (Jeansonne and Luhrssen 2008). He was active in the World Wildlife Federation and championed the rights of tribal populations in the Philippines, threatened by the encroachment of civilization. Controversy returned in the 21st century as memories of his earlier anti-Semitic and racist remarks were recalled. Although he expressed sympathy for the persecuted Jews of Germany in a speech he gave for America First, he went on to say that the "greatest danger to this country lies in their large ownership and influence in our motion pictures, our press, our radio, and our government" (Cole 1953, 144). He once spoke of Western technological superiority as "one of those priceless possessions which permit the White race to live at all in a pressing sea of Yellow, Black, and Brown" (Lindbergh 1939).

DEPICTION AND CULTURAL CONTEXT

The Lindbergh Kidnapping Case remains remarkable for its fidelity to facts and informed speculation. After a brief sequence of archival footage from Lindbergh's 1927 flight accompanied by a hit song lauding his accomplishment and establishing his place in American popular culture, the film proceeds chronologically from Charles Jr.'s disappearance on the night of March 1, 1931 at the Lindbergh's Highfields estate through Charles and Anne's self-exile in England five years later. *The Lindbergh Kidnapping Case*'s scenario, described as follows, is fully accurate except where noted.

Normally, the Lindberghs would not have been at their new home on the Tuesday night of the kidnapping. With work on Highfields still underway, they usually arrive on Saturday afternoon and depart Sunday night or Monday morning for the Morrow estate in Englewood, New Jersey. This time, they stay on because Charles Jr. has developed a cold. The film raises the question of whether the kidnapper had inside knowledge of the household. The British immigrant household staff, including butler Olly Whateley (1884–1933), maid Violet Sharp (1904–1932), and the baby's nurse Betty Gow (1906–?), underwent no background checks before being hired. As a result, the police suspect that one of them worked with the kidnapper, leading him to the room where the baby slept. Although Gow discovers the empty cradle and alerts the parents, she handles herself well under questioning. Sharp, however, falls under suspicion. She is evasive regarding her whereabouts on the evening of March 1, only gradually revealing details. Her responses to questions are nervous and erratic, and after her final interrogation, she commits suicide by swallowing cyanide. Sharp's suspicious behavior remains one of the case's loose threads.

After being alerted by Gow of the baby's disappearance, Lindbergh finds an envelope on the windowsill of the nursery and with "remarkable restraint, he left it unopened and told Whateley to call the Hopewell police and the New Jersey State Police" (Gardner 2004, 23).

The Hopewell police and state troopers search the grounds by flashlight, finding the ladder used to scale the wall and get into the nursery window along with footprints. The film omits the initial police report suggesting that the prints were left by more than one set of feet. The New Jersey state police superintendent, Colonel Norman H. Schwarzkopf (1895–1958), takes charge of the investigation, and like all parties in the case, he defers to Lindbergh. "Everyone who came to Highfields . . . obeyed Lindbergh's orders" (Gardner 2004, 23).

The ransom note left on the windowsill, demanding $50,000, is filled with spelling errors and ends with a curious symbol, two interlocking hollow circles with a small red solid circle, wavy vertical lines and three perforated holes. This is meant to be the "signature" identifying the kidnapper. It's the vital detail kept from reporters who swarmed across Highfields before the police could cordon off the property and establish an uncontaminated crime scene. The press is unrelenting throughout the case, in search of new story angles. Lindbergh called the publicity "so intense, so inaccurate and sensational, that it resulted in our suffering threats, extortion letters, and the presence of sight-seers in such numbers that I had to arrange for an armed guard to protect our second son" (Lindbergh 1977, 17). The New Jersey State Police sets up a command post in Lindbergh's garage and monitors all incoming calls and mail.

Along with the expected flood of cranks come several individuals who claim knowledge of the case or offer to serve as intermediaries. Some are underworld figures—including one mentioned in the film, gangster Al Capone (1899–1947)—who offer to assist in finding the child in exchange for commutation of their prison sentence. *The Lindbergh Kidnapping Case* focuses on two intermediaries. One is prominent Norfolk, Virginia businessman John Hughes Curtis (1887–1962), a fraud who guides Lindbergh on several wild goose chases. The other, Dr. John F. Condon (1860–1945), plays a vital if controversial role.

The film introduces Condon as he holds court at a Bronx diner. He learns of the kidnapping from a passing newsboy and decries it as "a crime against all Americans" because of his high esteem for Lindbergh. In reality, the semiretired educator was more eccentric than the movie depicts and led the investigation down several blind alleys (Gardner 2004, 67–73). However, the screenplay accurately draws the outline of Condon's involvement. He writes a letter to the *Bronx Home News*, a paper widely read in the borough, offering to pay $1,000 to the kidnappers if the Lindbergh baby is returned unharmed. The kidnapper responds, asking him to become the intermediary. Several versions of what happened next have been recorded. The film shows the version in which the kidnapper's response letter includes a sealed letter to Lindbergh along with instructions that Condon contact Lindbergh immediately. The sealed letter raises the ransom to $70,000 and is signed with the curious symbols found in the original ransom note (Gardner 2004, 60–62). Condon later receives the baby's sleeping garments by mail as further proof that he's in touch with the real perpetrator.

Condon claimed to have met the kidnapper twice in a cemetery but the film simplifies the account to a single night-time encounter at St. Raymond's Cemetery in the Bronx. While Lindbergh waits in the car, Condon goes into the graveyard and finds a masked man with a German accent. The kidnapper claims he couldn't bring the baby as promised but gives direction for finding Charles Jr. onboard a boat anchored off the Elizabeth Islands between Martha's Vineyard and Cape Cod. Condon renegotiates the ransom and hands the kidnapper $50,000 rather than $70,000. Afterward, Lindbergh flies a seaplane over the Elizabeth Islands with Condon at his side but finds no boat. Condon then places an ad in the *Bronx Home News* asking "What Is Wrong? Have You Crossed Me?"

When Condon's role as intermediary leaks to the press, he is besieged by reporters as well as accusations linking him to the kidnapping ring. Lindbergh is onboard a Coast Guard cutter still searching for the boat mentioned by the kidnapper when his son's body is discovered less than two miles away from Highfields, an area that had been thoroughly searched in the hours after the kidnapping (Gardner 2004, 86).

The film accurately depicts the New Jersey State Police's rivalry with the New York Police Department, represented by Lieutenant James J. Finn but ignores the tension between Schwarzkopf and J. Edgar Hoover. Schwarzkopf is loath to share evidence and eager to solve the case himself. Unexamined in the film is the FBI director's desire to intervene but ultimate refusal to act. He provided scant assistance to New Jersey authorities because he "didn't want to be anyone's errand boy, especially not Schwarzkopf," deemed by him as a "lightweight" (Cox 2021, 98). He also feared the case would end badly and didn't want to share the blame.

However, after Hauptmann's arrest, Hoover rushed to claim a share of the credit. The press believed him. Headlines such as "J. Edgar Hoover, Ace Kidnapping Solver, Never Gave Up Hope on Lindy Case" and "Hoover Stayed in Shadows to Lead Great Kidnap Hunt" promoted the perception that the FBI saved the investigation from failure. The word was out that "it was futile for criminals to try to thwart the invincible G-men" (Cox 2021, 246).

The film ignores the FBI but shows the New York police employing several experts in their investigation, including Arthur Koehler from the U.S. Forest Service who identifies the wood from the ladder found at Highfields with a Bronx lumberyard. By examining the ransom notes, Freudian psychiatrist Dudley Schoenfeld (1893–1971) concludes that the kidnapping is the work of a lone actor, a man of thwarted ego seeking to exert power over one of the world's famous people.

Bruno Hauptmann is finally arrested after a gas station owner, disgruntled by his behavior, gives the police his license plate number (Gardner 2004, 148–149). The police mount a stakeout of Hauptmann's house and follow him when he leaves. Accounts of the arrest vary. The film goes with the version in which Hauptmann, stuck in traffic behind a truck, is pulled from his car by the arresting officers. A large cache of the ransom money is discovered in Hauptmann's garage. (Gardner 2004, 150–151).

Public interest is unabated by the arrest. A crowd numbering in the thousands gathers outside the Fleming, New Jersey courthouse during the trial, including hawkers selling miniature "kidnapping ladders" as souvenirs. The courtroom is packed with reporters. Hauptmann's wife Anna (1898–1994) is present. New York's attorney general David Wilentz (1894–1988) leads the prosecution and his case is strong.

The courtroom drama rises with Wilentz's theatrical oratory. He brands Hauptmann as the worst sort of person not only for kidnapping a child but for taking money and spending it on luxuries, such as a $400 radio, during the Great Depression, a time of deprivation for most Americans. Hauptmann's attorneys mount an unconvincing defense and fail to follow up on discrepancies in the prosecution's case, including Condon's erratic account of his role. The jury finds Hauptmann guilty and Judge Thomas W. Trenchard (1863–1942) sentences him to die in the electric chair.

The Lindbergh Kidnapping Case touches on the reprieve granted by New Jersey governor Harold Giles Hoffman (1896–1954), which delayed the execution. The governor believes, with good reason, that Hauptmann had not acted alone and hopes the condemned man might implicate coconspirators if given time. Hoffman soon drops the matter for political expediency. Hauptmann is convicted in the court of public opinion and the public wants blood. The film concludes with the Lindberghs in England, where they took refuge. "Newspaper publicity intensified and continued after the conviction of the kidnapper. Life for my family became so difficult, disagreeable, and dangerous that I decided to take up residence abroad," Lindbergh explained (Lindbergh 1977, 18).

FURTHER READING

Cole, Wayne S. 1953. *America First: The Battle against Intervention, 1940–1941*. Madison: University of Wisconsin Press.

Cox, Carolyn. 2021. *The Snatch Racket: The Kidnapping Epidemic That Terrorized 1930s America*. Lincoln, NE: Potomac Books.

Denenberg, Barry. 1996. *An American Hero: The True Story of Charles A. Lindbergh*. New York: Scholastic.

Gardner, Lloyd C. 2004. *The Case That Never Dies: The Lindbergh Kidnapping*. New Brunswick, NJ: Rutgers University Press.

Hixon, Walter L. 1996. *Charles A. Lindbergh: Lone Eagle*. New York: HarperCollins College Publishers.

Jeansonne, Glen, and David Luhrssen. 2008. "Between Heaven and Earth: Lindbergh, Technology and Environmentalism." *History Today*, January 2008.

Lindbergh, Charles A. 1927. *WE*. New York: G. P. Putnam.

Lindbergh, Charles A. 1939. "Aviation, Geography and Race." *Readers Digest*, November 1939.

Lindbergh, Charles A. 1977. *Autobiography of Values*. New York: Harcourt Brace Jovanovich.

O'Connor, John J. 1976. "TV: 'Lindbergh Kidnapping Case.'" *New York Times*, February 26, 1976. https://www.nytimes.com/1976/02/26/archives/tv-lindbergh-kidnapping-case.html

Chapter 12

Kansas City (1996)

Kansas City was released on August 16, 1996, by Fine Line Features. The film was produced, directed, and cowritten by Robert Altman (1925–2006), one of the most prestigious directors to emerge from the "New Hollywood," a loose movement of mavericks that emerged in the late 1960s and enjoyed its greatest influence through the 1970s.

Altman was never afraid to ridicule or cast a subversive eye on any aspect of American life that met his disapproval. His first popular film, *MASH* (1970), was a comedy set near the frontlines of the Korean War (but interpreted at the time of release as satirizing U.S. policies in Vietnam). After winning five Oscar nominations for *MASH*, Altman enjoyed critical and popular success in the decade that followed with films such as the "revisionist western" *McCabe & Mrs. Miller* (1971) and the country music industry satire *Nashville* (1975). By the time of *Kansas City*, his years as a box-office hit director were years behind him but his films continued to appeal to select audiences and cinema buffs.

Kansas City draws from Altman's childhood memories of Missouri city and is cowritten with Frank Barhydt Jr. (1942–), a Kansas City–born journalist who had previously collaborated with the director on screenplays for *The Player* (1992) and *Short Cuts* (1993). With his reputation as a prestigious director, Altman had no trouble recruiting stars for *Kansas City*'s lead roles, Jennifer Jason Leigh (1962–) as Blondie O'Hara and Miranda Richardson (1958–) as Carolyn Stilton. Harry Belafonte (1927–), unseen in films since the 1970s, costars as the Black gangster Seldom Seen. Actors in supporting roles include Michael Murphy as Carolyn's politician husband Henry Stilton; Dermot Mulroney as Blondie's husband Johnny O'Hara, a smalltime criminal; and Steve Buscemi as Johnny Flynn, a political operator with ties to the city's mayor.

The film was notable for casting prominent 1990s jazz musicians as real-life musicians from Kansas City's flourishing Depression-era jazz scene. Among them are pianist Cyrus Chestnut (1963–) as Count Basie (1904–1984), tenor saxophonist Joshua Redman (1969–) as Lester Young (1909–1959), tenor saxophonist Craig Handy (1962–) as Coleman Hawkins (1904–1969), pianist Geri Adams (1957–2017) as Mary Lou Williams (1910–1981), and tenor saxophonist James Carter (1969–) as Ben Webster (1909–1973).

Kansas City follows Blondie as she seeks to secure the release of her husband Johnny from the hands of Seldom Seen. Blacking his face to disguise himself as African American, Johnny robs one of Seldom Seen's couriers. He is easily apprehended by the gangster and faces almost certain death. Blondie kidnaps Carolyn, hoping to leverage the influence of Mr. Stilton over the city's political machine with its close links to the underworld. The story focuses on the fragile, anxious relationship between Blondie and Carolyn, neither of them an attractive character. Blondie's face is drawn into a sneer as if frozen in the middle of a wisecrack and Carolyn, scatterbrained and entitled by wealth, is cold and aloof. Blondie is addicted to the era's pop culture and Carolyn to laudanum, an opium extract.

In the final scene, Johnny is returned to Blondie after being mutilated by Seldom Seen and dies on the floor of their home. Carolyn reaches for Blondie's gun, kills her, and returns to her husband.

The critics were sympathetic but much of their enthusiasm was reserved for the film's music and musical guest stars. The *Los Angeles Times* called *Kansas City* "a gorgeous period tapestry and a glorious celebration of jazz" that lacked "enough story to fill out so magnificent and broad a canvas" (Thomas 1996). The *Chicago Sun-Times'* Roger Ebert called the story "fairly thin; it might have held together for the length of a 1930s B-movie, which is probably what Altman was thinking of when he wrote it." He added that *Kansas City*'s story was less important than its evocation of a time and place, especially the city's jazz music, which he described as "terrific" (Ebert 1996). The *New York Times* praised the film but added that it fell short of Altman's best work (Holden 1996).

Belafonte won the New York Critics Award for Best Supporting Actor, but otherwise, the film took no trophies during awards season. Produced on a relatively modest $19 million, the film lost over $17 million at box offices during its theatrical release.

Most film historians concur with jazz scholar Nicolas Pillai's assessment that *Kansas City* is "somewhat forgotten as a Robert Altman film and as a jazz film," adding that it is "an exemplary instance of both" (Pillai 2020). Film historian David Thomson agrees. After disparaging most of Altman's later films, he called *Kansas City* "fascinating, not least in the way it was backed up by a very lively jam-session" (Thomson 2010, 15). Years later, Altman conceded that reception was muted for *Kansas City* because of its uncomfortable mix of crime and music, tragedy and satire, saying, "I probably overdid it" (Thomson 2020).

HISTORICAL BACKGROUND

In the early 20th century, Kansas City, Missouri, was a prosperous and rapidly expanding urban center. As wheat production increased on the plains, it became one of America's leading grain markets; adjacent to cattle country, its stockyards overflowed. By 1930, its population had grown to 399,746, with a segregated Black population accounting for nearly 10 percent of the inhabitants.

Like many U.S. cities in the century following the Civil War, Kansas City was dominated by a "political machine," one of many such systems of patronage and power usually operated by local Democratic Party leaders. New York City's Tammany Hall under the notorious William "Boss" Tweed (1823–1878) served as a model for an organization enmeshed in all levels of local politics, embezzling public money, dispensing measures of much-needed welfare in a society without safety nets, and relying on coalitions of ethnic voters. The machines were reviled by reformers as well as Anglo-Saxon Protestant elites—who viewed them as interlopers of immigrant, often Irish stock—but they often enjoyed genuine public support.

Known as Boss Pendergast, Thomas J. Pendergast (1872–1945), "a burly Irishman with a twinkle in his eye" (Driggs and Haddix 2005, 5), held sway over the political machine that dominated Kansas City during the Great Depression. Many details of his life are unclear and contradictory, including his education and even the date of his marriage to Carolyn Elizabeth Dunn (1887–1951).

Born in St. Joseph, Missouri, he followed his older brother Jim (1856–1911) to Kansas City in 1894. By the time Tom arrived, Jim had made a fortune as a saloon keeper in the West Bottoms, the city's district of bordellos and gambling dens, and was a Democratic Party functionary and alderman representing the ward where his businesses flourished. Jim laid the foundation for the political machine his younger brother would inherit and expand (Larsen and Huston 1997, 17–21).

Tom worked at odd jobs at first, including as a bouncer at his brother's bars, giving him "a reputation for violence that caused people to think carefully before crossing him" (Larsen and Huston 1997, 27). He periodically reinforced that reputation. Early in his political career he accosted an alderman who had challenged him, beating him up in his office (Reddig 1986, 84). Jim secured an appointment for Tom as deputy constable (bailiff) at a municipal court, followed by various appointments to city and county committees. The younger Pendergast also became Democratic Party precinct captain for one of West Bottoms' neighborhoods. "Tom learned how to get out the vote, along with such methods of stealing elections as counting ballots twice and cheating in filling out tally sheets" (Larsen and Huston 1997, 29).

Jim sought no office higher than alderman but exerted influence through helping elect presentable candidates with respectable backgrounds, such as Attorney James A. Reed (1861–1944), who with the Pendergasts' help was elected county prosecutor in 1898 and mayor in 1900. In exchange for their support, Reed ignored illegal gambling and prostitution in the West Bottoms.

Although the Democratic Party was the majority party in Kansas City, it was divided into two factions, the Goats and the Rabbits. The origin of their names remains uncertain. Jim ran the Goats and his rival, Joseph Shannon (1867–1943), precinct captain of the Ninth Ward southeast of downtown, led the Rabbits. Sometimes Goats and Rabbits ran rival candidates in the general election. Sometimes one faction or the other entered a temporary alliance with the Republican Party. Because Kansas City lacked a professional civil service, city employees served at the pleasure of public officials. Under the city's charter, all "the considerable number of patronage positions went to the victor, making the stakes very high" (Larsen and Huston 1997, 32).

The Goats operated out of the Jackson Democratic Club, an ample building located near Jim's properties and furnished with a bar, a billiard parlor, lunch and meeting rooms, and a 1200-seat auditorium. Establishing the template for his younger brother's career, Jim held no office in the Democratic Club but was the wire-puller running the show from behind the curtain.

Early in the new century, the Goats and Rabbits reached an uneasy accord, the "Fifty-Fifty" solution. If the factions could not agree in advance on a candidate for a given public office, they battled it out in the primaries but came together in the general election against their Republican opponent. If the Democratic candidate won, the patronage connected to his office was divided 50–50 between Goats and Rabbits (Dorsett 1968, 33–34). However, distrust continued between the factions and double crosses occurred, including under-the-table deals with the Republicans.

Mayor Reed appointed Tom, then 28, as the city's superintendent of streets, which included the responsibility for filling 250 jobs in his department. He was a hands-on boss, eager to prove himself, and legends gathered around him. "His figure is a familiar one on the streets, standing in a snow storm in winter, or the boiling sun in summer, superintending the work of his men," wrote an admiring biographer in a 1902 booklet, *Men Who Are Making Kansas City* (Larsen and Huston 1997, 35). "He was a familiar figure and something of a local hero in the saloons and bawdy houses of the West Bottoms," frequenting pubs and singing Irish songs (Larsen and Huston 1997, 39).

The city streets became the springboard to Tom's first elected office, Jackson County marshal, whose responsibility included running the jail.

A Republican editor, not normally disposed to supporting the Pendergast family, praised him for launching "a new era in penal progress. He stood for the Negro as well as the white man. No cruel treatment of prisoners" (Larsen and Huston 1997, 36).

Even so, he was voted out in 1904, defeated by a Republican challenger. Tom reemerged as superintendent of streets and increasingly devoted himself to the daily affairs of the growing Pendergast organization. With his health declining, Jim left the city council in 1910 and Tom won the seat easily. Jim died a year later, his successor at his bedside. With his brother's death, Tom Pendergast assumed control of a political organization that did not yet enjoy a monopoly of power over the Kansas City Democratic Party or the city. Step by step, Pendergast extended his influence until he became dominant.

From 1911 through 1914, Pendergast's Goats and Shannon's Rabbits maintained an uneasy truce. However, in January 1915, the 50–50 policy began to unravel as Kansas City mayor Henry L. Jolst (1873–1950) dismissed two Goats from important patronage-dispensing jobs and a Goat judge removed several Rabbits from office. On May 3, Pendergast abruptly resigned from the city council. The *Kansas City Post* predicted that his departure would bring an end to old-style politics in the city but praised Pendergast as an "easy boss" who helped "down-and-outers," feeding the poor in winter and providing lodging for the homeless (Larsen and Huston 1997, 55). His resignation was a dramatic coup that masked his intention to manipulate city politics from outside city hall.

The struggle between Goats and Rabbits broke into warfare over the 1916 mayoral election. The Rabbits backed another term for Jolst and when they booed and jeered Pendergast at the Democratic Party city convention, he retaliated by throwing his support behind the Republican candidate. Joe Shannon, by then the police commissioner, rounded up Pendergast campaign workers on flimsy charges, yet the Republican mayoral candidate won and all Rabbit candidates for city council were defeated. The Goats took five seats on the council. The day after election day, "Boss Tom emerged as the number one Democratic leader in Kansas City" (Larsen and Huston 1997, 57).

Later that year, the Goats gained control over Jackson County and helped elect Frederick Gardner (1869–1933) as governor of Missouri. The appreciative new governor replaced Shannon as police commissioner with a Goat. By then, Pendergast was boss at the poll places in every election in Kansas City and determined the outcome by any means necessary. "He formulated a harsh policy of using thugs, both local and imported," who lurked at polling places. "Roving bands of hoodlums moved throughout town frightening and intimidating honest voters." Police stationed at the polls assisted the thugs. "Outright election thievery saw the routine last-minute switching of real ballot boxes with similar-looking ones, right down to scratches and chipped paint, filled with illegal ballots" (Larsen and Huston 1997, 58).

After his brief tenure as alderman, Pendergast never held public office again but ran his machine as chairman of the Jackson County Democratic Party and through his subordinate, real estate developer Henry L. McElroy (1865–1939), who was appointed city manager of Kansas City in 1926. As McElroy once explained to a reporter for a national magazine, "Tom and I are partners. He takes care of politics and I take care of the business of Kansas City. He gives people jobs. I make them work" (Ferrell 1999, 12).

He could have added that the important decisions were made at the Jackson Democratic Club, not city hall. Supplicants who came to Pendergast's office found him to be quick and to the point but not always candid in his responses. "If necessary he gave visitors letters to public officials, signed with varicolored ink or pencil. Rumor had it that one color meant 'Do what I say' and another meant 'forget it'" (Ferrell 1999, 9). He was accessible, holding court at the Democratic Club three days a week.

Under the Pendergast machine, every ward in the city had its own Democratic club and some wards had one club for Goats and another for Rabbits, even though Pendergast had long tamed the latter faction. Wards were divided into some 800 precincts, each with its own captain. All of them paid dues to the Jackson Democratic Club and to their ward clubs and were expected to contribute to Pendergast's causes, including the election campaign of candidates he backed. Precincts were subdivided into blocks, each with their own captain. The Pendergast machine gave some Blacks authority in their precincts and extended its web into Republican neighborhoods (Larsen and Huston 1997, 92–93).

The machine's captains eagerly assisted newcomers to their districts. As Pendergast explained, the services rendered created a system of obligation— "Whenever you have any little troubles, the precinct captain takes care of them. Nothing is said about politics until a day or so before the election" (Larsen and Huston 1997, 93). That same system punished dissidents by raising their tax assessments and protected incompetent city employees as long as they remained loyal. The Pendergast machine might well have won many elections legitimately, but the boss could never be certain that his control would not be diminished and insisted on rigging the outcome.

During the 1930s, an estimated $11 million in municipal funds disappeared in Kansas City, much of it into the pockets of Pendergast supporters or to pay his growing debts from horse racing. But some of that stolen money trickled down to the needy as Pendergast provided food baskets and buckets of coal and paid medical bills for many constituents. In 1930, he hosted holiday meals that saw "more than three thousand homeless men of all races" forming "a line of several blocks" to receive their dinner. "Pendergast usually carried a pocketful of quarters that he handed out to broken-down derelicts out of generosity and in recognition of their election day services" (Larsen and Huston 1997, 73).

In the first years of the Great Depression, when Herbert Hoover held office and little help was expected from Washington, Pendergast anticipated the New Deal by launching a Ten-Year Plan of public works. He ordered his produce company to donate food to the municipal General Hospital and established General Hospital No. 2 for Blacks, widening the benefits of health care in the context of a segregated city (Larsen and Huston 1997, 73). Pendergast seemed genuinely concerned with providing good medical services. He told the physician appointed to administer the General Hospital to "run a clean hospital—and I don't mean the floors and windows. I mean don't have a scandal. Nothing costs more votes than a scandal at General Hospital" (Larsen and Huston 1997, 96).

During the Pendergast-McElroy period, Kansas City carried thousands of employees on the municipal payroll whose only responsibility was to collect their salary on Friday. Pendergast's legion of supporters enjoyed other unusual benefits. One involved a guarantee against the theft of their car tires, a common problem during the Depression. If a Pendergast man reported the theft to the police, the police called the gangster called Fat Willie, who controlled the tire-theft ring, and told him to return the tires (Ferrell 1999, 13).

With an organization capable of delivering at least 100,000 votes, Pendergast held the balance of power statewide and over Missouri's electoral votes. In 1932, Pendergast led the Missouri delegation to the Democratic National Convention and threw his support behind Franklin D. Roosevelt. That same year, his support helped elect Guy Brasfield Park (1872–1946) as Missouri's governor, bypassing an aspirant who would play a key role in ending his reign, Lloyd C. Stark (1886–1942). "Park was so grateful to Boss Tom for making him governor that he did almost anything he asked," including whitewashing flagrant abuses of power (Larsen and Huston 1997, 90).

Private interests advanced arm-in-arm with Tom Pendergast's political career. In partnership with Casimir Welch (1873–1936), the enforcer for the Rabbits and precinct captain of the First Ward, where most of the city's African Americans lived, Pendergast operated a messenger service. Along with delivering legitimate parcels, the company most likely ran numbers and provided other services for the West Bottoms gambling dens. Pendergast owned at least a half dozen saloons and at least one restaurant.

Before Prohibition, Pendergast forced many saloons to buy from his wholesale liquor distributor by threatening them with license and code violations. His construction companies received lucrative city and county contracts. His Jefferson Hotel was a popular spot for traveling salesmen with rooms available at hourly as well as daily rates, private poker games on the fifth floor and a basement nightclub featuring bands, burlesque, showgirls, and singers who flirted from table to table (Larsen and Huston 1997, 60–61).

With the imposition of Prohibition (1919), Pendergast sold the Jefferson Hotel to the city for a street-improvement project and reorganized his wholesale liquor company as a soft drink and medicinal water distributor. "Pendergast scrupulously avoided any direct or easily traced involvement in rum-running throughout Prohibition" (Larsen and Huston 1997, 62). With Prohibition's repeal (1933), he resumed liquor wholesaling using all the old coercive methods. Sometimes his company's trucks "simply delivered liquor to drinking establishments, whether ordered or not" (Larsen and Huston 1997, 85). His construction companies charged the city exorbitantly but contrary to rumor, they performed their tasks capably.

"As a result of elaborate methods of concealment and deception, such as using the names of others on corporation papers, there was no way of telling the true extent of Pendergast's holdings," which may have included everything from insurance companies to cigar sellers and the sanitation company with the city contract for garbage collection (Larsen and Huston 1997, 87).

Starting with Prohibition and continuing into the 1930s, Kansas City was a safe city for criminals from across the country, "the crown jewel on a gaudy necklace of lawless havens" (Wallis 2011, 226). "Pendergast, probably without design, contributed to the formation of a home-grown crime syndicate in Kansas City" through the machine's practice of "licensing" concessions to particular criminals, whether for running numbers, selling narcotics, or stealing tires. As occurred in many other cities, the ambitious sons of Italian immigrants, facing bigotry and deemed unassimilable by white Anglo-Saxon Protestants, formed a gang under Johnny Lazia (1897–1934).

In 1916 Lazia, convicted of highway robbery, was granted early release through the intervention of Missouri's pro-Pendergast lieutenant governor. He rose in the ranks of the Pendergast machine in the city's Little Italy and in 1928 overthrew the district's ward captain, an Irishman, claiming that he better represented the constituents. Pendergast negotiated a pact with Lazia, resulting in Kansas City's "double bureaucracy of public posture and the dark world of graft, threat and occasional violence" (Crouch 2013, 64).

In 1932, when an associate of Lazia became police director, the gangster recruited 60 recently released convicts for the Kansas City police department (Ferrell 1999, 14). For a price, the Kansas City police granted protection to fugitive criminals from elsewhere in the United States.

Lazia drew unwanted attention to Kansas City on June 17, 1933, when he helped the notorious bank robber Charles "Pretty Boy" Floyd (1904–1934) to free a fellow criminal, Frank "Jelly" Nash (1887–1933), traveling through Kansas City under FBI custody. In the parking lot outside Union Station, Floyd's gunmen opened fire with machine guns, killing three Kansas lawmen and one FBI agent. Nash died in the gunfight and his would-be rescuers escaped the city with Lazia's help. The "Missouri Massacre" gave FBI director J. Edgar Hoover (1895–1972) another opportunity to seek Congressional approval for expanding his authority. Less than a year later Lazia was assassinated and the ensuing investigation encountered much speculation while finding no evidence for who was responsible.

Although the Pendergast machine controlled or influenced much of the city's criminal activities, its leaders were not immune to crime. When

Pendergast's mansion was burglarized, the thieves made off with $150,000 in diamond jewelry. McElroy's daughter was kidnapped and released after he paid $30,000 in ransom.

By 1936, even before being diagnosed with coronary thrombosis, Pendergast's appearance had changed. "He was heavier and grayer, and his eyes carried a sick look . . . the marks of age were painfully visible on him, and within him was a great tension" (Reddig 1986, 278). He underwent other medical procedures that year and his grip weakened. In his absence, the 1936 primary and general elections were rigged so fraudulently, producing numbers so unbelievable, that a delegation of leading Democrats as well as Republicans approached federal judge Albert L. Reeves (1873–1971). He agreed to convene a grand jury at the end of 1936 alongside an investigation undertaken by U.S. attorney Maurice Milligan (1884–1959) with FBI assistance.

Like reformers elsewhere in the United States such as New York governor Thomas Dewey (1902–1971), Milligan depicted his investigation as a moral crusade. "If you want to see sin, forget about Paris and go to Kansas City," he declared, comparing the city's "sin industry" to seaports such as Singapore and Port Said (Milligan 1948, 12).

Although its grip on the city was weakening, the machine fought back. Threats were issued against potential witnesses and jurors and against Judge Reeves. "Milligan kept a revolver on his nightstand and developed the habit of searching his automobile and garage for explosive devices" (Larsen and Huston 1997, 126). The hearings proceeded in 1937 and into 1938 with 200 mostly low-level offenders convicted of engaging in voter fraud. The Pendergast machine paid their fines and legal expenses and kept imprisoned municipal employees on the payroll.

Reeves admitted that Pendergast "endeavored to checkmate his henchmen, minions, and representatives as against their open and too bold methods" but the criminals he assembled "were not satisfied with anything less than complete license to operate as their wild and reckless judgment might dictate to them. In other words, his machine was getting out of hand" (Larsen and Huston 1997, 127).

The machine was dealt a heavy blow when Gov. Lloyd Stark declared war on vice, gambling, and corruption. In a manifesto published on the front page of the *Kansas City Star*, he declared "that the gambling racket is carried on openly in defiance of the law and without protest from any official heads of the city's government; that houses of prostitution flourish within the very shadows of the courthouse and city hall" (Driggs and Haddix 2005, 181). Stark's agents raided brothels, gambling dens, and nightclubs, shutting many down and putting a chill on the city's hot jazz scene.

Not unlike other racketeers of the Depression era, including Al Capone (1899–1947), Pendergast was finally cornered for tax evasion. The Bureau of Internal Revenue joined Milligan's investigation in 1938, tracking the boss's finances. "They did such a thorough job that after his conviction Pendergast admitted that Milligan had a better grasp of the transactions than he did" (Larsen and Huston 1997, 139).

On April 7, 1939, Pendergast was indicted on two counts of tax evasion. Before the end of the month McElroy and other top Kansas City officials resigned. McElroy, facing his own indictment, died soon after from a heart attack. Facing the likelihood of additional indictments if the investigation continued, Pendergast pled guilty on May 22, 1939. He served 15 months at Leavenworth and was released under strict terms of probation.

"When he fell, his machine fell with him ... the political machines in Chicago and New York survived many leadership changes, but that was not so in Kansas City" (Larsen and Huston 1997, xii). Pendergast never reentered politics and lived the remaining years of his life in isolation.

While it's not clear if Kansas City weathered the Depression better than other cities, "the perception among most Kansas Citians of all races was that the policies of the Pendergast machine lessened the impact of the Great Depression in their city" (Larsen and Huston 1997, 181). He was a criminal with a social conscience who offered pragmatic politics in place of ideology. "What's government for if it isn't to help people?" he once said (Larsen and Huston 1997, 72).

The relationship between Harry S. Truman (1884–1972) and Pendergast has for long been the subject of speculation. With the aid of the Pendergast machine, Truman was elected as presiding judge of Jackson County in 1922, a position that gave him principal responsibility for administering the county. But despite ties to Pendergast, Truman was focused on infrastructure and determined to build rural bridges and roads with as little graft as possible. In 1927, he defied Pendergast by granting a road-paving contract to a South Dakota firm. "The boss let the incident slide ... and the judge was glad for that." Truman became a U.S. senator with Pendergast's blessing and "cooperated on patronage issues" but "did not involve himself in the illegalities and especially the financial dealings" of the Pendergast machine after going to Washington (Ferrell 1999, 4).

Before leaving for Washington, Truman had little choice but to work inside the system. He was vice president of the Jackson Democratic Club, with its 6,000 dues-paying members. However, in his bailiwick of eastern Jackson County, Truman acted with autonomy, appointing his own supporters to key positions (Larsen and Huston 1997, 92). "I am obligated to the Big Boss, a man of his word; but he gives it very seldom and usually on a sure thing," Truman said of Pendergast (Ferrell 1999, 18).

Despite conducting public policy as honestly as possible under the circumstances and refusing to intervene on Pendergast's behalf when the boss fell into legal trouble in 1939, Truman was branded "the Pendergast senator" by his opponent in the 1940 election. Missouri's ambitious governor

Stark, one of the politicians who eventually broke the Pendergast machine, was determined to link Truman to the corrupt Kansas City boss. When Pendergast's other foe, U.S. attorney Milligan, entered the Democratic primary, the anti-Pendergast vote was split, giving victory to Truman.

Established at the confluence of the Missouri and Kansas rivers, Kansas City was a crossroads town in frontier days, a role only enhanced with the coming of the railroads. "Commerce bred culture, and during the 1920s Kansas City blossomed into a cosmopolitan oasis of culture and entertainment, ranging from grand theaters and ballrooms to a thriving sin industry" (Driggs and Haddix 2005, 5).

Revenue flowed from the nightlife that "swirled around the hundreds of saloons and nightclubs liberally sprinkled from downtown south to 'out in the country,' just beyond the city limits." Despite Prohibition, liquor flowed freely throughout the city, unchecked by local authorities. "Clubs flouted state and federal laws against gambling" and when pressed, the police mounted raids for show, gently rounding up barkeepers and patrons. "Once downtown, the courts unceremoniously cut the suspects loose" and sent them back to saloons (Driggs and Haddix 2005, 113).

Jazz, the new music that defined the era, straddled both worlds. Through the 1930s, Black jazz bands donned white tuxedos, polished their acts and performed at the city's many ballrooms, including Paseo Hall, Fairyland Park, the Pla-Mor Ballroom, and the El Torreon. The audiences at those venues were largely white; the whites-only Harlem Night Club—ironically named—admitted Blacks only as kitchen help and entertainers.

But the well-heeled couples who danced to the music were only part of the story. The "sin industry" was especially hospitable to the flourishing of jazz, supporting many smaller venues with mostly Black clientele where the players honed their craft and discovered the expressive possibilities of their music. The illegal enterprises of prostitution, gambling, and (until 1934) alcohol provided shelter and money for jazz to grow in Kansas City's tolerantly corrupt political environment.

Because of the ready availability of paid work and its crossroads location, "bands from all over the South and Southwest, the Great Plains, and the Midwest passed through, some to play local dates, others to use the city as a stopover where they indulged in fierce cutting contests with local musicians" competing for speed, fervor, and proficiency on their instruments (Brooks 2000, 34).

The jazz groups working from there were called "territorial bands in recognition of the vast areas they toured," from Texas to Minneapolis and the Dakotas and west as far as Denver (Driggs and Haddix 2005, 62). Musicians playing regularly in Kansas City also had an opportunity for wider exposure through broadcasts from Fairyland Park on KMBC, picked up by the CBS radio network for distribution across 17 states (Driggs and Haddix 2005, 113).

Along with the musicians who passed through on their way to the next town came many who made Kansas City their home, with the most significant and internationally recognized among them being William "Count" Basie (1904–1984). The pianist from Red Bank, New Jersey, came to Kansas City to fill in for the city's most popular band leader, Bennie Moten (1894–1935). Moten stepped away from the piano to concentrate on conducting and arranging a powerhouse orchestra whose players became jazz legends, including electric guitarist Eddie Durham (1906–1982), bassist Walter Page (1900–1957), and tenor saxophonist Ben Webster (1909–1973).

The Moten band was seminal for its "exciting breakneck tempos, and impressive virtuosity" (Brooks 2000, 35). Riding on swinging rhythms, the soloists were in rapid dialogue with each other, pushing their band to the edge of music while remaining accessible to dancers and mainstream listeners. Basie held court at the Oriental-themed night club The Cherry Blossom but was also prominent in other sectors of the city's Black community. In 1934, he arranged the music for a program at Centennial African Methodist Episcopal Church, "The Negro and the New Deal," which featured the Moten orchestra.

With Moten's death from a failed tonsillectomy, Basie inherited most of his band and continued to follow Moten's musical vision. The great Black essayist Albert Murry compared the Basie orchestra to a locomotive roaring down the tracks (Murray 2016, 10). The prominent music critic Robert Palmer said that Basie's band "set the jazz world on fire when he brought it to New York from Kansas City in 1936" (Palmer 2009, 73–74).

COUNT BASIE (1904–1984)

Born Bill Basie in Red Bank, NJ, Count Basie found his sound—and his name—after moving to Kansas City. When he returned to the East Coast to play Harlem's Savoy Ballroom in 1937, he was a star, the leader of one of the greatest of the era's big bands. He may have lacked the orchestral imagination of his fellow nobleman of jazz, Duke Ellington, but as much as any band leader, he infused his swing with the sadness and optimism of the blues.

Basie got started playing piano in a traveling Black vaudeville show and was deeply impressed by the virtuoso stride playing of Fats Waller. However, once he found his own sound, his playing was almost minimal, a guiding signal for rhythmically orchestrated jazz that allowed soloists to soar within the space his music created. Basie's occasional Top-40 hits and exposure to the U.S. military during World War II through Armed Forces Radio made him one of the country's most widely known African Americans, yet he wore his fame lightly.

Basie worked hard throughout his life touring and recording. He earned many honors during his last decades, including Grammy awards, a royal command performance for Queen Elizabeth, and a Medal of Freedom awarded by Ronald Reagan.

Basie gained the ear of New York music producer, critic, and social activist John Hammond (1910–1987), who heard his band on a radio broadcast from Kansas City. Hammond signed the band leader to Decca Records in 1936 and enlisted Basie and other Kansas City acts, including the blues singer Big Joe Turner (1911–1985), to perform at a pivotal event, "From Spirituals to Swing." The 1938 Carnegie Hall concert organized by Hammond was an entertaining and much publicized lesson in the history and breadth of African American music. Basie and Turner would go on to enjoy long and successful careers as musicians.

Andy Kirk (1898–1992) led another prominent band from Depression-era Kansas City, the Twelve Clouds of Joy. Known for his "combination of drive and subtlety," Kirk scored several hits including "Take It and Git," the first record to reach No. 1 on *Billboard* magazine's Harlem Hit Parade (as their R&B chart was called when it debuted in 1942). He is also credited for the unusual choice at that time of employing a woman, Mary Lou Williams (1910–1981), in the key role of pianist (Brooks 2000, 35). Williams eventually joined Duke Ellington's orchestra and enjoyed a career performing at New York's prestigious Café Society, where she mentored the young generation of bebop musicians that emerged after World War II.

DEPICTION AND CULTURAL CONTEXT

Kansas City weaves together places, races, and social classes as well as politics, crime, and music for a well-knit mosaic of urban life during the Great Depression. Kansas City was notorious as a "wide-open city, thanks to the power of local gangsters and the corruption of Boss Tom Pendergast's regime" (Crouch 2013, 6). Given the puritanical values that continued to dominate American society, Kansas City's corruption fertilized a flourishing nightlife and jazz culture whose leading figures influenced music across the world. Musicians "had known no Depression in Kansas City, no lack of work. Throughout the late 1920s and the 1930s, they had been free to play, compete and party around the clock" (Crouch 2013, 6).

Kansas City "represents an exaggerated kind of memory of the time," Robert Altman said of his film. He explained that the character of the well-connected, seemingly respectable politician Mr. Stilton was "partly based" on his father. The stories he told his young son (Altman was nine years old in 1934, the year in which *Kansas City* is set) shaped his "glamorized teenage view of that world." Stilton's wife Carolyn was based on the mother of a friend (Thomson 2020).

Much of *Kansas City* seems directly inspired by events and personalities at the height of Pendergast's control over the city. The murder shown of a conscientious election official outside a polling place could have actually occurred. During the 1934 election, gangs of men recruited by the

Pendergast machine roamed the streets as the police stood by. Dozens of citizens were beaten and four were killed. Such was the impunity of Pendergast's enforcers that a reporter from the *Kansas City Star* "was chased from street to street until he managed to reach the safety of the building of his paper" (Ferrell 1999, 15).

Almost identical to the polling place scene in the film is an account from a witness who complained of long lines of voters who obviously were not residents of the district. "He was beaten unconscious, left bleeding from the nose and mouth. Witnesses carried him out, as the police watched impassively" (Larsen and Huston 1997, 58–59). Blondie stages her kidnapping on the night before election day because "all the cops are going to be out stuffing ballot boxes."

The persona adopted by *Kansas City*'s doomed protagonist, Blondie, was modeled after the popular culture of the Great Depression. Her peroxide hairdo was copied from Jean Harlow (1911–1937), the "blonde bombshell" of early 1930s Hollywood. Her snappy dialogue with its ring of criminality derives from one of Harlow's signature roles, as the "gun moll" (gangster's girlfriend) in *The Public Enemy* (1931). Blondie takes Carolyn to see a Harlow picture, *Hold Your Man* (1933). "All her life is based on the movies, including handling a gun," Altman explained.

Carolyn makes it clear that she regards Harlow as "low class" and "cheap." One of the few subjects on which the two women can agree is the Lindbergh kidnapping. Both believe that the Lindbergh servant who committed suicide, Violet Sharp, was complicit.

As shown in the film, Kansas City was racially segregated, more loosely than in the South but stricter than in the North. Hospitals, public schools, and jails were segregated, but not drinking fountains or rest rooms. Most Black Kansas Citians were confined to the Second Ward with covenants that excluded them from buying real estate in most other neighborhoods. The golf courses were whites-only but the municipal auditorium was open to all races. Blacks could shop in the downtown department stores but couldn't eat at the lunch counters. Blacks had low-level positions in the machine and welfare was distributed in a color-blind fashion (Larsen and Huston 1997, 104–105).

Kansas City's Black nightclubs and jazz scene are well represented in the film, constituting a milieu in which Blondie enters any time of day and finds musicians playing round the clock. "You could have a good time morning, noon, and night," wrote a jazz historian. "That's where the Kansas City swing came from. Those guys were playing *all* the time, long hours, and then they went out jamming and might not get home until the next afternoon" (Crouch 2013, 60).

The manager of bandleader Jay McShann (1916–2006) recalled, "In Kansas City, the joints didn't have locks on the door. Threw them away! Didn't need them. They were never closed anyway. Whatever you wanted, you could get it whenever you wanted it—girls, liquor, gambling, freak shows" (Crouch 2013, 60).

The pervasiveness of gambling is correctly shown in *Kansas City*. Poker and roulette wheels were a big—though illegal—business, employing as many as 3,000 bookmakers, dice throwers, and card dealers. The film depicts gambling in the Black neighborhood but not in the more expensive, exclusive setting where the city's businessmen and politicians mingled. Located one block from the federal courthouse, the Chesterfield Club offered roulette, dice tables, and dinner served by nude waitresses (Larsen and Huston 1997, 101). As in the film, cocaine, laudanum, and other illicit drugs were plentiful. Harry J. Anslinger (1892–1975), commissioner of the Federal Bureau of Narcotics, called Kansas City the drug distribution center of the Midwest and conducted several raids on the city's dealers.

Altman recalled a real gangster called Seldom Seen who "carried his money around in a cigar box" (Thomson 2020). However, the film character is likely a composite of Felix Payne and Walter "Piney" Brown, "the two Pendergast Negroes best known by musicians" who "made the Sunset Club hospitable to their efforts to master blues and swing" (Crouch 2013, 64). With its floating roster of top musicians and gambling at all hours in the backroom, the Sunset Club was one of the models for Seldom Seen's Hey Hey Club. Altman probably took the name from his memory of an actual Hey Hey Club, a speakeasy that may have been closed or renamed by the time of *Kansas City*'s setting. As in the film, Kansas City was home to a Black-operated taxi company, owned by Brown's brother.

Race and class are pervasive subtexts in *Kansas City* and are handled with period accuracy. When Blondie casually uses a racial slur, Carolyn replies, "In our house we say colored." The Stiltons employ a Black housekeeper and in a side plot, a league of upper-class women provide support for a home for pregnant "little colored girls." One of those girls is befriended by a 14-year-old boy called Charlie Parker (1920–1955), a name familiar to any jazz fan or student of American music. Parker grew up in Kansas City and, moving to New York as an adult, became one of jazz's most innovative saxophonists.

Seldom Seen mocks Johnny O'Hara for posing as a Black man in his bungled robbery, accusing him of copying *Amos'n'Andy*, a popular 1930s radio comedy starring white actors playing Black characters. For him, the show illustrates the whites' lack of understanding regarding Blacks and the falsity of the era's culture. "White people sit around all day thinking of these plots—and they believe it," he says.

Seldom Seen also scoffs at activist Marcus Garvey (1887–1940), who called for Black people to reclaim their heritage by returning to Africa. "What you going to do in Africa?" he asks one of his men. As for Franklin D. Roosevelt, he expects no New Deal for African Americans.

Kansas City is a work of historical fiction that gets its history right.

FURTHER READING

Brooks, Michael. 2000. "The Flourishing of Jazz." In *Jazz: The First Century*, edited by John Edward Hasse. New York: HarperCollins.
Crouch, Stanley. 2013. *Kansas City Lightning: The Rise and Times of Charlie Parker*. New York: HarperCollins.
Dorsett, Lyle W. 1968. *The Pendergast Machine*. Lincoln: University of Nebraska Press.
Driggs, Frank, and Chuck Haddix. 2005. *Kansas City Jazz: From Ragtime to Bebop, A History*. New York: Oxford University Press.
Ebert, Roger. 1996. "Kansas City." *Chicago Sun-Times*, August 16, 1996. https://www.rogerebert.com/reviews/kansas-city-1996
Ferrell, Robert H. 1999. *Truman & Pendergast*. Columbia: University of Missouri Press.
Holden, Stephen. 1988. "Dreaming of Gangsters in a Hotbed of Jazz." *New York Times*, August 16, 1988. https://www.nytimes.com/1996/08/16/movies/dreaming-of-gangsters-in-a-hotbed-of-jazz.html
Larsen, Lawrence H., and Nancy J. Huston. 1997. *Pendergast!* Columbia: University of Missouri Press.
Milligan, Maurice M. 1948. *Missouri Waltz: The Inside Story of the Pendergast Machine by the Man Who Smashed It*. New York: Scribner's.
Murray, Albert. 2016. *Murray Talks Music: Albert Murray on Jazz and Blues*. Minneapolis: University of Minnesota Press.
Palmer, Robert. 2009. *Blues & Chaos: The Music Writing of Robert Palmer*. New York: Scribner.
Pillai, Nicolas. 2020. "Dream Boogie: Visions of the Past in Robert Altman's Kansas City." In the booklet for Arrow Academy Blu-ray release of *Kansas City*.
Reddig, William M. 1986. *Kansas City and the Pendergast Legend*. Columbia: University of Missouri Press.
Thomas, Kevin. 1986. "Altman Visits a Jazz-Filled 'Kansas City.'" *Los Angeles Times*, August 16, 1986. https://www.latimes.com/archives/la-xpm-1996-08-16-ca-34611-story.html
Thomson, David. 2010. *The New Biographical Dictionary of Film*. New York: Alfred A. Knopf.
Thomson, David. 2020. "Altman on Altman." In the booklet for Arrow Academy Blu-ray release of *Kansas City*.
Wallis, Michael. 2011. *Pretty Boy: The Life and Times of Charles Arthur Floyd*. New York: W.W. Norton.

Chapter 13

Cinderella Man (2005)

Cinderella Man was released by Universal Pictures on June 3, 2005. Director Ron Howard (1954–) coproduced the film with Brian Grazer (1951–), his partner in Imagine Entertainment, the film and television production company they founded in 1985. Director and *Laverne & Shirley* star Penny Marshall (1943–2018) was also credited as coproducer. *Cinderella Man* was written by Cliff Hollingsworth and Akiva Goldsman (1962–), who condensed the life story of a real-life boxing champion, James J. Braddock (1905–1974), as it panned out during the Great Depression years. The film's title comes from the nickname bestowed on Braddock by New York columnist Damon Runyon (1880–1946), who compared the boxer's unexpected comeback to a fairytale story.

Howard had worked with Australian actor Russell Crowe (1964–) on the Academy Award–winning film *A Beautiful Mind* (2001) and tapped him for *Cinderella Man*'s lead role of Jim Braddock. Renée Zellweger (1969–) costars as his wife Mae (1906–1985) and Paul Giamatti (1967–) as his manager Joe Gould (1896–1950). Other cast members include Bruce McGill (1950–) as boxing promoter James Johnston (1875–1946) and Craig Bierko (1964–) as the champion Braddock must defeat, Max Baer (1909–1959).

In *Cinderella Man*'s opening scene, Jim Braddock defeats Tuffy Griffiths (1907–1958) in a 1928 championship-upset and returns home to Mae and their three children in suburban New Jersey. The film then jumps to 1933. Jim and his family have been reduced to poverty following the stock market crash and a series of accidents that have left him in poor condition to fight. They now live in the basement of a New Jersey tenement. Joe Gould arranges a fight which ends in a humiliating draw. So poor was his performance in the ring that Johnston arranges for the revocation of his boxing license.

As his poverty worsens, and with blue-collar jobs scarce, Jim is forced to accept public assistance for money to restore gas and electricity to his family's basement room. His fortunes change when Joe books Jim as the last-minute substitute in a bout with heavyweight Corn Griffin (1911–1973). To everyone's surprise, Jim wins.

Impressed by that victory, Johnston restores Jim's license and Jim returns to compete regularly in the ring. He beats John Henry Louis (1914–1974) and Art Lasky (1908–1980) and, in the climactic scene, Max Baer. Jim's reputation and livelihood are restored. *Cinderella Man* is an inspirational story of the determination and devotion of a man who gained a second chance at success.

Cinderella Man was shot on a budget of $88 million and reaped $108 million at box offices. It ranked No. 42 for movie ticket sales in 2005 (Box Office Mojo n.d.). Most reviews were favorable. Roger Ebert praised *Cinderella Man* as "a terrific boxing picture, but there's no great need for another one. The need it fills is for a full-length portrait of a good man." He goes on to praise Crowe's remarkable performance, comparing him to Spencer Tracy in his combination of good heartedness with physical toughness (Ebert 2005). *Variety* called the film "an almost impossibly perfect" underdog drama "with emotional gravitas, wrenching danger and a panoramic sense of American life during the Great Depression" (Koehler 2005). The *New Yorker* was more cynical, finding Crowe's characterization impossible to believe. "Even as Braddock is hoisted high on men's shoulders, you wonder if Howard hired a smile wrangler to approach the actor with a monkey wrench and jack up the corners of his mouth" (Lane 2005).

Cinderella Man received three Academy Award nominations: Film Editing, Makeup, and Supporting Actor (Paul Giamatti). It received numerous other nominations from other organizations, including the Golden Globes and BAFTA. Giamatti was the only winner, taking trophies for Best Supporting Actor from the Screen Actors Guild and the Critics' Choice Movie Awards.

Film historian David Thomson described *Cinderella Man* as "sincere and plodding" but "close to the rhythm of the real Jim Braddock" (Thomson 2010, 465). *Cinderella Man* ranked 41 out of the top 50 boxing films of all time in a recent survey (Newman 2020).

HISTORICAL BACKGROUND

According to archeological evidence, boxing was a familiar sport in ancient Mesopotamia and Egypt. The contests were described by Homer and taken up by the Romans. Boxing was known in Africa and Asia. The roots of the sport as a modern spectacle go back at least as far as 17th-century England, as aristocrats organized bouts between hardy servants with bets placed on the outcome. This provided the model for plantation owners in North America, who arranged contests between slaves for their own amusement. One slave, Bill Richmond (1763–1829), was freed by the British during the American Revolution and brought to England as the valet to a British general. He became a prominent boxer in his adopted homeland (Gems 2014, 1, 10–11, 15–16).

Little evidence for public prizefighting survives from the early years of the American republic. Not until 1824 was a fight covered extensively in the press. In that year, a New York paper reported on a match in Brooklyn between Dublin-born Ned Hammond and Liverpool-born George Kensett. At that moment, the Irish were an insignificant minority in a United States dominated by white Anglo-Saxon Protestants, yet their fight already played into a larger narrative of ethnic rivalry, "a recurring theme in American prizefighting" (Lang 2008, 15).

In the United States as in Great Britain, boxing was denounced by religious leaders and social reformers throughout the 19th century for its underworld association with gambling and prostitution as well as its violence. The violence was not always contained and often overspilled the ring. In 1833, Louisiana's governor sent the militia to suppress widespread mayhem following a boxing match. Crimes were also committed within the ring. In 1842 when a bout lasting 181 rounds in upstate New York ended with the death of one contestant, organizers were arrested on charges ranging from disturbing the peace to manslaughter (Lang 2008, 16).

According to one historian, "The anti-prizefighting movement might have ultimately succeeded if not for Ireland's potato famine" (Lang 2008, 17). From 1845 to 1852, Ireland's staple crop was blighted by a fungus, worsening a system of poverty and religious oppression against Ireland's majority Roman Catholic population. One million Irish died and another million left the island, many of them pouring into the United States. The first wave of Irish arriving in America included many young men seeking work with the hope of sending for their fiancées and their families after gaining a foothold in the New World. The "bachelor subculture" of Irish men—focused on drinking, gambling, and physical prowess—found parallels in other immigrant histories. However, "unweddedness was especially pronounced among the Irish immigrants, who would dominate pugilism in their new country" for many years (Lang 2008, 17).

America's newly arrived Irish population provided a deep pool of boxers and attracted resentment from nativists who feared they would erode America's ethnic, religious, and social norms. White Anglo-Saxon Protestant boxers wanted to fight them and prove their superiority. The 1847 bout in Maryland between the Irishman called Yankee Sullivan (1811–1856) and the American-born Tom Hyer (1819–1864) was "the first to transcend American working-class boundaries, commanding the attention of a wide spectrum of the population" (Lang 2008, 17–18). The match exploited ethnic friction. Younger, heavier, and taller than his opponent, Hyer defeated Sullivan in the first of many matches that were really about ethnic and racial dominance in the United States.

Boxing enabled some Irish immigrants to survive anti-immigrant violence on the streets and in the ring. In 1855, Irish-born John Morrissey (1831–1878), who had won an American boxing championship two years earlier against Yankee Sullivan, encountered Bill Poole (1824–1855), leader of a violent gang of Know-Nothings, as the xenophobic secret society was popularly called. The fight that broke out between them in a New York saloon led to Poole's death. Nativists considered Poole "a martyr to the cause" and turned out by the tens of thousands for his funeral procession (Gems 2014, 49).

Morrissey evaded punishment and began to fight his way upward in American society. He became one of many Irish "shoulder-hitters," intimidating voters and disrupting opposition rallies, for Tammany Hall, the organization that dominated New York politics. His rise in Tammany Hall allowed him to run gambling operations without police interference. Three more murder charges against him were dismissed for lack of evidence. He continued to fight in the ring, winning an 1858 bout staged on the Canadian side of Lake Erie because boxing remained illegal in New York State, and was elected in 1866 to the U.S. House of Representatives, where he served two terms (Lang 2008, 18–19).

"New York City remained the nerve center of prizefighting until the last decade of the [19th] century." While few celebrated high-stakes, bare-knuckled contests were staged in Manhattan, "it was there, in sparring matches, that unknown fighters built their reputations" (Lang 2008, 20). Their acclaim was spread by widely circulated sporting publications based in the city, including the *National Police Gazette*, "which catered to the working class and bachelor subculture with lurid stories of crime, scandal, and debauchery" (Gems 2011, 26).

The fight crowd hung out in the Bowery—fertile ground in those years for lowbrow entertainment—and gravitated to a saloon called Harry Hill's. Many profitable matches were conceived there, including fights held by kerosene light on barges up the Hudson River beyond the jurisdiction of local police. Others were staged in far-flung places. The 1880 title fight between Englishman Joe Goss (1837–1885) and the Irish American contender Paddy Ryan (1851–1900) took place in Colliers, West Virginia, a hamlet at the border of Ohio and Pennsylvania, "to ease potential escapes if authorities should intervene" (Gems 2014, 26).

Ryan lost his title two years later in another clandestine fight, a bare-knuckler but held under London Prize Fight Rules in Mississippi City, Mississippi. The winner, John L. Sullivan (1858–1918), was crucial to elevating boxing to a more respectable level in American society. More than anyone in the United States, Sullivan sold boxing's old guard "on the idea that the so-called Manly Art could survive—nay thrive" under the rule book emerging in Great Britain (Lang 2008, 31).

The violence and illegality of boxing, and the greater profit to be made if the sport could be staged publicly in more accessible settings, led the English Pugilistic Benevolent Association to adopt a set of rules in 1853 to standardize the size and configuration of boxing rings, stipulate the presence of "corner men" to give water and other aid to boxers, and define the authority of referees. The self-regulation by the boxing industry was further codified under the influence of John Sholto Douglas (1844–1900), Marquis of Queensberry, in the 1867 guidelines named for him. The Marquis of Queensberry Rules called for boxing gloves instead of bare fists, set the length of rounds, mandated rest periods, and banned "below the belt" and other foul moves.

The United States was slow to embrace the rules and Sullivan's advocacy was crucial. He was a star who came up the hard path, fighting on wooden platforms or earthen clearings. He could last hours in the ring, sometimes fighting to a draw but seldom losing. Comparable to the world champion of the 20th century, Muhammad Ali (1942–2016), Sullivan "inspired both adulation and loathing" early on and as with Ali, public opinion gradually shifted in his favor (Lang 2008, 30).

Promoters came to understand that boxing with gloves reduced the legal jeopardy from death in the ring. Perhaps more important was the realization that reform was "needed to make the sport palatable to the masses, in particular the burgeoning middle class" (Lang 2008, 26).

The hostility shown toward the sport by American jurisprudence can be seen in an 1876 decision by a Massachusetts court which ruled that boxing matches "serve no useful purpose, tend to breaches of the peace, and are unlawful even when entered into by agreement." By 1880, prizefighting had been banned in 30 states (Gems 2014, 25).

But in the United States, the statutory status of boxing was always a patchwork of conflicting laws in states and municipalities. Some jurisdictions permitted boxing matches only in private clubs, a barrier easily evaded by selling one-day memberships. Other jurisdictions banned bare-knuckle fights but permitted boxing with gloves. Some cities tried to cap the weight of contenders to reduce injury. Some states mandated "no-decision" matches to undermine gambling. "Although referees were required to leave the ring without designating a winner, fights continued to attract betters," albeit not as profitably for bookmakers (Lang 2008, 50).

The mood among lawmakers shifted as boxers began to play by the English rules. The first heavyweight championship fight in the United States under the Marquis of Queensberry's regime occurred in 1892 when Gentleman Jim Corbett (1866–1933) defeated John L. Sullivan. Corbett exemplified the faster, younger breed of fighters who prized finesse over brute force.

New York State's 1920 boxing statute became a model for other jurisdictions. Under its provisions, everyone deriving an income from the sport was licensed by and accountable to a boxing commission appointed by the governor. This included vendors, promoters, managers, "ring doctors," and referees as well as boxers. The commission was empowered to approve matches, assign referees, collect fees, and levy fines and suspensions. The law limited fights to 15 rounds and exempted boxers and promoters from legal jeopardy but allowed ring doctors and referees to stop fights to prevent serious injury or death.

The statute was popularly known as the "Walker Law" for its author, New York State senator James J. Walker (1881–1946). "By 1934, boxing was legal in every state in the union, although not legal in every county." Boxing advocates promoted legalizing the sport as a revenue-generating "sin tax" (Lang 2008, 54). Sinful or not, boxing's image was polished with the advent of Golden Gloves. In 1926, Paul Gallico (1897–1976), sports editor of the *New York Daily News*, organized a citywide youth boxing contest. Spectators for the final session filled Madison Square Garden and the winner earned a set of golden gloves. In 1928, Gallico collaborated with the *Chicago Tribune*'s Arch Ward (1896–1955) on an intercity contest that grew into the annual nationwide amateur tournaments. In 1930, the Catholic Youth Organization began its own boxing tournaments. During the Depression era, they were joined by similar events hosted by the YMCA and a variety of ethnic, political, and civic organizations. Boxing was promoted as a means of social control and teaching discipline to restless, aggressive male youth (Gems 2014, 67).

By the end of the 19th century and into the first decades of the 20th century, the larger social story of boxing competitions became less about Protestant versus Catholic and more about white against Black. The 1892 championship contest between Corbett and Sullivan was stimulated by Sullivan's public challenge that he could defend his title against any "Caucasian" challenger. "Mixed matches were viewed, with some justification, as the stovewood of racial discord" (Lang 2008, 32). Some said the real reason Sullivan drew the color line was to avoid fighting Peter Jackson (1861–1901).

Born in the Danish West Indies (now the U.S. Virgin Islands), Jackson honed his skills in Australia where he won a championship in 1886. From there he traveled to the United States where, in 1891, he fought Corbett in a 61-round match that ended in a draw. Despite this, racist preconceptions prevailed. The *Sporting and Theatrical Journal* editorialized that "colored pugilists" were "usually quick quitters" (Gems 2014, 76).

By the end of the 1892 "Carnival of Champions" in New Orleans, the Black Canadian featherweight George Dixon (1870–1908), known as "Little Chocolate," defeated Irish American Jack Skelly (1870–1953). The victory was celebrated by Crescent City's Blacks and resented by whites nationwide. The *Chicago Tribune* reported that "white fans winced every time Dixon landed on Jack Skelly." In an editorial, the *New Orleans Times-Democrat* worried that "among ignorant negroes the idea has naturally been created that it was a test of the strength and fighting powers of Caucasian and African," adding, "because of his victory they are far more confident than they ever were before of the equality of the races, and disposed to claim more for themselves than we intend to concede" (Gems 2014, 79).

Joe Gans (1874–1910) was the first Black born in the United States to win the world title. "He developed the footwork, defense, and punching combinations that formed the basis for modern boxing techniques" (Gems 2014, 80). Like the Irish boxers who preceded him, Gans learned the rudiments of his trade on the streets. Working as an oyster shucker, he had to fight for his place on the Baltimore docks. In his hometown, "Black boys were often subjected to the spectacle of battle royals, which consisted of white men rounding up black youths and corralling them in a ring, often blindfolded, in which they fought to the finish for the amusement of whites." The last one standing "might be lucky to garner some coins for his efforts" (Gems 2014, 81).

Gans was so often the winner in those gladiatorial contests that a white manager took interest and aided his ascent as a professional boxer while stealing some of his earnings. In 1900, Gans lost to featherweight champion Terry McGovern (1880–1918) in a Chicago fight widely denounced as fixed. As a result, Chicago banned prizefighting for several years and Gans's reputation suffered. Nevertheless, he fought Frank Erne (1875–1954) in 1902 and became the lightweight champ after knocking out his opponent in the first round. The fight took place in Canada "due to the racial tensions of the times and the outcry after the Dixon-Skelly match" (Gems 2014, 82).

Gans successfully defended his title 17 times over the next several years, including a 1906 challenge by Battling Nelson (1882–1954), the Danish-born fighter "who had captured the imagination of the public with his aggressive style, tremendous stamina, [and] a well-deserved reputation for bending the rules" (Lang 2008, 41–42). The fight lasted two hours with Gans outboxing the "Durable Dane" and winning the sympathy of the crowd. Gans had little choice but to fight on with a broken hand and win. So much money rode on the outcome that his manager had threatened to have him killed if he lost (Gems 2014, 83). Racists struck back after Gans's victory, even resorting to a white race riot in Atlanta that killed a dozen Blacks and destroyed many homes and businesses. Despite that, the fight was seen by African Americans as a victory for social justice. According to the Rev. Francis Grimke (1850–1937), a prominent Black pastor, even the life's work of educator and reformer Booker T. Washington (1856–1915) "never did one-tenth to place the black man in the front rank as a gentleman as has been done by Joe Gans" (Aycock and Scott 2008, 6–7).

The most notorious boxing promoter of the early 20th century, George "Tex" Rickard (1870–1929), smelled money in racial conflict. In 1910, Rickard mounted a heavyweight championship in Reno, Nevada, one of the few places where prizefights were fully legal, pitting Black fighter Jack Johnson (1878–1946) against white champion Jim Jeffries (1875–1953).

Johnson embodied the call for a more aggressive stand issued by activist W. E. B. DuBois (1868–1963) in his 1903 essay *The Souls of Black Folk*: "We are men! We shall be treated as men. And we shall win!" (DuBois 1980, xx). Born in Galveston, Johnson was subjected to brutal battle royals at the hands of white men before embarking on his boxing career in 1897. Confrontational in society as well as in the ring, he taunted opponents, wore flashy jewelry and clothes, and drove fast cars in the company of white women. Johnson gained his first acclaim in Australia where he defeated the reigning heavyweight champ, a Native American from Canada, Tommy Burns (1881–1955), at the end of 1908. Short documentary films on the fight reached Africa and Asia where "indigenous residents reveled in his victory" (Gems 2014, 83). Evidently, Burns' indigenous identity was overlooked.

Johnson made politically provocative statements. "Do you think it is to go on forever, this domination of the millions of people of color by a handful of white folks? I think it is not . . . the time will come when the black and the yellow man will hold the earth, and the white man will be regarded just as the colored man is now" (Runstedtler 2012, 63–64).

With Johnson's win the search began for the "Great White Hope" who would reestablish white supremacy in the ring. Johnson demolished five white challengers in 1909 and flaunted his triumph, hiring white chauffeurs and valets (Gems 2014, 86–87).

Rickard's 1910 promotion in Reno brought Jeffries out of retirement with the explicit purpose of winning a racial war. "I realize full well just what depends on me, and I am not going to disappoint the public," Jeffries declared. "That portion of the white race that has been looking to me to defend its athletic superiority may feel assured that I intend to do my best" (Roberts 1983, 103–104).

Reporters from across the United States were among the 20,000 spectators who descended on Reno to watch the spectacle. Jeffries was knocked down three times before conceding. His loss triggered race riots and a rash of lynchings (Gems 2014, 87–88). Although Johnson was greeted by a crowd of 10,000 when he celebrated his victory in Chicago, he faced death threats and became too controversial for American promoters. He toured the British vaudeville circuit instead and after returning to the United States, he was convicted for violating the Mann Act, the charges arising from his relations with his white teenage secretary. He went into exile to avoid prison.

Despite or perhaps because of the troubles he faced, Johnson's status among African Americans only grew taller. In 1922, Black nationalist Marcus Garvey (1887–1940) said, "The age for turning the right cheek if you are hit on the left is past. This is a Jack Johnson age, when the fittest will survive" (Runstedtler 2012, 236).

The next great Black fighter, Joe Louis (1914–1981), was the Golden Gloves champion of 1934. He attracted the attention of a Detroit businessman who promoted his professional career under strict guidelines. Dubbed the "Brown Bomber" by the Black press, Louis would be the opposite of Johnson, "never gloating over a defeated foe, never being seen with a white woman" (Gems 2014, 106). A dignified hero for African Americans who received continual coverage in the Black press, Louis's humility never blunted his power inside the ring. He won 22 bouts in 1935, 18 with knockouts. His trainer advised him, "It's mighty hard for a colored boy to win decisions. The dice is loaded against you. You gotta knock 'em out . . . Let your fist be your referee" (Roberts 2010, 23).

Ethnic rivalry remained at the forefront. By the 20th century, the once-despised Irish had risen in social status. Now it was the Italians' turn to occupy the lowest rung among European immigrants in the minds of white Anglo-Saxon Protestants. Before the arrival of Italian heavyweight champion Primo Carnera (1906–1967), Italian boxers hid under Irish-sounding names. His success was a source of Italian American pride (Lang 2008, 92).

JOE LOUIS (1914–1981)

The Alabama-born Joe Louis began boxing professionally in 1934. In a career that ended with his retirement in 1951, Louis lost only 3 fights, winning 66, 52 of them by knocking out his opponents. He earned the longest reign as heavyweight champion in boxing history.

Louis embraced his nickname, "the Brown Bomber," at a time when Black athletes were usually invisible in professional sports. His sharecropping family was part of the northward Great Migration of Southern Blacks fleeing Ku Klux Klan violence and seeking economic opportunities. Louis spent his teenage years in Detroit where, like many boys of his era, he learned to box at a neighborhood community center.

His victories on the amateur circuit attracted the interest of a Black Detroit entrepreneur, John Roxborough. At a time of intense racial tension, Roxborough groomed Louis for success as a model of decorum and sportsmanship, knowing that any misstep in or out of the ring would bring derision from fans and sportswriters. Louis was lionized in Black communities but continued to be treated disrespectfully by a news media that wanted him to lose.

Louis's most famous bouts—when he defeated Italy's Primo Cavera (1935) and lost to Germany's Max Schmeling (1936)— had overtones of racial and national conflict. In a rematch against Schmeling in 1937, set amid rising apprehensions of a second world war, Louis beat Schmeling in two minutes as white Americans cheered.

After enlisting in the U.S. Army as a private in 1942, he was elevated to heroic status by the media. His stature opened the door to Jackie Robinson and the desegregation of American sports.

In 1935, Louis defeated the six-foot-six Italian champ, against the backdrop of Mussolini's invasion of Ethiopia. Louis defeated Carnera after six rounds at Yankee Stadium before a mixed-race audience of 62,000. Celebrations erupted in Black neighborhoods across the United States but in Harlem, Italians attacked Black residents in acts of vengeance (Gems 2014, 106).

Coverage of the event included undisguised racism. One sportswriter wrote, "Something sly and sinister, and perhaps not quite human came out of the African jungle last night to strike down and utterly demolish a huge hulk that had been Primo Carnera, the giant" (Roberts 2010, 80–81).

Louis's winning streak continued as he defeated former champ (and Braddock opponent) Max Baer in a fight witnessed by 88,000 fans at Yankee Stadium. According to Black novelist Richard Wright (1908–1960), "Negroes poured out of beer taverns, pool rooms, barber shops, rooming houses and dingy flats and flooded the streets. They chanted 'Louis!' 'Louis!' 'Louis!' throwing their hats into the air" (Roberts 2010, 95). Actor Ossie Davis remembered, "Joe was our avenging angel . . . He was spiritually necessary to our sense of who we were, to our manhood" (Roberts 2010, 101).

In 1936, Germany's Max Schmeling (1905–2005) came to the United States to challenge the undefeated Brown Bomber in an encounter with even greater political significance. Tensions with Nazi Germany were rising, putting most Americans on Louis's side except for German Americans and many Southern whites. Sixty million Americans listened to the radio as Schmeling delivered Louis's first defeat at the end of 12 rounds. However, in the 1937 rematch at a packed Yankee Stadium, Louis prevailed before the end of round one.

Many awkward moments occurred behind the scenes of the second Louis-Schmeling fight. Schmeling's American manager, Joe Jacobs (1898–1939), was Jewish and in an awkward position. American Jews were demanding a boycott of all German imports as the pitch of anti-Semitism rose under the Nazis. Jacobs lobbied behind the scenes to let his promotion of the fight proceed without interference. In the end, the contest between his client and Louis lasted barely two minutes.

When the broadcast concluded, celebrations broke out once again in Black communities. In Detroit, Louis's fans waved a banner reading "JOE LOUIS KNOCKED OUT HITLER." Louis, along with many other professional boxers (including Braddock), enlisted in the military when the United States entered World War II.

The importance of boxing—relative to other sports—during the Great Depression can be measured by the salaries of the brightest stars. In 1935, Max Baer made $215,000 fighting Joe Louis, while the highest-paid baseball player, the New York Yankees' Lou Gehrig (1903–1941), made only $40,000 for the entire season. "In a sports landscape lacking international basketball stars, soccer stars, and Formula One race-car drivers, the heavyweight champion wasn't just the best-paid or the most significant athlete in the world; he was—with the possible exception of a few world leaders, such as Stalin and King George V—the most famous person on the planet" (Schaap 2005, x–xi).

Professional boxing continued on a high plateau of popularity throughout the 1930s. In 1938, New York City counted more than a thousand licensed fighters who performed weekly at seven boxing clubs, while amateurs "fought as often as every other day for prizes that could easily be pawned." By the mid-1950s, only 241 professional boxers and one club remained in New York City (Anasi 2004, xii). By this time, the *New Yorker* essayist and sportswriter A. J. Liebling (1904–1963) declared professional boxers "an endangered species," blaming this on the popularity of television (despite televised boxing matches) and the cultural shift caused by the growth of suburbia.

"In postwar America, boxing was losing its audience for the same reasons cities were losing their inhabitants . . . When white Americans left the cities, they left boxing as well" (Anasi 2004, xiii–xiv). The shift among white Americans coincided with changes in the status of immigrant groups. Before World War II, Irish, Italian, and Jewish fighters as well as Black contestants represented their communities in a battle for respect. "When they assimilated and prospered, they stopped boxing" (Schaap 2005, 18).

DEPICTION AND CULTURAL CONTEXT

The film skips Jim Braddock's early life. He was born in New York's tough Hell's Kitchen "where he got an early introduction to fighting in the neighborhood battles" (Gems 2014, 147). His family later moved across the river to New Jersey where he won two state amateur boxing championships before turning pro in 1926.

Instead, *Cinderella Man* opens with the November 1928 main bout at Madison Square Garden between heavyweight Tuffy Griffiths and Braddock. The Garden was packed with 19,000 fans who expected to watch Braddock fall given the hyperbole of sportswriters who called Griffith "the second coming of Dempsey" (Schaap 2005, 69). The reference was to Jack Dempsey (1895–1983), who reigned as heavyweight champion from 1919 through 1926. Griffiths charged like a bull but Braddock remained surefooted, parrying his opponent's punches, waiting for the moment to deliver the blow that sent Griffiths to the ropes.

The victory brought Braddock close to winning the heavyweight title. He is encouraged afterward by his enthusiastic, supportive manager, Joe Gould. The film veers from reality, however, when Braddock returns to his comfortable New Jersey home where Mae and their children wait for his return. In reality, Braddock didn't marry Mae until 1930.

Cinderella Man trims a more complicated history to an acceptable running time of just under two-and-a-half hours. It doesn't show how Braddock "hit the skids, beginning with a loss to light heavyweight champion Tommy Loughran in 1929" (Lang 2008, 113). By jumping from 1928 to 1933, the screenplay implies that Braddock had been relatively inactive in the ring since the Great Depression began and fell immediately into the poverty of the North Bergen, New Jersey basement where he now lives with Mae and their three children. However, aside from many omissions, many of them in the interest of brevity, most of the details are correct as shown.

Braddock lost the money he earned in prizefighting in the early years of the Depression from a series of failed investments. Crisscrossing the United States, he also lost a string of fights in the early 1930s, including one to Black heavyweight John Henry Louis (1914–1974), who would later become world champion. Braddock was written off as a has-been by many sports writers and wanted to quit, but "kept fighting in part because Mae was now pregnant with their first child" (Schaap 2005, 115). The movie accurately depicts Gould as Braddock's cheerleader, encouraging him to continue when everyone else lost faith.

The screenplay correctly references a car accident as another link in the chain of Braddock's bad luck. With his ribs aching, he continued to fight and continued to lose. *Cinderella Man* shows the 1933 bout between Braddock and Abe Feldman (1912–1980) in Mount Vernon north of the Bronx. Feldman was younger and considered a hopeful. The film accurately stages the bush-league dressing room and the derisive mood of the crowd. Both fighters were mediocre that night and slogged at each other for six futile rounds. "Finally, as the jeering crowd reached a crescendo, the referee waved his hands" and ended the fight (Schaap 2005, 130–131). The state boxing commission revoked Braddock's license out of concern for his poor health but also to open the schedule for boxers considered more bankable, more likely to put on a good fight.

Braddock broke his right hand in the Feldman bout. "The injury was a double whammy as his day job unloading cargo from ships required two good hands" (Lang 2008, 113). With his boxing career apparently over and nothing but physical strength to fall back on, Braddock did, as shown in the movie, seek work each morning in Hoboken and Weehawken on the New Jersey waterfront. He walked three miles and stood outside the gates of the port, hoping to be picked by the foreman from among the crowd of desperate faces for a one-day stint on the docks. Sometimes he walked home without finding work. On days when he was chosen, despite a broken right hand, he worked with his left, which was good training for the fights to come. His left hook proved as powerful as it was unexpected. On the docks, Braddock "developed a reputation as someone who was willing, indeed eager, to do his share and more" (Schaap 2005, 160). Like other longshoremen, he sometimes treated himself to a nickel beer at a waterfront bar on his way home.

Although Braddock and his family live in one basement dwelling throughout the film, in reality their status declined when their cramped apartment became too expensive, forcing them to move to the basement of the same building. Even there, months would pass before Braddock could pay the rent. Gas and electric service was cut and the milkman refused to deliver when the bills were unpaid. Hunger was never far away. "The Braddocks lived on bread and potatoes" (Schaap 2005, 161).

Cinderella Man dramatizes the shared plight of most Americans during the Great Depression. When Mae begs the electric company man not to shut off their lights, he replies that his job is on the line. "Lady, I got kids too," he says. Mae and Jim scrape coins together to pay bills and sleep together with their three children for warmth when there is no heat. They are forced to improvise, tearing apart sign boards for firewood.

As in the film, Mae briefly sent the children to live with relatives who were better off. When times worsened, Jim "made the most difficult decision he had ever made" by applying for public relief but he eventually paid the money back to the State of New Jersey (Schaap 2005, 164–165).

Cinderella Man accurately renders Braddock's surprise comeback. With only two days' notice, Gould secured a fight for him with Corn Griffin scheduled for June 14, 1934. Although he hadn't fought in nearly nine months, Braddock knew that if he could beat Griffin, "the toast of the boxing writers and trainers, he would set himself up for a bigger payday against one of the top challengers" (Schaap 2005, 188). He knocked out Griffin in the third round.

The film chronicles the key fights that followed and Braddock's comeback, including the November 16, 1934 victory over John Henry Lewis and the March 22, 1935 victory over Art Lasky on the way to the climactic scene, the celebrated bout on June 13, 1935 between Braddock and Baer.

While *Cinderella Man* displays the pride and excitement of Braddock's local Irish Catholic community in his achievement, it fails to acknowledge the wider context. The screenplay and visual direction ignore the racial and ethnic rivalry that drove many fans to the bleachers or their radios to follow the fights. Braddock's victory over Lewis was a blow to Black pride and his defeat of Lasky was lamented by Jews. Although Baer wasn't raised as an observant Jew, his father was Jewish and pride of heritage fueled his defeat of Schmeling. He took to the ring with a Star of David on his trunks while Braddock wore a shamrock on his.

The film accurately conveys Baer's image. He was a sharp-dressed man with matinee good looks and a sharp tongue quick with quotable putdowns. With the defeat of Schmeling under his belt, he enjoyed an additional level of celebrity after being cast as the star of *The Prizefighter and the Lady* (1933). The Hollywood melodrama concerns a boxer who falls in love with a nightclub singer (Myrna Loy, 1905–1993), marries her, and cheats on her but finds redemption in the ring. Other famous boxers were given supporting roles, including Jack Dempsey, Jess Willard, James J. Jeffries, and Primo

Carnera. Always a ladies' man, Baer was, as *Cinderella Man* depicts, seldom seen in public without a bevy of beautiful women in tow. "Chasing women around is the best exercise I know," he told reporters. "They're harder to catch than washed-up Irishmen" (Schaap 2005, 207).

Baer was a powerful fighter who acted as if he didn't take the sport of boxing seriously even though his fists resulted in the death of two opponents. He was the son of an immigrant father and raised in modest circumstances, but his wealth and celebrity were contrasted in the public imagination with Braddock, an ordinary and hard-pressed American determined to feed his family. The film tends to vilify Baer and imply that he was widely disliked, when in reality he "had captured the imagination of tens of millions of people around the world," not only Jews, with his charisma as well as his punching power (Schaap 2005, 185).

However, "throngs of hopeful Irishmen easily outnumbered the Jews supporting Baer" among the 30,000 fight fans who witnessed the battle at Madison Square Garden. Braddock's comeback story of determination resonated widely among Americans suffering from the Great Depression. "Although millions of people across the country would be listening on the radio and cheering for Braddock, few of his supporters thought he would actually win" (Schaap 2005, 246–247). As in the film, Braddock's win with seconds left in the fight was a glorious surprise to fans as well as family and friends, who expected the fast-footed Baer to treat Braddock the way a matador handles his bull. With Braddock's underdog victory, and his comeback from failure as a boxer and the failure of the American Dream, essayist and chronicler of hustlers, Damon Runyon (1880–1946), dubbed him the "Cinderella Man."

The aftermath of Braddock's boxing career and his later success as a business owner is accurately summarized in the closing credits.

Cinderella Man gives a sideways glance to the political responses of everyday people to the Great Depression. Braddock's friend on the docks, Mike Wilson (Paddy Considine, 1973–), declares "We need to organize unions" and gives the suspicion that he's the sort of disgruntled worker looked to by the era's active Communist Party. Braddock shrugs, expressing the vague sense of many Americans that Franklin D. Roosevelt would get the job done.

FURTHER READING

Anasi, Robert. 2004. Foreword to A. J. Liebling, *The Sweet Science*. New York: North Point Press.

Aycock, Colleen, and Mark Scott. 2008. *Joe Gans: A Biography of the First African American World Boxing Champ*. Jefferson, NC: McFarland & Company.

Box Office Mojo. n.d. "Domestic Box Office for 2005." https://www.boxofficemojo.com/year/2005/

DuBois, W. E. B. 1989. *The Souls of Black Folk*. New York: Penguin.

Ebert, Roger. 2005. "Good Guys Pack Strong Punch." *Chicago Sun-Times,* June 2, 2005. https://www.rogerebert.com/reviews/cinderella-man-2005

Gems, Gerald R. 2014. *Boxing: A Concise History of the Sweet Science*. Lanham, MD: Rowman & Littlefield.

Koehler, Robert. 2005. "Cinderella Man." *Variety*, May 19, 2005.

Lane, Anthony. 2005. "Cinderella Man." *The New Yorker*, May 29, 2005.

Lang, Arne K. 2008. *Prize-Fighting: An American History*. Jefferson, NC: McFarland & Company.

Newman, Christina. 2020. "The 50 Best Boxing Movies of All Time." *Paste*, November 12, 2020. https://www.pastemagazine.com/movies/boxing-movies/the-50-best-boxing-films-of-all-time/

Roberts, Randy. 1983. *Papa Jack: Jack Johnson and the Era of White Hopes*. New York: Free Press.

Robert, Randy. 2010. *Joe Louis: Hard Times Man*. New Haven, CT: Yale University Press.

Runstedtler, Theresa E. 2012. *Jack Johnson, Rebel Sojourner: Boxing in the Shadow of the Global Color Line*. Berkeley: University of California Press.

Schaap, Jeremy. 2005. *Cinderella Man: James J. Braddock, Max Baer, and the Greatest Upset in Boxing History*. Boston: Houghton Mifflin Company.

Thomson, David. 2010. *The New Biographical Dictionary of Film*. New York: Alfred A. Knopf.

Bibliography

Adler, William M. 2011. *The Man Who Never Died: The Life and Times of Joe Hill, American Labor Icon*. New York: Bloomsbury USA
Alter, Jonathan. 2006. *The Defining Moment: FDR's Hundred Days and the Triumph of Hope*. New York: Simon & Schuster.
Anasi, Robert. 2004. Foreword to A. J. Liebling, *The Sweet Science*. New York: North Point Press.
Anbinder, Tyler. 1992. *Nativism and Slavery: The Northern Know Nothings and the Politics of the 1850s*. New York: Oxford University Press.
Aycock, Colleen, and Mark Scott. 2008. *Joe Gans: A Biography of the First African American World Boxing Champ*. Jefferson, NC: McFarland & Company.
Beckert, Sven. 2014. *Empire of Cotton: A Global History*. New York: Vintage Books.
Berlin, Ira. 1998. *Many Thousands Gone: The First Two Centuries of Slavery in North America*. Cambridge, MA: The Belknap Press of Harvard University Press.
Birdwell, Michael E. 2000. *Celluloid Soldiers: The Warner Bros. Campaign Against Nazism*. New York: New York University Press.
Bogle, Donald. 2016. *Toms, Coons, Mulattoes, Mammies, and Blacks: An Interpretive History of Blacks in American Films*. New York: Bloomsbury Academic.
Bogle, Donald. 2019. *Hollywood Black: The Stars, The Films, The Filmmakers*. Philadelphia: Running Press.
Breen, Patrick H. 2015. *The Land Shall be Deluged in Blood: A New History of the Nat Turner Revolt*. New York: Oxford University Press.
Calabria, Frank M. 1993. *Dance of the Sleepwalkers: The Dance Marathon Fad*. Bowling Green, KY: Bowling Green State University Popular Press.
Callow, Simon. 2000. *The Night of the Hunter*. London: British Film Institute.
Chalmers, David M. 1965. *Hooded Americanism: The First Century of the Ku Klux Klan*. Garden City, NY: Doubleday.
Cole, Wayne S. 1953. *America First: The Battle Against Intervention, 1940–1941*. Madison: University of Wisconsin Press.

Cox, Carolyn. 2021. *The Snatch Racket: The Kidnapping Epidemic that Terrorized 1930s America*. Lincoln, NE: Potomac Books.
Crouch, Stanley. 2013. *Kansas City Lightning: The Rise and Times of Charlie Parker*. New York: HarperCollins.
Davis, Mike. 1990. *City of Quartz: Excavating the Future in Los Angeles*. London: Verso.
Denenberg, Barry. 1996. *An American Hero: The True Story of Charles A. Lindbergh*. New York: Scholastic.
Denning, Michael. 1996. *The Cultural Front: The Laboring of American Culture in the Twentieth Century*. London: Verso.
DiBattista, Maria. 2001. *Fast Talking Dames*. New Haven: Yale University Press.
Dickson, Paul, and Thomas B. Allen. 2004. *The Bonus Army: An American Epic*. New York: Walker & Company.
Dickstein, Morris. 2009. *Dancing in the Dark: A Cultural History of the Great Depression*. New York: W.W. Norton.
Dorsett, Lyle W. 1968. *The Pendergast Machine*. Lincoln: University of Nebraska Press.
Dorsett, Lyle W. 1991. *Billy Sunday and the Redemption of Urban America*. Grand Rapids, MI: W. B. Eerdmans.
Driggs, Frank, and Chuck Haddix. 2005. *Kansas City Jazz: From Ragtime to Bebop, A History*. New York: Oxford University Press.
DuBois, W. E. B. 1989. *The Souls of Black Folk*. New York: Penguin.
Duncan, Dayton, and Ken Burns. 2012. *The Dust Bowl: An Illustrated History*. San Francisco: Chronicle Books.
Eaton, Michael. 1998. *Chinatown*. London: British Film Institute.
Eichenbaum, Rose. 2014. *The Director Within: Storytellers of Stage and Screen*. Middletown, CT: Wesleyan University Press.
Ferrell, Robert H. 1999. *Truman & Pendergast*. Columbia: University of Missouri Press.
Fogelson, Robert. 1967. *The Fragmented Metropolis: Los Angeles 1850–1930*. Cambridge, MA: Harvard University Press.
Fonda, Jane. 2006. *My Life So Far*. New York: Random House.
Foner, Eric. 1988. *Reconstruction: America's Unfinished Revolution, 1863–1877*. New York: Harper and Row.
Gardner, Lloyd C. 2004. *The Case That Never Dies: The Lindbergh Kidnapping*. New Brunswick, NJ: Rutgers University Press.
Gates, Henry Louis, Jr. 2019. *Stony the Road: Reconstruction, White Supremacy, and the Rise of Jim Crow*. New York: Penguin Press.
Gates, Henry Louis, Jr. 2021. *The Black Church: This is Our Story, This is Our Song*. New York: Penguin Press.
Gems, Gerald R. 2014. *Boxing: A Concise History of the Sweet Science*. Lanham, MD: Rowman & Littlefield.
Gordon, Linda. 2017. *The Second Coming of the KKK: The Ku Klux Klan of the 1920s and the American Political Tradition*. New York: Liveright Publishing.
Green, Donald J. 2010. *Third-Party Matters: Politics, Presidents, and Third Parties in American History*. Santa Barbara, CA: Praeger.
Grubbs, Donald H. 1971. *Cry from the Cotton: The Southern Tenant Farmers' Union and the New Deal*. Chapel Hill: University of North Carolina Press.

Guthrie, Woody. 1975. *Woody Sez*. New York: Grosset & Dunlap.
Guthrie, Woody. 1983. *Bound for Glory: The Hard-Driving, Truth-Telling Autobiography of America's Great Poet-Folk Singer*. New York: Plume.
Halker, Clark D. 1991. *For Democracy, Workers, and God: Labor Song-Poems and Labor Protest, 1865–1895*. Urbana: University of Illinois Press.
Hatch, Nathan O. 1989. *The Democratization of American Christianity*. New Haven: Yale University Press.
Heimert, Alan. 1966. *Religion and the American Mind: From the Great Awakening to the Revolution*. Cambridge, MA: Harvard University Press.
Hickcock, Lorena. 1962. *Reluctant First Lady*. New York: Dodd, Mead.
Hixon, Walter L. 1996. *Charles A. Lindbergh: Lone Eagle*. New York: HarperCollins College Publishers.
Hofstadter, Richard. 1948. *The American Political Tradition*. New York: Alfred A. Knopf.
Hurt, R. Douglas. 1981. *The Dust Bowl: An Agricultural and Social History*. Chicago: Nelson-Hall.
Jackson, Kenneth T. 1992. *The Ku Klux Klan in the City, 1915–1939*. Chicago: Ivan R. Dee.
Jeansonne, Glen. 2012. *The Life of Herbert Hoover: Fighting Quaker 1928–1933*. New York: Palgrave Macmillan.
Jeansonne, Glen, with David Luhrssen. 2017. *Herbert Hoover: A Life*. New York: New American Library.
Johnson, Paul. 1991. *Modern Times: From the Twenties to the Nineties*. New York: HarperCollins.
Kazin, Michael. 2006. *A Godly Hero: The Life of William Jennings Bryan*. New York: Alfred A. Knopf.
Kennedy, David M. 1999. *Freedom from Fear: The American People in Depression and War, 1929–1945*. New York: Oxford University Press.
Kerr, Elizabeth M. 1979. *William Faulkner's Gothic Domain*. Port Washington, NY: Kennikat Press.
Kingsbury, Paul, and Alanna Nash, eds. 2006. *Will the Circle Be Unbroken: Country Music in America*. London: DK.
Klein, Joe. 1980. *Woody Guthrie: A Life*. New York: Alfred A. Knopf.
Lang, Arne K. 2008. *Prize-Fighting: An American History*. Jefferson, NC: McFarland & Company.
Larsen, Lawrence H., and Nancy J. Huston. 1997. *Pendergast!* Columbia: University of Missouri Press.
Leuchtenberg, William E. 2009. *Herbert Hoover*. New York: Times Books.
Lewis, David Levering. 1993. *W.E.B. DuBois: Biography of a Race, 1868–1919*. New York: Henry Holt and Company.
Lewis, Tom. 2015. *Washington: A History of Our National City*. New York: Basic Books.
Lindbergh, Charles A. 1977. *Autobiography of Values*. New York: Harcourt Brace Jovanovich.
Lisca, Peter. 1978. *John Steinbeck: Nature & Myth*. New York: Thomas Y. Crowel Company.
Luhrssen, David. 2015. *Secret Societies and Clubs in American History*. Santa Barbara, CA: ABC-CLIO.

Luhrssen, David, with Michael Larson. 2017. *Encyclopedia of Classic Rock*. Santa Barbara, CA: Greenwood.
Malham, Joseph M. 2013. *John Ford: Poet in the Desert*. Chicago: Lake Street Press.
Marchand, B. 1986. *The Emergence of Los Angeles: Population and Housing in the City of Dreams 1940–1970*. London: Pion.
Marling, William. 1986. *Raymond Chandler*. Boston: Twayne.
Marsden, George M. 1980. *Fundamentalism and American Culture: The Shaping of a Twentieth Century Evangelicalism 1870–1925*. New York: Oxford University Press.
Martin, Carol. 1994. *Dance Marathons: Performing American Culture in the 1920s and 1930s*. Jackson: University Press of Mississippi.
Masur, Kate. 2021. *Until Justice Be Done: America's First Civil Rights Movement, from the Revolution to Reconstruction*. New York: W.W. Norton.
Maurer, David W. 1974. *The American Confidence Man*. Springfield, IL: Charles C. Thomas.
Mayo, Morrow. 1933. *Los Angeles*. New York: Alfred A. Knopf.
McElvaine, Robert S., ed. 1983. *Down & Out in the Great Depression: Letters from the Forgotten Man*. Chapel Hill: University of North Carolina Press.
McWilliams, Carey. 1942. *Ill Fares the Land*. Boston: Little, Brown.
Morris, George. 1936. *The Black Legion Rides*. New York: Workers Library Publishing.
Payne, Stanley G. 1995. *A History of Fascism 1914–1945*. Madison: University of Wisconsin Press.
Pizzitola, Louis. 2002. *Hearst Over Hollywood: Power, Passion, and Propaganda in the Movies*. New York: Columbia University Press.
Reading, Amy. 2012. *The Mark Inside: A Perfect Swindle, A Cunning Revenge, and a Small History of the Big Con*. New York: Alfred A. Knopf.
Reddig, William M. 1986. *Kansas City and the Pendergast Legend*. Columbia: University of Missouri Press.
Rice, Arnold S. 1972. *The Ku Klux Klan in American Politics*. New York: Haskell House.
Roberts, Randy. 1983. *Papa Jack: Jack Johnson and the Era of White Hopes*. New York: Free Press.
Roberts, Randy. 2010. *Joe Louis: Hard Times Man*. New Haven, CT: Yale University Press.
Sann, Paul. 1967. *Fads, Fallacies and Delusions*. New York: Bonanza Books.
Santelli, Robert, and Emily Davidson, eds. 1999. *Hard Travelin': The Life and Legacy of Woody Guthrie*. Middletown, CT: Wesleyan University Press.
Sarris, Andrew. 1998. *"You Ain't Heard Nothin' Yet": The American Talking Film History and Memory, 1927–1949*. New York: Oxford University Press.
Sbardellati, John. 2012. *J. Edgar Hoover Goes to the Movies: The FBI and the Origins of Hollywood's Cold War*. Ithaca, NY: Cornell University Press.
Schaap, Jeremy. 2005. *Cinderella Man: James J. Braddock, Max Baer, and the Greatest Upset in Boxing History*. Boston: Houghton Mifflin Company.
Schatz, Thomas. 1988. *The Genius of the System: Hollywood Filmmaking in the Studio Era*. New York: Pantheon.
Schlesinger, Arthur M., Jr. 1957. *The Age of Roosevelt: Crisis of the Old Order 1919–1933*. Boston: Houghton Mifflin.

Seeger, Pete. 1972. *The Incomplete Folk Singer*. New York: Simon & Schuster.
Smith, Margarita G., ed. 1972. *The Mortgaged Heart*. New York: Bantam Books.
Speir, Jerry. 1981. *Raymond Chandler*. New York: Frederick Ungar.
Standiford, Les. 2015. *Water to the Angels: William Mulholland, his Monumental Aqueduct, and the Rise of Los Angeles*. New York: Ecco.
Stanton, Tom. 2016. *Terror in the City of Champions: Murder, Baseball, and the Secret Society that Shocked Depression-Era Detroit*. Guilford, CT: LP.
Strausbaugh, John. 2006. *Black Like You: Blackface, Whiteface, Insult & Imitation in American Popular Culture*. New York: Jeremy P. Tarcher/Penguin.
Striner, Richard. 2006. *Father Abraham: Lincoln's Relentless Struggle to End Slavery*. New York: Oxford University Press.
Swindell, Larry. 1975. *Screwball: The Life of Carole Lombard*. New York: William Morrow.
Szwed, John. 2010. *Alan Lomax, The Man Who Recorded the World: A Biography*. New York: Viking.
Taylor, S. J. 1990. *Stalin's Apologist: Walter Duranty, The New York Times's Man in Moscow*. New York: Oxford University Press.
Terkel, Studs. 1970. *Hard Times: An Oral History of the Great Depression*. New York: Pantheon Books.
Thomson, David. 2008. *"Have You Seen...?" A Personal Introduction to 1,000 Films*. New York: Alfred A. Knopf.
Thomson, David. 2009. *Humphrey Bogart*. New York: Faber and Faber.
Wallis, Michael. 2011. *Pretty Boy: The Life and Times of Charles Arthur Floyd*. New York: W.W. Norton.
Watkins, T. H. 1993. *The Great Depression: America in the 1930s*. Boston: Little, Brown.
Weaver, John D. 1980. *Los Angeles: The Enormous Village 1781–1981*. Santa Barbara, CA: Capra Press.
Worster, Donald. 1979. *Dust Bowl: The Southern Plains in the 1930s*. New York: Oxford University Press.
X, Malcolm, with Alex Hailey. 1965. *The Autobiography of Malcolm X*. New York: Grove Press.

Index

Abolitionism, 84–86, 125
Adams, Geri, 152
Addie Pray, 95
Agee, James, 54, 64
Airhart, James, 80
Akins, Zoe Byrd, 13
Alexander, Denise, 135
Ali, Muhammad, 171
Allen, Sian Barbara, 135
Almanac Singers, 128
Alonzo, John A., 90
Altman, Robert, 151, 152, 163, 165
Alviso, Chad, 72
America First, xxxi, 145
Anslinger, Harry J., 165
Anti-Semitism, 113, 117, 145
Arliss, Dimitra, 98
Armstrong, William H., 79
Arnold, Eddy, 124
Asch, Moses, 129
Ashby, Hal, 121
Auer, Mischa, 14, 15

Baer, Max, 167, 168, 176, 179, 180
Bakalyan, Dick, 110
Balbo, Italo, 6
"Bank holiday," xxi
Barhydt, Frank, Jr., 151

Barnum, P. T., 100–101
Bartlett, John Henry, 21
Basie, William "Count," 152, 162–163
Beatles, The, 129
Bedelia, Bonnie, 68
Belafonte, Harry, 151
Benny, Jack, 106
Best, James, 80
Bierko, Craig, 167
Big Con, The, 98, 105
Bill, Tony, 97
Black Legion, film, x, xxx, 27–40
Black Legion, organization, 34–39
Black Mask, 111
Black Monday/Black Thursday, xvii, xxvii
"Blaxploitation" films, 80, 90
Blumofe, Robert F., 121
Bogart, Humphrey, 27–28
Bogdanovich, Peter, 95–96, 97, 105
Bonnie and Clyde, xi, 109
Bonus Army, xix, xxvii, 18–22
Bound for Glory, film, 121–134
Bound for Glory, memoir, 121, 129–130
Bowdon, Dorris, 42
Bowron, Fletcher, 117
Braddock, James J., 167–168, 176, 177–180
Braddock, Mae, 177–179

Brady, Alice, 14, 15
"Brain Trust," xx
Brandon, Henry, 27
Brown, Joe David, 95
Brown, John, 85
Brown, Roscoe, Jr., 80
Brown, Walter "Piney," 165
Bruce, Sally Jane, 54
Bryan, William Jennings, 61–63
Burns, Tommy, 174
Buscemi, Steve, 151
Buttons, Red, 68
Byrd, Richard, 138
Byrds, The, 129

Capone, Al, 106, 147, 159
Carnera, Primo, 175, 176, 179–180
Carradine, David, 121, 130, 133
Carradine, John, 42
Carter, James, 152
Carter Family, 122, 124, 128
Cass, Gerson, 140–141
Chambers, Whittaker, 43
Chandler, Harry, 117
Chandler, Raymond, 109, 111, 112, 116
Chapin, Billy, 54
Chaplin, Charlie, 4, 67
Chaplin, Sydney, 67
Chartoff, Robert, 67
Chestnut, Cyrus, 152
Child, Francis James, 123, 124
Chinatown, x, 109–120
Churchill, Winston, xxxi, 6
Cinderella Man, xi, 167–181
Civil War, 31–32, 85–86, 123
Civilian Conservation Corps (CCC), xxi, xxiv, xxvii, 47
Collier, John, xxiv
Collins, Thomas E., 51
Columbus, Christopher, 81
Communist Party, xx, 19, 21, 36, 124, 127, 128, 129, 131, 180; Hollywood blacklist, 79
Condon, John F., 135–136, 147–148
Coolidge, Calvin, xvi, 140
Coppola, Francis Ford, 96
Corbett, Gentleman Jim, 171, 172
Cotton, Joseph, 135

Coughlin, Father Charles, xx, 38
Cox, Ronny, 121
Crandall, Milton D., 70–72
Crowe, Russell, 167, 168
Crowley, Aleister, 9
Cukor George, 96
Curtis, John Hughes, 147

Darien, Frank, 42
Darrow, Clarence, 63
Darwell, Jane, 42
Davis, Jefferson, 87
Davis, Noel, 138
Davis, Ossie, 176
Dean, Dayton, 34–35, 36, 37, 38
Dempsey, Jack, 177, 179
Dern, Bruce, 68
Dewey, Thomas, 159
DeYoung, Cliff, 135
Dillon, Melinda, 121
Dixon, George, 172
Dixon, Jean, 15
Dixon, Thomas, 32–33
Donat, Peter, 135
Douglass, Frederick, 85
Du Bois, W.E.B., 87, 174
Dunaway, Faye, 109, 110
Dunn, Carolyn Elizabeth, 153
Duranty, Walter, 9–10
Durham, Benny, 162
Durning, Charles, 98
Dust Bowl, 42–51, 115–116, 121, 128, 130, 131
Dylan, Bob, 124, 129

Eaton, Fred, 117, 118
Edwards, Jonathan, 57
Effinger, Virgil "Bert," 35
Elcar, Dana, 98
Elder, Lonne, 79, 81, 92
Ellington, Duke, 162, 163
Erne, Frank, 173
Evans, Hiram Wesley, 33
Evans, Robert, 109, 112
Evans, Walker, 64, 90

Faulkner, William, 53
Feldman, Abe, 178

Fine Line Features, 151
Finkel, Abem, 27
Fitzgerald, F. Scott, 22
Flint, Helen, 28
Floyd, Charles "Pretty Boy," 158
Fonck, René, 138
Fonda, Henry, 42
Fonda, Jane, 67–68, 69, 109
Foran, Dick, 28
Ford, Henry, xvi
Ford, John, 41, 44
Forest, Nathan Bedford, 32
Franco, Francisco, 7
Frankfurter, Felix, xxiv
Franklin, Benjamin, 58

Gabriel Over the White House, xxviii, 1–12
Gallico, Paul, 172
Gans, Joe, 173
Gardner, Frederick, 155
Garrison, William Lloyd, 84
Garvey, Marcus, 87, 165, 174
Gehrig, Lou, 176
George V, 177
Giamatti, Paul, 167, 168
Gish, Lillian, 54
Glassford, Pelham D., 19, 21
Gleason, James, 55
Golden Gloves, 172
Goldsman, Akiva, 167
Goodman, Benny, 76
Gordon, C. Henry, 2
Goss, Joe, 170
Gould, Joe, 167, 177
Gow, Betty, 135, 146
Grapes of Wrath, The, film, x, xxxi, 41–52, 128, 132
Grapes of Wrath, The, novel, xxxi
Grapewin, Charlie, 42
Graves, Peter, 54
Grazer, Brian, 167
Great Awakening, 57–58, 59
Great Migration, xvi, 35, 88, 175
Greeley, Horace, 86
Green, Johnny, 77
Greenblatt, Marjorie, 128–129
Greer, Will, 132

Gregory, Paul, 53
Gretchell, Robert, 121
Griffin, Corn, 168, 177, 179
Griffith, D. W., 33, 54
Griffiths, Tuffy, 167, 177
Grimke, Francis, 173
Grubb, Davis, x, 53, 65
Guggenheim, Harry, 140
Guthrie, Arlo, 128
Guthrie, Charles Edward, 130
Guthrie, Jack, 122, 132
Guthrie, Nora Belle Sherman, 130
Guthrie, Woody, 44, 121–134; early life, 130–131; influence of, 129; political views, 121–122, 127, 129, 131–133; songwriter, 127–128, 129, 131

Haines, William Wister, 27
Hamlin, Reno, 102–103
Hamlisch, Marvin, 107
Hammer, Armand, 7–8
Hammett, Dashiell, 112
Hammond, John, 163
Handy, Craig, 152
Harburg, Yip, 105
Harding, Warren G., 2
Harlow, Jean, 164
Hatch, Eric S., 13, 15
Hauptmann, Anna, 136, 145, 148
Hauptmann, Bruno, 136, 148–149
Havoc, June, 72
Hawkins, Coleman, 152
Hawks, Howard, 96
Hays Office. *See* Hollywood Production Code
Hearst, William Randolph, 1–2, 10, 11
Hill, George Roy, 98, 107
Hill, Joe, 127
Hitler, Adolf, xxiv, xxvii, 4, 6, 131, 176
Hobos, 17, 132
Hoffman, Harold Giles, 136, 149
Hollingsworth, Cliff, 167
Hollywood Production Code, xxix, 2, 13, 42, 43
Holodomor, 8
Hong, James, 110
Hooks, Kevin, 80

Hoover, Herbert, xxvii, 2, 7, 72, 143, 156; Bonus Army, 22; career of, xvi–xvii, 5; Great Depression, response to, 16; misrepresentation of, xvii; 1932 election, loss of, xix–xx; Republican convention 1932, xviii
Hoover, J. Edgar, 144, 145, 148, 158
Hoovervilles, x, 17–18, 20–21, 24
Hopkins, Anthony, 136
Houston, Cisco, 132
Howard, Ron, 167–168
Hurley, Patrick J., 21
Huston, John, 110
Huston, Walter, 2
Hyer, Tom, 169

Immigration Act of 1924, xv, xxiv, 35
"Indian New Deal," xxiv

Jackson, Peter, 172–173
Jacobs, Joe, 176
Jeffries, Jim, 174, 179
Jennings, Mary, 130
Jenson, Roy, 110
Jim Crow, 81, 88, 122
Johnson, Andrew, 86
Johnson, Hugh S., xxii
Johnson, Jack, 174
Johnson, Nunnally, 41
Johnston, Eric, 43
Johnston, James, 167, 168
Jones, Robert Earl, 98
Jones, Samuel P., 60
Joplin, Scott, 107

Kahn, Madeleine, 96, 97
Kansas City: history of, 153–163; music scene, 161–163; political corruption, 153–161
Kansas City film, xi, 151–165
Karch, Charles A., 143
Keelley, Dee, 142–143
King Kong, x, xxvii
Kirk, Andy, 163
Know Nothings, 31, 58, 170

Ku Klux Klan, 31–34, 38, 87–88, 125, 175; *Birth of a Nation, The*, 33; Black Legion, connections with, 35
Kulik, Buzz, 135

La Cava, Gregory, 1, 13, 15
Landau, David, 2
Landon, Alf, xxiv
Lang, Christa, 136
Lange, Dorothea, 50, 90, 131
Larman, Joseph "Legs," 141–142
Lasky, Art, 168, 179
Laughton, Charles, 53, 54, 56
Lazia, Johnny, 158
Lead Belly, 125–126
Ledbetter, Huddie. *See* Lead Belly
Lee, Robert E., 87
Legion of Terror, 27, 39
Leigh, Jennifer Jason, 151
Lenin, Vladimir, 4–5, 8, 9
Lerner, Max, xx
Leventhal, Harold, 121, 132
Lewis, John Henry, 178
Lewis, Sinclair, 29
Liebling, A.J., 177
Lincoln, Abraham, 86
Lindbergh, Anne Morrow, 135, 140–141
Lindbergh, Charles: Atlantic flight, 136, 139–140; celebrity of, 136, 139–141; controversies surrounding, 136, 145; early life of, 136–138; kidnapping case, xxvii, 135–136, 143–149
Lindbergh, Charles, Jr., 141, 143–144, 146
Lindbergh Kidnapping Case, The, x–xi, 135–149
Lindbergh Law, 144
Lippmann, Walter, 10
Lloyd, Norman, 67
Lloyd George, David, 1
Lomax, Alan, 124–126, 127–128, 129
Lomax, John, 124–126
Lombard, Carol, 13, 14, 15
Lombardo, Guy, 76
Long, Huey, xx, xxix
Lopez, Perry, 110
Lord, Robert, 27
Loughran, Tommy, 178

Louis, Joe, 175, 176
Louis, John Henry, 168, 178, 179
Lowell, James Russell, 123
Loy, Myrna, 179
Lucas, George, 95
Luckinbill, Laurence, 136
Lupp, Arthur, 38
Lynch, Harold J. "Shorty," 137

MacArthur, Douglas, xix, 20, 21–22
Malcolm X, 37
Marks, Benjamin, 101
Marquis of Queensberry Rules, 171
Marshall, Frank, 95
Marshall, Penny, 167
Marx, Karl, 5
Matthews, Carmen, 80
Maurer, David, 98, 101, 105, 106
Mayo, Archie, 27
Mayo, Morrow, 115
McCarthy, Joe, 129
McCoy, Horace, 67
McElroy, Henry L., 156, 157, 159, 160
McGill, Bruce, 167
McGovern, Terry, 173
McLean, Evalyn Walsh, 19
McPherson, Aimee Semple, 61
McShann, Jay, 164
Mead, Margaret, 105
Mellon, Andrew, xvii
Melville, Herman, 100
Memphis Minnie, 91
Mencken, H. L., 63
Metro-Goldwyn-Mayer Studios, 1
Miller, JP, 135
Milligan, Maurice, 159–160
Millikan, Robert A., 115
Mills, Shirley, 42
Mitchell, Billy, 3
Mitchell, Grant, 43
Mitchum, Robert, 54, 55
Molly Maguires, 31
Morgan, J.P., 140
Morgenthau, Henry, xxiv
Morley, Karen, 2
Morrissey, John, 170
Morrow, David, 140
Moseley, George Van Horn, 20

Moten, Bennie, 162
Muench, Nellie Tipton, 142–143
Mulholland, William, 116–119
Mulroney, Dermot, 151
Murphy, Michael, 151
Murry, Albert, 162
Mussolini, Benito, 4–5, 6–7, 11, 131, 176
My Man Godfrey, x, xxx, 13–25

Nash, Frank "Jelly," 158
National Relief Administration, xxii, xxix
Nelson, Battling, 173
New Deal, xx–xxiii, xxv, 7, 11, 47, 49, 62, 124, 127, 157, 165
Newman, Paul, 95, 98
Nicholson, Jack, 109
Night of the Hunter, 53–66
Norfleet, J. Frank, 102–104

O'Brien-Moore, Erin, 27
O'Day, Anita, 72
O'Neal, Ryan, 95, 96
O'Neal, Tatum, 96, 97
Orteig, Raymond, 138
Otis, Harrison, 117

Pace, John T., 19
Page, Walter, 162
Pallette, Eugene, 14
Palmer, Belinda, 110
Paper Moon, film, 95–97, 105–106
Park, Guy Brasfield, 157
Parker, Charlie, 165
Parker, Dorothy, 9
Parker, Jean, 3
Parks, Gordon, 90
Patman, Wright, 18
Patrick, Gail, 14
Payne, Felix, 165
Pearl Harbor, xxv, xxxii, 43, 145
Peer, Ralph, 124
Pelley, William Dudley, 29
Pendergast, Jim, 153–154, 155
Pendergast, Thomas J., 152–161, 163–164; fall of, 159–161; political machine, 153–161; race relations, 156, 157, 164

194 Index

Perkins, Frances, xxiii
Phillips, Julia, 97
Phillips, Michael, 97
Pidgeon, Walter, 136
Plessy, Homer, 88
Poe, James, 67, 69
Polanski, Roman, 109, 111, 119
Pollack, Sydney, 67, 69
Poole, Bill, 170
Poole, Charles, 34, 38
Popular Front, 124
Porter, Cole, 6
Potter, John C., 116
Powell, William, 13, 14, 15
Presley, Elvis, 63, 92
Prohibition, x, xvi, xxi, xxviii, 97, 106, 144, 157, 161
Protestantism, history in U.S., 56–63
Public Enemy, The, x

Quakers, *Sounder*, 84
Qualen, John, 42
Quigley, Martin, 43
Quillan, Eddie, 42

Racism, 29–34, 60, 64, 113, 114–115, 131–132, 145, 164, 172–175. *See also* Black Legion; Ku Klux Klan; Slavery
Radnitz, Robert B., 79
Randolph, Thomas Jefferson, 84
Reagan, Ronald, 162
Reconstruction, 86–88
Redford, Robert, 95, 98
Redman, Joshua, 152
Reeves, Albert L., 159
Remarque, Erich Maria, 114
Rice, Thomas Dartmouth, 88
Richardson, Miranda, 151
Richmond, Bill, 168
Rickard, George "Tex," 173–174
Ritt, Martin, 79, 90
Roberts, Tony, 136
Robinson, Jackie, 175
Rodgers, Jimmie, 122, 124
Rogers, Charles R., 13
Rogers, John, 143
Rogers, Will, 133

Roman Catholicism, prejudice against, 30–31, 33, 58, 113, 169–170
Roosevelt, Eleanor, xxiii–xxiv, 23
Roosevelt, Franklin D., x, xxiii, xxvii, 1, 6, 47–48, 56, 73, 115, 125, 180; biography of, xviii–xix; Democratic Convention 1932, xix, 157; Fireside Chats, xxi–xxii, xxviii; foreign policy, xxv, 10; *Gabriel Over the White House*, 2, 10–11; "Hundred Days," xx–xxii; inaugural address 1933, xx; plots against, 37; president elect, as, xx; racial views, xxiv, 165; television, xxxi
Roosevelt, Theodore, xviii
Rose, Billy, 105
Rosenman, Harold, 122
Ross, Harold, 9
Rothstein, Arthur, 50
Runyon, Damon, 167, 180
Ryan, Paddy, 170
Ryskind, Morrie, 13, 15

Salazar, Antonio de Oliveira, 7
Sargent, Alvin, 95
Sarrazin, Michael, 68
Sawyer, Joseph, 27
Schmeling, Max, 175, 179
Schoenfeld, Dudley, 148
Schwarzkopf, Norman, 135, 146, 148
"Scopes Monkey Trial," 61
Screwball comedy, 13–14, 23
Seeger, Pete, 122, 125, 127, 128, 133
Shannon, Joseph, 155
Sharecropping, x, 54, 79–80, 87, 89–90, 92
Sharp, Cecil, 123, 124, 125
Sharp, Violet, 135, 146
Shaw, Robert, 98
Sheridan, Ann, 28
Silver Shirts, 29
Simpson, Russell, 42
Skelly, Jack, 172
Skelton, Red, 72
Slavery, 81–87
Smith, Al, 10
Smith, Bessie, 91
Smith, Joseph, 59–60
Smith, Truman, 145

Social Security Act, xxiii, xxiv
Soubier, Clifford, 28
Sounder, film, 79–93
Sounder, novel, 79
Southern gothic, 53–54, 65
Spielberg, Steven, 96
Spirituals to Swing, 76, 163
Stalin, Josef, 4, 7–8, 9, 11, 177
Stanton, Billy, 35
Stark, Lloyd C., 157, 159, 161
Starling, Edmund W., 19
Steinbeck, John, x, xxxi, 41–42, 48, 51
Sting, The, 95, 97–99, 105–106
Sullivan, John L., 170–171
Sullivan, Yankee, 169, 170
Sully, Frank, 42
Sunday, Billy, 60–61

Taj Mahal, 80, 91
Tammany Hall, 153, 170
Tennessee Valley Authority, xxi, xxviii
Terkel, Studs, xxi
They Shoot Horses, Don't They?, film, 67–78
They Shoot Horses, Don't They?, novel, 67–68, 73–74
Thomas, Lowell, 6
Thompson, Robert E., 67, 69
Thompson, William, 99–100
Thoreau, Henry David, xx
Tilbury, Zeffie, 42
Tone, Franchot, 2
Torrio, Johnny, 106
Towne, Robert, 109, 112, 116, 119
Trenchard, Thomas W., 136, 148
Trotsky, Leon, 9
Truman, Harry S., 160–161
Tugwell, Rexford, xx
Turner, Big Joe, 163
Turner, Nat, 60, 84
Twain, Mark, 100
Tweed, Thomas Frederick, 1
Tyson, Cicely, 79–80, 81

Underground Railroad, 85

Vesey, Denmark, 84

Walker Law, 172
Wall Street Crash, xvii, 9, 15–16, 45
Wanger, Walter, 1
Ward, Arch, 172
Ward, David S., 97–98
Washington, Booker T., 87, 173
Washington, George, 58
Waters, Walter W., 18–19, 20
Watterson, Mark, 118–119
Weavers, The, 128, 129
Webster, Ben, 152, 162
Welch, Casimir, 157
Welles, Orson, xxx
West, Nathaniel, 115
Wexler, Haskell, 121, 122
Whateley, Olly, 146
Whitehead, O. Z., 42
Whitney, Eli, 83
Wilentz, David, 148
Wilkie, Wendell, xxv
Willard, Jess, 179
Williams, Hank, 124
Williams, Mary Lou, 152
Wilson, Carey, 2
Wilson, Woodrow, 10
Winfield, Paul, 80
Winkler, Irwin, 67
Winters, Shelley, 54
Woodville, Kate, 135
Woollcott, Alexander, 9
Works Progress Administration (WPA), xxiii, xxiv, 38, 105, 124
World War I, 45
World War II, xxxi–xxxii, 48
Wright, Richard, 176

York, Susannah, 68, 69
Young, Brigham, 60
Young, Gig, 68
Young, Lester, 152

Zanuck, Darryl F., 41
Zellweger, Renée, 167
Zwerling, Darrell, 109

About the Author

DAVID LUHRSSEN is managing editor and film critic of the Shepherd Express newspaper in Milwaukee. He lectured at the University of Wisconsin-Milwaukee and the Milwaukee Institute of Art and Design. He is author of ABC-CLIO's *World War II on Film, The Vietnam War on Film, Encyclopedia of Classic Rock*, and several other books.

www.ingramcontent.com/pod-product-compliance
Lightning Source LLC
Chambersburg PA
CBHW060951230426
43665CB00015B/2148